CW00432269

CHRIST

THE CLASSICS

Christian Theology: The Classics is a vibrant introduction to the most important works of theology in the history of Christian thought. Exploring writings from the origins of Christianity to the present day, it examines some of the most influential theologians of all time, considering the context in which they were writing and the lasting significance of their work. It covers thirty-one theological classics such as:

- Augustine of Hippo, *On the Trinity*
- Martin Luther, *Commentary on Galatians*
- John Calvin, *The Institutes of The Christian Religion*
- Jonathan Edwards, *Religious Affections*
- Thomas Aquinas, *Summa Theologiae*

With a glossary and outlines of the key criticisms of each text, this book is the perfect starting point for anyone interested in theology and the history of Christian thought.

Shawn Bawulski is an assistant professor of theology at LCC International University in Klaipėda, Lithuania. His PhD thesis (University of St Andrews) was awarded the Samuel Rutherford Prize for best doctoral thesis in Divinity. His research interests include various topics in eschatology and philosophical theology.

Stephen R. Holmes is senior lecturer in theology, director of teaching, and deputy head of school at the School of Divinity, University of St Andrews. He has written extensively on historical theology, treating patristic, Reformation, early modern, and contemporary theology in different publications.

CHRISTIAN THEOLOGY

THE CLASSICS

Shawn J. Bawulski and Stephen R. Holmes

Routledge
Taylor & Francis Group

LONDON AND NEW YORK

First published 2014
by Routledge
2 Park Square, Milton Park, Abingdon, Oxon OX14 4RN

And published in the USA and Canada
by Routledge
711 Third Avenue, New York, NY 10017

Routledge is an imprint of the Taylor & Francis Group, an informa business

© 2014 Shawn J. Bawulski and Stephen R. Holmes

The right of Shawn J. Bawulski and Stephen R. Holmes to be identified as authors of this work has been asserted by them in accordance with sections 77 and 78 of the Copyright, Designs and Patents Act 1988.

All rights reserved. No part of this book may be reprinted or reproduced or utilised in any form or by any electronic, mechanical, or other means, now known or hereafter invented, including photocopying and recording, or in any information storage or retrieval system, without permission in writing from the publishers.

Trademark notice: Product or corporate names may be trademarks or registered trademarks, and are used only for identification and explanation without intent to infringe.

British Library Cataloguing in Publication Data
A catalogue record for this book is available from the British Library

Library of Congress Cataloging in Publication Data
A catalog record for this book has been requested

ISBN: 978-0-415-50190-3 (hbk)
ISBN: 978-0-415-50187-3 (pbk)
ISBN: 978-1-315-81644-9 (ebk)

Typeset in Bembo
by Taylor and Francis Books

MIX
Paper from
responsible sources
FSC
www.fsc.org   FSC® C013604

Printed and bound by CPI Group (UK) Ltd, Croydon, CR0 4YY

From Shawn: For Kate and Charlotte, whose arrivals into the world were most welcome interruptions to this project.

From Stephen: For Nigel Wright, my first doctrine tutor, whose retirement coincided with the submission of this manuscript.

CONTENTS

Preface   ix

Introduction: the story of Christian theology   1

1 Irenaeus of Lyons, *Against All Heresies*   14
2 Origen of Alexandria, *On First Principles*   21
3 Athanasius, *On the Incarnation*   29
4 Basil of Caesarea, *On the Holy Spirit*   38
5 Creeds and Conciliar Documents   45
6 Augustine of Hippo, *On the Trinity*   54
7 Anselm, *Why the God-Man?*   61
8 Thomas Aquinas, *Summa Theologiae*   70
9 Julian of Norwich, *Revelations of Divine Love*   78
10 Martin Luther, *Commentary on Galatians*   86
11 John Calvin, *Institutes of the Christian Religion*   95
12 The Canons and Decrees of the Council of Trent   103
13 The Anglican Formularies, *The Book of Common Prayer,*
   The Thirty-Nine Articles, and *The Homilies*   112

14 The Westminster Standards, *The Westminster Confession*, *The Shorter Catechism*, *The Larger Catechism*, and *The Book of Common Order*   121

15 Jonathan Edwards, *The Religious Affections*   130

16 John Wesley, *A Plain Account of Christian Perfection*   138

17 Friedrich Schleiermacher, *The Christian Faith*   147

18 John Henry Newman, *Essay on the Development of Doctrine*   157

19 Ludwig Feuerbach, *The Essence of Christianity*   165

20 Søren Kierkegaard, *The Philosophical Fragments*   173

21 Adolf von Harnack, *What is Christianity?*   182

22 Karl Barth, *Church Dogmatics*   191

23 Dietrich Bonhöffer, *The Cost of Discipleship*   199

24 Rudolf Bultmann, *New Testament and Mythology*   207

25 H. Richard Niebuhr, *Christ and Culture*   216

26 Karl Rahner, *The Trinity*   224

27 The Second Vatican Council, *Lumen gentium*   233

28 John Howard Yoder, *The Politics of Jesus*   242

29 Rosemary Radford Ruether, *Sexism and God-Talk*   250

30 Gustavo Gutierrez, *A Theology of Liberation*   258

31 George Lindbeck, *The Nature of Doctrine*   267

Glossary   276

Index   280

PREFACE

In *Changing Places*, one of his humorous novels about academic life, David Lodge invents the parlour game 'Humiliation'. In the novel, it is played by members of an English faculty of a Californian university, but a group of theologians could easily have a go. Each player in turn is required to name a book he or she has not read and scores a point for each other player who has read the book. In effect, one wins the game by admitting to not having read central texts in the discipline. Our definition of a 'classic' for this book owes something to Lodge's game. We have not tried to choose the 'best' works of theology, in our estimation, or the most historically significant, but those which would lead to raised eyebrows or worse if, in the present state of the academy, one admitted to not having read them. There is thus something of a bias towards recent books, and the effects of contemporary fashion are felt on the list, as is the broadly Protestant bias of much contemporary theological education. There are important works that have been left out, certainly, and any such list will always involve drawing difficult lines. However, these are the books that, in our estimation, undergraduates are most likely to encounter in the course of their studies in a mainstream British or American university today.

In selecting our 'classics', we also adopted the principle that we would have no more than one work by any one author. There are places we were tempted to go in a different direction – Augustine's *City of God* alongside *On The Trinity*; Luther's *Babylonian Captivity* – and/or his *Bondage of the Will* – alongside his *Commentary on Galatians*; Barth's *Commentary on Romans* alongside *Church Dogmatics* – but we finally judged it more appropriate to allow more voices to be heard.

The chapters in this book are, of course, no substitute for reading these primary texts. Ideally, reading this book will encourage reading (or re-reading!) of the works treated. We hope students and readers will use this book as a springboard into the wealth and treasures of the classics in Christian theology. Each chapter attempts to make the covered work more accessible and understandable, to set it in its historical context, and to sketch its influence on Christian theology. Our goal for each chapter has been to make the reader eager and interested to read the great works themselves.

An asterisk (*) has been used to indicate that words in the text appear in the Glossary; two asterisks (**) have been used to show that a source in the text appears as a chapter within the book.

INTRODUCTION
THE STORY OF CHRISTIAN THEOLOGY

Christian theology begins in earnest with reflection on the significance of the claim that Jesus of Nazareth, crucified by the Roman occupiers, has risen from the dead. What does this mean about who Jesus is, or about the way divine power is active in the world? What does it mean about the nature of deity and what it is to be human? Questions like these, and suggested answers that were offered, criticized, and refined, began the work of Christian theology.

These reflections did not happen in an intellectual vacuum, of course. Jesus lived and taught in the context of a particular moment in the development of the ancient faith of Israel. The ancient people, who understood themselves to be particularly chosen and blessed by God, had been exiled across the Ancient Near East about five centuries before Christ and had been living under occupation, first by Greek empires (Alexander the Great and his successors) and then by Rome, except for a brief period of independence under the Maccabbees. The religious and cultural traditions that Jesus knew, as a result, were shaped by encounter with, and in some cases resistance to, these broader cultural currents.

After Jesus, the early Christian communities very quickly had to make sense of his teaching in the broader eastern Mediterranean context of a vibrant and developing inheritance of Greek philosophical ideas, which offered various schools, all devoted to answering questions concerning what the world is really like and how to live well within it. For many, particularly those amongst the more leisured classes, attention to one or another philosophical school and its advice on what a well-lived life looked like was a determinative aspect of personal existence. Another result of this context was the very widespread use of Greek as a trade language across the region and as far west as Rome itself.

At the same time, the Holy Land and the wider eastern Mediterranean world knew well the reality of Roman empire. Imperial Rome had brought stability – Rome called it 'peace' – but at a price, both financial (i.e. taxation) and cultural. Palestine felt the burden of taxation very heavily: we have records of an appeal to the Emperor for a lessening of the tax burden, and when, a few decades after Jesus' death, the Jewish people revolted against Rome, taxation was at the heart of their grievances. Roman peace, however, brought advantages: travel was possible and relatively safe; where Greek was not spoken, Latin was.

The Jewish context meant that Christian reflection was, from the start, uncompromisingly monotheistic: one God only is to be confessed and worshipped. This God is the one Jesus called 'Father'. Christian practice from the earliest times ranked Jesus with the Father, however: Jesus was honoured and worshipped as God. There was some precedent for this in ancient Jewish religion: the Hebrew scriptures (received as authoritative by the early church) spoke of the 'Spirit of God' or the 'angel of the Lord' in terms that suggested both an identity with God and a degree of separate existence. This was all very fuzzy, however, and working out how properly to speak of Jesus' relation to the Father (and the place of the Holy Spirit) was a problem that the theological tradition worked on for some centuries.

The earliest theological developments, however, were more directed towards problems posed by Roman empire and Greek philosophy than those posed by Jewish doctrine. Christians attracted suspicion from the imperial authorities; early Christian writers sought to dispel this suspicion and to turn aside persecution. The earliest sustained genre of Christian writing is thus the 'apology': an account of Christianity that stresses how unthreatening it is, and so pleads for toleration from the authorities. We have not included any examples of this apologetic literature in this volume, but it marks a significant early flowering of Christian theology.

Our first classic text, Irenaeus of Lyons' *Against All Heresies*, nonetheless carries echoes of this period. Irenaeus' work as Bishop of Lyons took place in the context of active persecution. He writes, though, not against the imperial powers that threatened the church from the outside, but against misrepresentations of Christian teaching which made the faith more acceptable in the broad intellectual climate shaped by Greek philosophy. Irenaeus' great point is the goodness of God's creation, a point affirmed in the Jewish Scriptures and necessary for Christian faith and devotion, but at odds with at least some developments of Greek thinking.

Origen of Alexandria, the greatest mind of the first few centuries of the church, faced similar issues. Here we have not his direct responses, but an ambitious summary of the whole of Christian doctrine he produced, *On First Principles*. Origen faces perennial questions of the origins of evil and the fairness of God's providence; there can be no doubting the brilliance of his theological imagination, even if his answers proved sufficiently strange for the later tradition to declare them heretical. Origen's life, like that of Irenaeus, was marked by persecution; he was not martyred himself, but suffered nonetheless and knew many who became martyrs for the faith.

Persecution by the Roman Empire came to a formal end (barring one brief relapse) as a result of the Emperor Constantine professing conversion in 312; suddenly, emperors were interested in theological questions – not least because they wanted a united church as a social glue to hold the Empire together. As Constantine professed conversion, the final stages of the debate over how to speak of Jesus in the same breath as speaking of the Father, without compromising monotheism, were beginning. Athanasius of Alexandria was the crucial controversialist on what was to become the successful side of the debate in its first few decades; his *On the Incarnation* is an early and non-polemical text which lays out the genius of the theological vision he was to spend his life defending. Later in the fourth century, the question of the place of the Holy Spirit in the developing account of God's life would come to the fore; here we have a classic contribution to that debate, Basil of Caesarea's *On the Holy Spirit*. Basil laid the foundations for the Trinitarian settlement that was finally to triumph at the Council of Constantinople in 381.

Many councils and synods had met previously, but imperial interest in theological conformity led to a new stage of theological work marked by great councils of bishops, called by the Emperor, or at least called with the Emperor's approval, and tasked with establishing unity on disputed points of doctrine or practice. Examples include the Council of Nicaea, where Athanasius was present, and the Council of Constantinople, which built on Basil's teaching. The early councils addressed the Trinitarian question, enshrining the ideas defended by Athanasius, Basil, and others; the later councils turned to the question of how Jesus can be both truly human and truly divine. Councils issued their own decrees and also recommended as orthodox the writings of key theologians. Here we include a selection of conciliar decrees and documents to give the flavour of these central theological texts, which are still crucial touchstones of historic orthodoxy in Christian doctrine.

The debate over the doctrine of the Trinity was declared settled at Constantinople, and the main energies of theological debate turned elsewhere. Not all were satisfied with the settlement, however, and there was a lasting need to expound the doctrine in ways that helped others to understand it. Augustine of Hippo had, without question, one of the greatest theological minds in history, which he applied to every significant theological problem of the day, and in every case provided works of lasting influence; of these many works, we have included his account of the Trinity as our representative classic here. He does not want to disagree with the Constantinopolitan settlement, but he nevertheless wants to propose certain different ways of reading biblical texts and to discuss certain theological formulations that sounded different in Latin than they had in Greek.

Our next writer, Anselm of Canterbury, recognizably stands in the tradition of Augustine, but dates from six centuries later. The historical gap requires explanation: theological exploration did not, of course, cease in the intervening period. It is arguable that it did go into decline, particularly in the Latin-speaking Western part of the Roman Empire, which was overrun in a series of invasions and which largely collapsed as a result. There were individual thinkers of great brilliance (John Scotus Eriugena particularly stands out), but there was not the general culture to encourage the flourishing of learning, except in very brief flashes – the school brought together by Charlemagne at Corbie, for instance. The Eastern part of the Empire survived longer and produced some truly great theologians: Maximus the Confessor, John of Damascus, and Symeon the New Theologian are all first-rank thinkers, without question, and their works would unquestionably be regarded as theological classics in the context of a culture influenced by Eastern Orthodox Christianity; in English-speaking theological study, which traces its core history through the Western churches, they are generally relegated to being more peripheral figures, however, and so we have chosen not to include them here.

Anselm was formed by the monastic school at Bec, in France, which came to prominence at the beginning of arguably the most sustained period of serious philosophical and theological thought that Christian Europe has yet seen. Between Anselm's birth, in 1033, and the Reformation about five hundred years later, an astonishing number of great theological minds flourished, addressing themselves to questions which, if we find them irrelevant or abstruse now, nonetheless demanded serious intellectual effort to understand, let alone unravel. Anselm himself demonstrates remarkable logical skill over a series of treatises, seeking to defend the rationality of Christian doctrine. Here we include his work on the atonement, *Why the God-Man?*, where he offers perhaps the first extended treatment of the question: 'How does Christ's life and death lead to salvation for Christian people?'

Our next writer, Thomas Aquinas, has come down in theological folklore as the greatest of the medieval theologians; whether he was the most acute is a question that might reasonably be debated, but the work he left has unquestionably been enormously influential. The *Summa Theologiae*, although left unfinished by Aquinas and completed on the basis of his notes after his death, stands unchallenged as one of the two or three greatest accounts of Christian theology ever written. It offers an account of Christian practice based on a rich vision of Christian doctrine that might be argued to be unsurpassed still.

Aquinas lived in a particular intellectual context, however. His Western European society had lost touch with significant parts of classical culture with the collapse of the Roman Empire centuries before; when the Islamic North African empires invaded Spain, they brought with them a rich literature, particularly the works of Aristotle – and also a developed Islamic tradition of commentating on those works. It is hard for us to imagine what a shock this must have been to Europe: works that were far in advance of anything they knew in philosophy, geography, zoology, botany, and several other disciplines were suddenly all available – and were being interpreted in ways that were incompatible with elements of the Christian faith. At the heart of Thomas Aquinas' theological achievement was a careful and critical assimilation of this new Aristotelian knowledge to the doctrines of the faith.

Alongside the scholastic traditions of the middle ages, exemplified by Aquinas, there was a parallel – and connected – development of mystical literature and theology. Julian of Norwich stands a little outside of the mainstream of this tradition, but her *Revelations of Divine Love* remains powerful and contains some fascinating themes that make it a very popular text in modern university programmes, notably a focus on feminine images for God and a concern for the wholeness of creation. Her theology is based on visions granted to her when near to death, but she works out the meaning of those visions in the light of the faith of the church.

Eventually, the unity of the medieval Western church splintered. Movements protesting against corruption in the church hierarchy had been growing for decades; what was new about Martin Luther's protest was that he gained local political backing, and so was protected from the harsh treatment experienced by other would-be reformers. As a result, the Protestant Reformation began, launching new church traditions – Lutheran; Reformed; and Anabaptist – that remain significant to the present day. Luther was concerned about various practical and ethical abuses that he observed, but at the heart of his protest was a theological belief: that salvation came by faith alone, not as a result of anything we did or anything the church did for us. His *Commentary on Galatians* is a classic expression of that belief, influential throughout Protestant history, and is our choice of a classic text here.

The Protestant movement itself soon splintered, with different strands committed to different patterns of church government and different theological emphases. The first split was between the Lutherans and the Reformed, a division which began with some questions over the eucharist, between German (Lutheran) and Swiss (Reformed) Protestants, but later hardened into a more profound division encompassing several different emphases. John Calvin was not the first Reformed theologian, but he was without doubt the greatest of the early period – perhaps the greatest yet. His *Institutes of the Christian Religion*, our chosen classic, was written to be a brief summary of doctrine to help readers of his biblical commentaries, but nonetheless stands as another of the truly classic summaries of Christian faith alongside Thomas Aquinas' *Summa Theologiae*.

The Roman Catholic Church, of course, responded to the challenge of the Reformation. There were various reforms of abuses and renewals of devotional life. In doctrinal terms, the crucial response came in the Council of Trent, which addressed many of the claims of the Reformers and offered responses. A number of doctrines that had been generally held but never formally taught by the church were codified at the Council of Trent; in other areas the Council clarified doctrine or terminology that had previously been more confused or simply undefined. The Decrees and Canons of the Council of Trent are here included as representing a crucial moment in the development of Roman Catholic dogma.

We have already noted the intimate connection between the success of Protestantism and the support of local rulers; one natural result of this was the formation of several 'national churches' immediately after the Reformation. The Church of England stood a little apart from the Lutheran-Reformed controversies of mainland Europe, although in its early years it tended to the Reformed side and developed its own distinctive tradition encapsulated in its authorized liturgy, *The Book of Common Prayer*; its statement of faith, *The Thirty-Nine Articles*; and a set of model sermons called *The Homilies*. Because of the importance of the Anglican tradition in the English-speaking world, we have included these three documents here. Together, they capture something of the genius of Anglicanism, and so deserve the status of a theological classic.

In seventeenth-century England, a bitter dispute arose between King and Parliament, eventually resulting in the English Civil War. Anglicanism became entwined with the English monarchy, which was removed for a brief period after the Civil War. The Parliamentarian side in the Civil War gathered support from many minority Christian traditions that had developed in England; it gave them all a chance to become established (the organized existence of denominations such as Baptists, Congregationalists, and Quakers dates from this period), but its centre of gravity was Presbyterian, the British version of the Reformed tradition of mainland Europe. (The Church of Scotland was Presbyterian from its beginnings, and Scotland supported the anti-monarchist cause in England.) A new liturgy and statement of faith was needed, and so Parliament called together an 'assembly of divines' to write them. The resulting documents, *The Westminster Standards*, were adopted by the Church of Scotland, soon crossed the Atlantic to the American colonies, and have been enormously influential in worldwide Presbyterianism ever since.

The brief period of relative religious tolerance in England under the Protectorate was framed on either side by active persecution of non-Anglicans; many chose exile, often either to the Netherlands or to the new colonies in North America, where they could practise their religion freely. The greatest theologian to be born in colonial America is without doubt Jonathan Edwards, who inherited a developed tradition of Reformed theology from European writers, and who – perhaps as Aquinas had done in regard to Catholic theology and Aristotle – reframed it in the light of the new philosophical traditions of the eighteenth century. Edwards was involved in the beginnings of the Great Awakening, a significant revival of religious fervour that swept across colonial America. The Awakening provoked controversy, not least over questions of the appropriateness of heightened emotional response in the context of Christian worship; Edwards used his theology, and his understanding of new traditions of psychology, to offer a series of interventions on this question. The last of these works, entitled *The Religious Affections*, remains one of the classic texts of applied theology and is included here.

In Britain, a similar event to the Great Awakening happened and was called the Evangelical Revival. The outstanding leaders of Evangelicalism were John and Charles Wesley and George Whitefield. John Wesley was a powerful preacher with a genius for organization: the worldwide Methodist movement owes its origins to his work. He believed that the crucial teaching that God had entrusted to him, and to other Methodists, was 'Christian perfection' – the idea that believers could, after conversion, be completely sanctified by the Holy Spirit, so that they no longer committed any sins. Wesley wrote repeatedly on the subject of perfection throughout his life; here we have included a text summarizing his various writings, namely, his *A Plain Account of Christian Perfection*.

Edwards and Wesley both successfully offered a vision of Christian belief and practice that made sense in the light of the changing culture of the eighteenth century, particularly the Enlightenment; in France and Germany, however, more radical versions of the Enlightenment offered a serious attack on Christian faith, and no comparable figure rose up to respond to it. Enlightenment philosophy stressed a lack of respect for tradition, particularly for inherited privilege, and a belief that mathematical or mechanistic theories would be sufficient to explain all things; the latter belief was inhospitable to classical modes of theological argument: where Christianity was identified with inherited privilege, the critique could seem devastating. Arguably, the eighteenth century posed the most serious challenge to Christian thought that it had ever faced.

Across Europe, Enlightenment ideas were attacked by a new cultural movement known as Romanticism. In Britain, the classic early figures of this movement were poets like Samuel Taylor Coleridge and William Wordsworth, while in Germany they were composers like Ludwig van Beethoven and painters like Caspar David Friedrich. The Romantics rejected the predominantly mechanistic pictures of the world offered by Enlightenment thinkers, and instead discovered a world that was organic and alive with feeling. The great German theologian Friedrich Schleiermacher gave himself to making Christianity comprehensible and attractive in this new cultural moment; towards the end of his life, he produced a summary of Christian doctrine which took this task seriously, but which also offered a profound restatement of the whole of Christian theology in a new idiom. Whether or not one agrees with his approach or his conclusions, there can be no doubt that Schleiermacher's *The Christian Faith* more than deserves the status of a classic.

The English theologian John Henry Newman was influenced by Romanticism in a very different way. He became concerned with questions of historical fidelity and church authority, finally coming to believe that only the Roman Catholic Church, with its claim to unbroken continuity from the time of the apostles down and its account of an infallible teaching authority, could be authentic. Before coming to this conclusion, he had been enormously influential in reshaping the Church of England, arguing that it had a truly 'catholic' identity. Here we have included his *Essay on the Development of Doctrine*, the work where he most fully works out his account of why Roman Catholic doctrines that do not appear directly in Scripture must nonetheless be accepted as authoritative.

The general theological response to the challenges of the nine-teenth century was not a return to Roman Catholicism, however. Schleiermacher's pattern of a radical recasting of Christian faith to make it comprehensible and acceptable in the new context was far more common. In Germany, and much of Protestant Europe, those who did not follow Schleiermacher followed Hegel and developed a vision of Christianity that stressed the ongoing evolution of the world towards perfection.

We have selected for our next two classics the works of two nineteenth-century theologians who were, from different direc-tions, deeply critical of these moves. This is not because we think the criticisms are right, necessarily, but because the two writers offer alternative visions to the mainstream, visions which seem to us to be important and which have been generative for later theological work.

Ludwig Feuerbach's *The Essence of Christianity* caused scandal in the original and in its English translation (made by the celebrated novelist George Eliot). Schleiermacher had argued that our sense of the givenness of the most precious things – one, Romantic, exam-ple might be natural beauty – implied that there was a giver, a God who delighted in giving us good things. Feuerbach argues, simply, that this logic assumes the universe is rational and that we have no reason (unless we already believe in God on some other basis) to assume that this is the case. Therefore, Schleiermacher's argument for faith fails.

Søren Kierkegaard's *The Philosophical Fragments* launches a similar frontal assault on Hegel. Kierkegaard assumes that Hegel teaches some sort of universal access to truth and denies, on that basis, the particularity of Christian revelation. *The Philosophical Fragments* contains the argument that this is meaningless: either we already know all things, or knowledge comes to us as the gift of a Redeemer who chooses to share our station in order to enable us to understand. Kierkegaard thus wants to defend traditional Christian doctrines of revelation against Hegelian assumptions; like Feuerbach, he attacks the popular form of Christianity of his day. Feuerbach, however, does it to destroy any possibility of Christian belief; Kierkegaard does it to re-establish the possibility – necessity, even – of traditional Christian belief.

Notwithstanding these critiques, the 'liberal' tradition of theolo-gical work continued in Germany. One of its greatest products was

Adolf von Harnack, who offered, over many books, a vision of the development of Christianity which assumed that the simple, ethical religion of Jesus had somehow become corrupted by mystical accretions. *What is Christianity?* spells this out in simple and brief terms, and so is a deeply influential text; behind it lie several serious engagements in historical work that von Harnack published.

The 'liberal' Christianity of von Harnack, developed out of Schleiermacher's ideas, was enormously positive about the potential of the human being and of human culture. The upwards development of humanity towards perfection was absolutely axiomatic. As a result, the outbreak – and conduct – of the First World War appeared to some to be a profound challenge to the whole intellectual system. Most famously, the Swiss-German pastor and theologian Karl Barth was sufficiently horrified at the way his former teachers supported militarism that he began to look for a new theological system; he was not the only one, and the school of 'neo-orthodoxy' flourished in the first half of the twentieth century.

Barth was, without question, the greatest mind in this movement, and his massive, uncompleted *Church Dogmatics* remains one of the great summary texts of Christian belief. Many others, however, followed. Dietrich Bonhöffer was closely associated with Barth, particularly in organizing church opposition to the rise of Hitler; whilst Barth was exiled to his native Switzerland, Bonhöffer was executed in a Nazi concentration camp, a martyr for the faith. Several of his writings have remained influential, but, perhaps because of the witness of his life, *The Cost of Discipleship* stands out as our classic text.

Two more 'neo-orthodox' theologians make an appearance: the German New Testament scholar Rudolf Bultmann developed his thought in a different direction, stressing the existential, immediate encounter of Christ with the believer as a way of preserving a living Christianity in the face of biblical criticism. His greatest works may have been his commentaries, but here we have included *New Testament and Mythology*, a programmatic work in which he spells out his ideas. Finally, an American theologian, H. Richard Niebuhr, whose *Christ and Culture* asked hard questions about how the church should relate to the broader culture if it was to be faithful to Christ. The uncritical support of militarism in the First

World War and the cosy assumptions that church and state should support each other were beginning to unravel in serious ways.

From the Reformation down, there had been a radical tradition of Christianity that believed in the separation of church and state, and believed that Christians should be pacifists. John Howard Yoder had his roots in this, Anabaptist, tradition, but succeeded in interpreting it for the wider academy. His classic work, *The Politics of Jesus*, offered a critically informed engagement with the biblical text in order to defend a radical Christian ethic of non-violent resistance to state power. It has been enormously influential.

A different theological development after the Second World War was associated particularly with Yale Divinity School; an interest in Christian practice, the function of narrative in the Bible, and the formulation of Christian belief led to the growth of 'postliberal theology', a movement that is still very influential. From the thinkers and books associated with this school, we have chosen George Lindbeck's *The Nature of Doctrine* as exemplifying the concern with thinking through how theology actually functions in the lives of the churches and reconsidering the nature of the discipline – what we do when we make doctrinal claims.

Roman Catholic theology produced a number of great thinkers, and challenging ideas, in the second half of the twentieth century. Karl Rahner was perhaps the greatest individual theologian; one amongst many significant works, *The Trinity* was hugely influential in sparking the twentieth-century Trinitarian revival. He was also a theological contributor to the Second Vatican Council (1962–1965), which was instrumental in a major renewal of Catholic life and thought. From the conciliar documents, we have selected *Lumen gentium*, the dogmatic constitution on the church, as a representative classic.

The Second Vatican Council was widely understood to be reorientating Catholic theology to be more open and responsive to the particular conditions of the cultures to which the church found itself ministering; in Latin America, this led to a group of theologians asking what Christian theology looked like from the perspective of the poor and oppressed. The answer they developed, known as 'liberation theology', was one of the major theological movements of the late twentieth century. Gustavo Guttierez's *A*

Theology of Liberation was the most careful and complete statement of the methodology of liberation theology.

Many other contextual theologies followed after liberation theology, asking similar questions: how can the gospel be reinterpreted as good news for people in this particular situation or context? Feminist theology, predicated on the demand that the gospel be good news for women, has been the most widespread and lasting of these movements. Rosemary Radford Ruether's *Sexism and God-Talk* is our representative classic text from this tradition; it is one of two or three major books, and we recognize that other authors might have chosen to include Mary Daly's *Beyond God the Father* instead of or in addition to Ruether's volume.

If the story of the last half-century seems fragmented, that is only because we do not yet have the benefit of historical distance: some things that seem important now will no doubt pass into obscurity; thinkers that seem diametrically opposed now will, in a century's time, seem obviously to share the same assumptions and working practices, and to be part of the same tradition. This is true of any lively discipline.

Christian theology remains a vital and fascinating subject, as these classic texts demonstrate. In these pages, we find profound thinkers, leaders who changed the course of history, courageous martyrs who died rather than surrender their convictions, and indeed powerful churchmen who imposed their beliefs on others. Not every figure is a hero, by any means, and it is certainly true that not every idea in these pages is right – many of the texts contradict each other. The texts, however, stand as several monuments to the seriousness and intellectual power of the discipline of Christian theology.

IRENAEUS OF LYONS
AGAINST ALL HERESIES

INTRODUCTION

Irenaeus was probably born around 130, although estimates have varied from 98 to 147. His place of birth is uncertain, but he tells us that, when he was young, he heard the martyr Polycarp (who died in 155/156) teaching in Smyrna, a town on the western coast of modern Turkey. He moved at some point to Lyons in France, and he was there during the persecution of 177. He carried a letter from the church there to Rome, where he evidently had connections. The Bishop of Lyons, Pothinus, died in prison in 177, and Irenaeus was elected his successor. He may have died a martyr in 202/203, but this tradition is uncertain.

Apart from *Against All Heresies* (hereafter *AH*), we have one other work by Irenaeus, a shorter book called *The Demonstration of the Apostolic Preaching*. We know he wrote several other works that have been lost. All his writings can be dated to the last two decades of the second century. Much of his work was controversial, particularly attacking various versions of a movement known as Gnosticism, which got its name from *gnosis*, a Greek word meaning 'knowledge'.

Gnosticism describes a movement, or perhaps a loose collection of movements, that arose in the early Christian centuries. We do not have enough evidence to be sure about what the various groups actually thought or how they were connected. What information we do have often comes from Christian writers criticizing the Gnostics: Their works might not be accurate, and they almost certainly do not offer a fair assessment of the movements.

We can, however, describe what Irenaeus thought he was opposing and leave aside questions of whether he was right or wrong in his accusations. We can also describe how the groups he targeted related to others we know about from other sources. In *AH* Irenaeus targeted a group called the Valentinians, which got its name from a Gnostic teacher of an earlier generation called Valentinus. Irenaeus describes their teaching in detail in Book 1 of *AH*. At the heart of it seems to be a fundamental dualism: matter is evil and opposed to spirit; secret knowledge – 'gnosis' – is the route for the spiritual part of humanity to escape its present imprisonment in a material body.

Irenaeus describes this knowledge, a complex mythology that describes the coming into being of all sorts of spiritual beings. The Valentinians claimed that this mythology was the real, secret truth of the biblical texts, particularly the gospels. For an example, we might take the story in Luke, where Simeon takes Jesus, still a baby, into his arms and says, 'Master, now you are dismissing your servant in peace …' (2:29, NRSV*). Irenaeus says the Valentinians read this as teaching that a spiritual principle called the 'Demiurge' learned that he would be removed by the coming of another spiritual principle called the 'Saviour', and gave thanks to the highest spiritual principle (*AH* 1:8).

Irenaeus' initial aim, then, was to combat the Valentinian reading of Scripture. He is worried that people will be convinced by this so-called 'secret knowledge' and turn away from true Christianity. *AH* is a classic because its author does much more than offer a simple refutation: he devotes one book to describing the Valentinian myth, one to rebutting it, and three books to constructing an account of Christian belief which stresses the goodness of matter and God's near presence with the churches in the world.

SYNOPSIS

As noted above, Book 1 is mostly devoted to describing Valentinian beliefs. It begins with the eternal, stable Pleroma, a complete collection of thirty spiritual principles arranged in male-female pairs. It begins with the (male) Pro-Father and his female partner Thought emitting the Only-Begotten, also called Father, who comes with Truth. From the Only-Begotten and Truth come Logos (male) and Life (female), and so on. The last of these thirty principles is Sophia, who is seized by a desire to commune with the Father, rather than with her own partner. She is restrained by the principle Order, but her misplaced desire was conceived and began to exist itself; the Valentinians call it, or her, 'Achamoth'. Achamoth is cast out of the Pleroma, but is in turn healed of her wrong desires and becomes generative. She gives birth to three substances called 'pneumatic', 'psychic', and 'hylic', respectively. She shaped these substances in order to make an image of the Pleroma as an act of worship.

Achamoth made the Demiurge out of the psychic substance. The Demiurge is the creator of heaven and earth, the one called 'God' in the Old Testament. The Demiurge is ignorant of his own creation by Mother Achamoth, and he is also ignorant of the highest of the three substances she brought forth, the 'pneumatic' or spiritual substance. He makes human beings, unknowingly inserting the pneumatic/spiritual substance into some of their souls.

There are three classes of human beings, corresponding to the three substances that came forth from Achamoth. The lowest, hylic, people are destined only for destruction in the coming fire which will destroy all material things. Psychic people have free will to choose to embrace faith or reject it; those who embrace faith and good works will be united with the Demiurge in the space outside the Pleroma, where Achamoth currently resides. Pneumatic, or spiritual, people will be united with Achamoth and received into the Pleroma. They have no need of faith or good works; their nature is divine and will guarantee their destiny. Irenaeus suggests that the Valentinians identify themselves as the pneumatics and the rest of the church as the psychics. They are the elite, who have no need to obey the church's rules or any other moral code.

Irenaeus' response to this bizarre scheme begins with a claim that the church's faith is united, whereas the beliefs of the Gnostics are endlessly varied (*AH* 1:10–21). The united faith of the church is summed up in the 'Rule of Faith'*, which Irenaeus expounds upon in *AH* 1:22 before offering a genealogy of Valentinian belief. He suggests that Gnosticism can be traced back to Simon Magus, who tried to buy the apostles' power in Acts 8, and then traces the descent of the Valentinians through various heretical groups (*AH* 1:23–31).

In *AH* 2, Irenaeus sets out to refute the Valentinian myth comprehensively. He begins with the suggestion that the God who created the heavens and the earth is a lesser being, indeed, the broken remnants of the misplaced desire of a fallen principle. Irenaeus exalts the majesty of the Creator before offering a series of arguments which essentially attempt to prove that the idea of a 'Pleroma' above the Creator is incoherent. For instance, he argues that if the Pleroma, or one within it, is omnipotent, then the failure of the Creator to make everything good is incomprehensible (a version of the standard argument from evil that has generally been deployed against Christianity).

He then turns to the notion of spiritual principles being 'emitted' from other principles. He claims that the reason for the profusion of spiritual principles is the Valentinians' desire to create distance between the perfection of a highest 'god' and the evil that is the act of creation. Irenaeus claims that this fails, however: if a spiritual principle emits a principle equal in perfection to itself, a series of emissions, however long, cannot solve the problem: if the act of emission introduces imperfection, then the problem is at the start of the chain, not way down at its end (*AH* 2:17).

Next, Irenaeus looks at the ways in which the Valentinians use Scripture, focusing particularly on their use of seemingly incidental numbers in the gospel narratives, which they take to be hidden symbols of their system. This sort of numerology was more popular in antiquity than it is today, and so these arguments, and the fact that Irenaeus takes them seriously, can seem strange to contemporary readers. His point is essentially that the Valentinians are very selective as to which numbers they pick out of the texts; they highlight the ones that can be made to conform to some aspect of their system, and they ignore the rest.

Irenaeus then turns briefly to the Valentinian account of salvation. His basic concern is with the different levels of salvation, which are linked to different substances. Why, he asks, can the various Valentinian gods not save material things? Is this not a clear limitation of their power? This focus on the goodness of matter is central for Irenaeus. As the book closes, he turns to other Gnostic groups, claiming that his refutation of the Valentinians will refute them all. This is because they all imagine a separation between the highest god and the creation, and suggest that the creator of material things was not the highest god (*AH* 2:31).

This focus on the goodness of creation, and on the closeness of God to creation, will be at the heart of Irenaeus' construction of his own account of Christian belief in the final three books. He begins *AH* 3, however, with a discussion of authority. How do we know that the Valentinians are wrong and that the church is right? Irenaeus stresses the authority of Scripture and acknowledges the authority of the tradition passed down by the apostles. There is a problem, however: the Valentinians appeal to the same Bible, and they also appeal to tradition. Irenaeus appeals to the direct line that bishops can trace back to the apostles, citing in particular the case of the Roman church, where Eleutherius, Bishop of Rome in Irenaeus' day, is the twelfth in line from the church's foundation by Peter and Paul (*AH* 3:3). There is a visible succession of doctrine going back to the apostles through the line of bishops.

To a modern reader, this passage can seem very 'Catholic': the orthodoxy of the church depends on an unbroken succession of bishops. Irenaeus may not have meant that, however: his point might be simply that the tradition, and the interpretations of Scripture to which he is appealing can be shown to be in visible continuity with the apostles, and so are to be preferred to other interpretations. A Protestant reader might interpret this passage by suggesting that the fact that the continuity runs through a line of bishops is incidental; it is the continuity in doctrine which actually matters. It is also worth noting that the line of succession sketched by Irenaeus appears inexact in several particulars when compared with other historical sources; he presumably believed it to be accurate, perhaps on the testimony of others, but in fact, simple lines of succession (or even, at times, the existence of a single recognized bishop) are not easily found in the earliest period of the church.

What, then, is the sound doctrine to which Irenaeus holds? There is one God, who is Creator of all. Irenaeus has a doctrine of the Trinity, although it is of course not developed with the precision worked out in the fourth-century debates. Irenaeus notes that

Scripture gives the name 'God' to the Father and to the Son, and similarly with the title 'Lord'. His point is not to understand how Father and Son (and Spirit, although the point is not made explicit here) can be one God, but to refute the multiplicity of deities in the Gnostic systems. So he is more interested in pointing out that 'the gods of the nations' (Ps. 96:5) are not real gods than in confronting the problem that Trinitarian belief raises for monotheism.

Nothing is above God, and God did not need or use any intermediaries in creating the world. Simply, God likes physical stuff, loves it enough to create it. In *AH* 3:16–19, Irenaeus cites the incarnation* as the ultimate truth of this: the Son of God became truly human, took a material, fleshy body to himself; how then can the Valentinians dismiss matter as evil and always separated from God? Elsewhere (e.g. *AH* 4:17) he will appeal to the sacraments on a similar basis: the highest mysteries, the most holy acts, of Christian religion involve washing in water, eating bread, and drinking wine; given this fact, how can we regard material things and processes (washing, eating, drinking) as evil?

In *AH* 4, Irenaeus insists on the unity of the Old Testament and the New Testament, and that the God who creates in Genesis is the same God who sends Jesus to save. This part of *AH* is rich in biblical theology, tracing themes and linkages between the two testaments. Early in the book, he focuses on Jesus' relationship to the Old Testament: he obeyed the law, cited its teaching as authoritative, and so on. He then turns to look at the Old Testament prophecies in order to show how they are fulfilled in Jesus. The two testaments are intimately bound together.

AH 5 is about salvation. Its central message is that salvation is physical: we are not saved from flesh, but our flesh is saved. Again, the polemical intent is clear, but Irenaeus is offering positive teaching to carry his polemic. Since God came in flesh in the incarnation, his intention must have been to redeem our flesh; the Bible clearly teaches the resurrection of the body. Along the way, Irenaeus pauses to consider difficult verses, such as 1 Cor. 15:50, 'flesh and blood cannot inherit the Kingdom', and to discuss the ordering of eschatological events as he looks forward to the final resurrection. Irenaeus also deploys and develops (as he has in passing in the previous two books) his famous idea of 'recapitulation': just as Adam was head of the human race, and led the whole race into ruin through his fall, so Christ becomes the new head of the human race and leads all who are 'in him' into paradise through his ascent.

CRITICISMS

We have known more than one student who, having heard of Irenaeus, has opened *AH* eagerly at Book 1 only to get totally discouraged somewhere around the account of the first Ogdoad emitting a new spiritual principle to complete the Pleroma! *AH* is highly contextual, and the context is (at first sight) utterly foreign to anything a twenty-first-century reader might encounter. Further, on many themes – such as the Trinity – Irenaeus witnesses to an early and fascinating, but undeveloped, form of the doctrine; the fourth-century writers give us much fuller and more satisfying accounts. Is *AH*, then, of merely historical interest?

Irenaeus' great points throughout *AH* are the unity of God and the goodness of the material world. These are points of perennial concern for Christian doctrine, and his treatment of them – on the latter point at least – may be unsurpassed. The most famous quotation from the book captures this theme well: 'the glory of God is the human person, fully alive' (*AH* 4:20). Being human, being enfleshed, being physical, is not a tragedy to be escaped from, for Irenaeus; it is the glorious state in which God created us. Fallenness is a problem, of course; death has entered the world, and our bodies tend to decay and dissolve – but Christ's recapitulation has changed all that and given us the promise of bodily resurrection and a future kingdom of human persons fully alive in him for all eternity.

The temptation to spiritualize Christian faith, and so to denigrate the material and bodily, has been constant through Christian history. The pressing ethical problems and issues for theology, even at the beginning of the twenty-first century, seem to cluster around the question of the goodness of creation: global warming and other issues of environmental concern; trade, justice, and economic development; and even human sexuality – these cannot be considered without a robust and serious account of the goodness of creation. In strange style, from the second century, Irenaeus still speaks.

2

ORIGEN OF ALEXANDRIA
ON FIRST PRINCIPLES

INTRODUCTION

Origen (c. 185–c. 254) was possibly the greatest thinker of the early period of the Christian church. He wrote an enormous amount and was a huge influence on those who came after him. However, there were always those who doubted his orthodoxy – and those who passionately defended it. His lasting reputation is as a brilliant and passionate, but difficult and questionable, thinker.

Origen was born and raised in Alexandria, one of the great intellectual centres of the ancient world, with a particularly vibrant tradition of Platonic philosophy*. He was born into a Christian family and raised in a church that had struggles with Gnosticism*, which intermittently knew persecution, and which upheld an ethically rigorous practice of Christianity focused on celebrating martyrdom as the ultimate demonstration of Christian commitment. All these influences can be seen in Origen: his theology has a distinctly Platonic cast; there are lengthy repudiations of Gnosticism in his work. He also wrote an *Exhortation to Martyrdom* – his father was martyred when he was 17, and his own death was the result, in part, of the torture he suffered in the Decian persecution.

Origen's great work, however, was his commentary on Scripture. He was trained as a teacher of literature, a respected occupation in

Greek culture. He took the methods long used for studying Homer and other Greek authors, and applied them to the biblical texts. These methods began with textual criticism – an important discipline at a time when every copy of a text was handwritten, and so potentially different from every other copy in certain respects. One of Origen's great achievements, the *Hexapla*, was a six-column comparison of the Hebrew Bible with several different Greek translations, which attempted to establish a best Greek text.

In commenting on the Bible, Origen would establish the meaning of the text, considering disputed points at some length, and then engage in application. Alexandria had a tradition of Jewish allegorical readings* of the Hebrew Bible, which had been used in part to harmonize biblical teaching and Greek philosophy; Origen borrowed freely from such reading practices to develop his own distinctive approach to interpreting and applying the Bible. At times this allows him to deal with (what he regards as) obvious difficulties in the biblical accounts: when Jesus is said to be shown all the kingdoms of the world from a high mountain, Origen argues that this is not literally possible and that the reader must be meant to find a figurative or allegorical interpretation. Origen's commentaries were sometimes on a grand scale – Book 1 of his *Commentary on John*, which runs to nearly fifty pages in English translation, covers only the first five words of the gospel!

Origen's biblical commentary was so valued that a patron, Ambrosius, paid for scribes and stenographers to take down his lectures and to copy them out so that many copies might be in circulation as books just one day after Origen had given the lecture. This, of course, spread Origen's fame and perhaps stoked the fires of controversy: whatever he said would rapidly be heard by many, including many who had no opportunity to ask for clarification or to suggest amendment.

Alongside the commentaries, Origen preached homilies on biblical texts read in the context of worship, many of which were transcribed and have survived. He also wrote many occasional works addressing one or another issue that became of interest to him or that he was challenged about. There are two major works to mention, however. First, towards the end of his life, Origen was sent a copy of an attack on Christianity by a Pagan controversialist, Celsus; it was not a new work (Celsus was long dead), but it was being newly discussed and analysed. Origen's response, *Against Celsus*, is the longest single work of his that we have, and so an important witness to his thought; it is also a careful and brilliant negotiation of the differences between Christianity and the traditions of Greek philosophy.

Finally, from earlier in his career, *On First Principles* is the closest text we have to a summary of Origen's theological vision. It was written around 229, and so represents Origen's mature thought. We will summarize the book below. For now, it is important to note the context and the state of the text. Although this work was not cast as controversial, it seems clear that Origen had the need to refute Gnostic ideas in his mind as he wrote it. It is a positive statement of his own beliefs, but it is written with the intention of refuting the Gnostics along the way. The text we have is, unfortunately, incomplete, at least in the original Greek; we do have a complete Latin translation, prepared by Rufinus, which is unfortunately not entirely accurate, as we can see when we compare the Latin to those bits of the Greek we do have.

Origen's reputation suffered as a result of two controversies after his death. In the last years of the fourth century, he was attacked as the real source of the Arian* doctrines that had been the source of so much controversy over that century. Rufinus defended Origen's memory, and in his translation of *On First Principles* clearly softened some of the more challenging or original ideas to make the text more palatable to his contemporaries. In 543, the emperor Justinian revived this charge and ordered the destruction of all copies of Origen's books on the grounds they were heretical and dangerous; the fact that we have no copies of so many of his books – and the problems with the text of *On First Principles* – is a direct result of this action.

SYNOPSIS

The Greek title translated *On First Principles* is a deliberate pun, only inadequately captured in the English translation. 'First principles' could mean 'elementary teachings', or it could mean 'fundamental truths'; Origen intends both meanings. The book will summarize the elementary teachings of Christianity, but it will also explore what lies behind and beneath these elementary teachings, namely, the fundamental truths of theology.

Accordingly, the book begins with an account of the Rule of Faith*, stressing one God, who created all things; Jesus Christ, 'born of the Father before all things'; the Holy Spirit, who is named with the Father and the Son; the existence and life of the soul and the resurrection of the body; the coming judgement and destruction of the present world; the inspiration, and multiple senses, of Scripture; and the existence of both devils and angels.

Origen suggests that the apostles taught these things very clearly because they were necessary to salvation; however, even here we are often merely given assertions. There is space for those who are eager to progress in knowledge of truth to investigate why these things are true, what lies behind them, and how they interrelate. At the same time, the apostles stayed silent on many other matters; amongst other examples, Origen lists whether the Holy Spirit was begotten or not; whether the soul is created at conception or exists earlier; and how and when angels were created. These are areas in which the theologian may legitimately propose answers that are faithful to Scripture.

Origen is very clear that his programme is of the nature of a 'research project': he is proposing ideas which may or may not be right, but which represent his best understandings or thoughts at the time. He is not proposing his more speculative ideas as settled dogma. This is important and is at least a part of the reason for his being misunderstood by later generations, who have often heard a claim that 'it might be a bit like this ...' as a claim that 'this is the truth!'

After the Preface, in which the Rule of Faith is outlined, *On First Principles* is divided into four books. This, however, obscures the real structure, which is based around repeated treatments of a theological narrative that begins with the doctrine of God, moves through Christology* and pneumatology*, addresses the creation and nature of rational creatures, and finally treats the material world. There are two short versions of this narrative, in the Preface and in the last chapter of Book 4 – the end of the whole work. The majority of the book is taken up with two longer versions of the same narrative, one running from the start of Book 1 to the third chapter of Book 2, and the other running from the fourth chapter of Book 2 to the third chapter of Book 4.

The first of these longer treatments is a continuous connected exposition of the various topics, offering a full summary of

Christian doctrine; the second is less connected, offering discussions of a series of important disputed topics, but laid out in the same order as the first narrative. In Origen's day, philosophical treatments of 'physics' – discussions of 'first principles' in the sense of 'fundamental truths' – often adopted a structure like this, with a brief introduction and a brief conclusion, and a central narrative exposition followed by treatments of disputed issues in the same order.

Given this structure, rather than work through the book in sequence, it makes sense to pull together the four repetitions of the narrative and to summarize Origen's thought on each subject raised in turn. His theological narrative begins with God the Father, who is pure spirit, simple, eternal, and immutable. Against the Gnostics, he insists that the God who creates the world and gives the Law in the Old Testament is the same as the one Jesus calls 'Father' in the New Testament. Origen emphasizes strongly the immateriality of God, suggesting that he was concerned to oppose the idea that God has a body of some sort, an idea which may well have been current in Alexandrian Christianity. God is spirit, utterly and completely, or so Origen wanted to insist.

The Son is the Logos*, the divine Wisdom who was with the Father in the creation of all things (Prov. 8). The Son is truly divine, but he is a separate existence from the Father – not just a different mode of existence of the same God. The Son is 'generated'* or begotten* from the Father; generation means the Son shares all the essential characteristics of the Father – like gives birth to like. Origen introduces the idea of 'eternal generation': the Son has his origin from the Father, being 'generated', but this happens in eternity, not at some point in time. This distinguishes the Son from all other beings; it also preserves the immutability of God – at no point in time does God become Father; this is who God eternally is.

The Son is not simple, but plural, and mediates various perfections, not unlike Platonic forms*, to the created order. The Logos provides the world with its rationality, its life, and so on. The Son here is clearly different from, and inferior in perfection to, the Father. Origen affirms the incarnation of the Logos, which he explains as the union of a (perfect, pre-existent – see below) human soul with the Logos, which then implies incarnation when that soul is united with a body.

The Holy Spirit is a third divine existence, subordinate to the Son. The Spirit's work is to mediate truth to believers and to make them holy. In particular, the Spirit inspired the writers of Scripture, enabling them to record the very words intended by God. The Spirit also inspires the readers of Scripture, enabling them to see the deep truths hidden therein. Origen offers an account of reading the Bible towards the end of *On First Principles*, and we will deal with it at the end of this exposition.

After discussing God, the divine triad, Origen turns to rational creatures. Following Plato, Origen believed that rational souls are naturally immortal; God's original creation was the creation of these rational spiritual beings. These beings were given free will, namely, to choose or reject the perfection of God. All but one – which united with the Logos and became the human soul of Jesus Christ – chose to reject God to some degree or another, and so fell from perfection. Those that fell least are now angels; those that fell furthest demons; and between the two are human souls. All these beings remain free and can choose to fall further or to return to God. Origen believed that, eventually, all creatures would return – this is the biblical hope that God will be all in all.

The material creation, and the union of human souls with bodies, is both a punishment for our fall and the means by which we can be brought back to God. The diversity of human stations – some born slaves; some royalty – is both appropriate justice for our various spiritual failures and the perfect medicine to induce us to return to God. We need inducing, however, because we still possess free will. God never coerces us; he always invites and entices us.

The first three chapters of Book 4 contain a discussion of biblical interpretation. The Bible is divinely inspired in every aspect – each word is divinely intended, each thought perfectly crafted. Biblical texts have a literal, surface meaning (which Origen never fails to take seriously – even when commenting on the Song of Songs, he reads the eroticism of the text straightforwardly); more importantly, they have a deeper, spiritual meaning which speaks, always, of Christ and his redemption. The literal sense may contain apparent factual errors (Origen points to the creation story, where 'evening' and 'morning' exist before the sun does); these are invitations to seek the more spiritual sense, which is the true meaning of the Bible.

CRITICISMS

Origen's immediate influence, before the controversies that permanently damaged his name a century or so after his death, was immense. Whilst his biblical interpretation was his most celebrated work, the Trinitarian ideas expressed in *On First Principles* (and elsewhere, especially in his *Commentary on John*) were one of the starting points for the debate that would run through the fourth century and finally issue in the creedal form of the doctrine of the Trinity. Excerpts of his teaching on spirituality were incorporated into the *Philocalia*, a collection of spiritual teachings still highly valued in the Eastern churches.

Nonetheless, Origen has been much criticized; the early condemnations mentioned above focused on his doctrines of creation, particularly the pre-existence of a spiritual creation, and on his teaching that all things, including the demons, would be reconciled to God in the end. Clearly, his doctrine of the Trinity does not accord with later orthodoxy; whilst he can perhaps be forgiven for not anticipating the technical debates and resolutions of the fourth century, his clear teaching that the Son is a lower being than the Father looked difficult even in his own day. His biblical interpretation is often brilliant, but equally often profoundly speculative.

Much of the criticism arguably comes from a misreading of Origen's purpose. He is clear that his theological constructions are speculation, interesting proposals that arise out of his 'research project'; to take them as settled teaching – and to assume that, had Origen been challenged, he would have defended his ideas strongly and not have modified them – might be argued to be a mistake, a failure to understand what he himself said he was doing in *On First Principles*.

That said, Origen's theology clearly offers a system, and it is a system that owes much to the developing Platonic philosophies of his native Alexandria. The early years of Christianity were marked by a need to negotiate the intellectually dominant traditions of Greek philosophy; if Tertullian's angry demand, 'What has Athens to do with Jerusalem?' marks one end of the spectrum of offered responses, stressing the distance between revealed truth in Christianity and the speculations of the philosophers, Origen (in common with other Alexandrian theologians, notably his contemporary, Clement) stressed the continuity that can be found between the two. With the benefit of historical distance, we might accuse him of surrendering too much, particularly on issues such as the Trinity and the goodness of the material creation, but his attempt to make Christianity comprehensible in the context of the best thought of his day remains remarkable.

On First Principles might be the earliest text that deserves the name 'systematic theology' – although Irenaeus'** *Against All Heresies* predates it and is similarly encompassing. Origen is much more self-aware of methodological questions: he offers an account of how the Bible should be read and a sophisticated distinction between dogma that must be believed and theological opinions that may be entertained. His reputation as the greatest theological mind of the pre-Nicene church is well-deserved; *On First Principles* shows him at his theological best.

3

ATHANASIUS
ON THE INCARNATION

Who is Jesus? The question was very important in the early centuries of the church and it still is today. Was Jesus just a man, a good moral teacher, but nothing more? Was he God, who merely appeared as a man, but who was not truly human? Just like many ask the question today, so did many in Athanasius' day – who is Jesus, and what is his relationship to God? Athanasius gives an answer to this question that proves to be foundational to the way the church after him would understand Jesus' identity.

INTRODUCTION

Athanasius, c. 295–373, was Bishop of Alexandria for most of his adult life. Not much is known about his early years, however. As best we can tell, he was born some time between 295 and 298 to wealthy parents. He was born an Egyptian, but he was educated as a Greek. He studied Scripture from an early age and had a classical Greek education; both of these facts profoundly shaped his identity, despite his Egyptian heritage. As a youth, he experienced many of his friends and teachers go off to a martyr's death, and this influenced him greatly. Throughout his life, he had a friendship with St Antony, an important figure in the monastic movement.

After writing *On the Incarnation*, Athanasius quickly rose to pro-minence. He was present at the Council of Nicaea in 325 but in a non-voting role. He was elected to be Bishop of Alexandria in 328. Some contested his election on the grounds that he was not the required age of 30, but these protests were misguided. He died still holding that title in 373. His time as bishop was anything but calm. He was repeatedly exiled and restored as emperors changed power and sometimes just changed their minds, switching between being sympathetic to his theological positions and being opposed to them. During this time of political and theological strife, the church swung between the Nicene faith* and Arianism*. During this time of difficulty and turmoil, Athanasius displayed political shrewdness as a bishop.

On the Incarnation is the second of two related works, the first being *Contra Gentiles* (*Against the Heathen*). Both were written to a man called Macarius, a friend and recent convert. Both are apolo-getic works, defending the Christian faith by showing that it is not irrational. In *Contra Gentiles*, Athanasius argues against the idols and Paganism of his day and explains how it is possible for the human soul to know God. In *On the Incarnation*, he puts forth the content of the Christian faith as he learned it. Yet he knew this was not a complete work – it was instead designed to be an entry point to lead the reader to study more.

The English translation divides *On the Incarnation* into nine chapters. Chapter 1 discusses creation and the fall. Chapters 2 and 3 address the problem the fall raises for God and the solution to that problem: the incarnation. Chapter 4 deals with the death of Christ, Chapter 5 his resurrection. Chapters 6 through 8 answer objections from the Jews (Chapter 6) and from the gentiles (Chapters 7 and 8). Finally, Chapter 9 concludes his discussion by briefly mentioning the second coming of Christ. Following the plotline of Scripture, Athanasius moves from creation to problem to solution. He does this showing that Christ was not an afterthought, but the one who holds all of these things together.

In *On the Incarnation*, Athanasius is trying to show that the incarnation is consistent with who God is and with how God relates to his creation, even from the very beginning. It is through God's goodness that the incarnation happens; the incarnation hap-pens in order to prevent creation – and particularly mankind – from amounting to a waste. The incarnation is not a new principle, because God was always present to creation and was always lovingly in control over it. *On the Incarnation* is designed to show the consistency between the doctrines of creation, the incarnation, and God.

Athanasius' understanding of the relationship between God and creation is a major theme in his whole theology, and is perhaps the heart of it. It explains his view of history and his view of ontology*, as well as his view of man, of Christ, and of salvation. God is very much involved in the world, in creation, and in the incarnation. Yet God does not stop being 'wholly other,' transcendent* from creation. This relationship between God and the world is one that is seen through the Word – the Word (that is, the Son) is in the world, but it is still fully God and thus is other than the world. Nearness and transcendence are not opposites, and in the incarnation, God is both.

Athanasius is often only remembered for his role in the Arian* controversy (and for the creed which bears his name, but which was not written by him). His battle with Arianism was fierce, and *On the Incarnation* shows his thinking on the subject, so a brief explanation is in order. Arianism is the theological teaching that God the Son did not exist eternally with the Father. Instead, he was created, but he did share in the divine nature. Since the Son was created, he must be distinct from God the Father. The Son is a second-order divine being, who does not participate in the essence of the Father. In this view, even before the incarnation Christ was a created being – 'there was a time when the Word did not exist,' Arius would say. The Council of Nicaea in 325 condemned Arianism and insisted that the Father and the Son are 'of one being.' (See Chapter 5, Creeds and Conciliar Documents, for more details.) Also, Athanasius' Christology was very influential on the statement on the person of Christ from the Council of Chalcedon in 451: Christ is one person with two natures, making him fully human and fully divine.

On the Incarnation was likely written before the Arian controversy, or at least before the controversy became very heated (dates range from 318 to the 350s). Nonetheless, it demonstrates the framework which Athanasius would use in his famous theological battle. He relates Jesus and God so closely that he even repeatedly referred to him as 'God the Word'. For Athanasius, there was no hint that the Son was anything but fully God. The Son was not created, but, in fact, the Son was the one through whom creation was brought into existence. If the Word is not fully God, as Arius said, then he could not save us and could not give us knowledge of God.

SYNOPSIS

On the Incarnation starts with creation, emphasizing that the redemption and renewal of creation will come through the same one who made it in the beginning: the Word, Jesus Christ. Thus the Christian doctrines of creation and salvation are not inconsistent. Athanasius argues against the wrong ideas of creation that humans have concocted. He denies that the universe just came into existence automatically, because a mindless act of creation would not have the variety and order we see in our world. He denies that the universe was made out of stuff that already existed, because then God would just be a craftsman like a carpenter and not a creator. He also insists that Scripture requires that God be the creator, and not someone else. In place of these misguided ideas, Athanasius says that God creates out of nothing, through Christ. Further, God gave mankind a special place in the world, making these creatures in the image of God. In grace, God breathed his own life into them. God gave humans the option of obeying him and staying in paradise to live in eternal happiness or turning astray from God and dying. Since mankind has a free will that could rebel and since that is just what happened, God has a problem. God's original plan for humans was in danger of being lost. Mankind was horribly corrupted and was now completely under the control of death. God made them out of nothing into something; now they were on the path of returning to nothing because of their corruption.

At this point, God has a dilemma. What was happening to mankind was not fitting for a race that God created and blessed so richly. God's plan for mankind could not amount to a failure: God knows better than to start a doomed project, and his goodness means that he will not just scrap the whole thing. No, that is not who God is. Yet God cannot go back on his word and take away the penalty of death for sin. So what was God to do? God could ask men to repent, but repenting alone would only stop sin from continuing. It would not remove the penalty of death for previous sinning and would not remove the corruption that came upon the entire race. No, something more was needed to salvage the human race from ruin.

This 'something more' is the incarnation. The Word made everything out of nothing. Now he would remove the corruption of the human race, saving it from going back to nothing and restoring it to what God had designed it to be. Out of love and pity, the one who created the world and who holds it together would enter the world in a new way, in a human body. Since he took a human body like ours, it could die; He gave his body over to death so that in his death all might die and be delivered from the power of death. Athanasius gives an illustration: when a king visits a city, he stays in one house, but the whole city benefits from his presence. Likewise, the Word takes on one human body, and all of humanity is saved. The Word, perfect and incorruptible, died in the body in exchange for us all so that we might have our corruption removed. This is the *why* of the incarnation.

This is the basic *why* of the incarnation, but Athanasius gives an additional and supporting reason for the incarnation: because mankind should know God. God created them to do so, making them in the image of the Word so that through him they might know the Father. But in turning away from God, they lost their understanding of God and turned to made-up idols. They gave these idols the worship and honour they should give only to God. They worshipped other men, they bowed down to evil spirits, and they lost the knowledge of God. Not only did God make man in his image so that man could know him, but God can be known through the works of creation. Further, despite their sin and corruption, God gave them the Law and sent them prophets. So even if they did not know God through his image or through creation, they had the Law and other men as messengers. God sent these ways of knowing to sinful men in his goodness and love, but men ignored them.

So again, what was God to do? If he let men continue on in their ignorance and worshipping of idols, he would be like a king who ignores the lands that he has conquered: those lands get taken over by other rulers. God could never allow such a thing! He, being God, must restore mankind to a position where they would know him again. How could he do this? Not by something a human might do, because humans are just *made* in his image. Not by something angels might do, for they are not in his image. Only the image of the Father himself, the Word of God, could restore man, who was made in that image. Only by the incarnation, where he would defeat death and corruption, could men know God again.

Athanasius answers a tricky question about the incarnation. How is the Word everywhere, holding all things together, and also located in the flesh at a particular place and time? Athanasius says that he is present to all of creation, but not contained by it; his being is still distinct from it. In the same way, the Word gives life to his human body, but is not contained by it. His body was not a limitation, but rather an instrument. He was at the same time in it and in all things because he solely exists in the Father. This is the wonder of the incarnation: that at the same time he was living a human life as man, holding all things together as the Word, and was in unbroken union with his Father as the Son. Athanasius says that his incarnation did not change him in any way. He was united with his body in such a way that he was *as a man* eating and drinking and casting out demons and healing people and everything else, but at the same time *as the Word* was holding all things together. As a man, the Word was doing all these signs and wonders to restore mankind to knowledge of the Father.

Athanasius next turns to the very centre of the Christian faith: the death of Christ. God became incarnate to remove man's corruption and restore to the race eternal life and the knowledge of God. To accomplish this, death was necessary. He died in the place of all so that mankind could be lifted from the debt of death. By proving victorious over death, he secured our defeat over it. The body of the Word, because it was *his* body, was free of corruption and was not liable to death. In this way, his death could be the death of all, paying the debt of all. This means that believers no longer die as a penalty for sin, but die in anticipation of a better resurrection. Our death has no sting because Christ took on the full sting of death in our place.

He then turns to the next step in the story: the resurrection. Because of the resurrection, believers no longer fear death, something important to Athanasius, as he witnessed so many martyrs in his early years. Christ's resurrection secures our resurrection, and because of this, believers do not fear death, but prepare themselves to die for the faith. This demonstrates that death has been defeated. Further, the truth of Christ's resurrection is shown in his current influence in the world. Athanasius says that even now Christ is working to bring people to faith and to obey him. If he were dead, how could he be currently working in people's lives in this way?

In several different places, Athanasius explains the reason for certain details of the life and death of Christ. Why did he live for thirty-three years and why did he have a three-year public ministry? Why not die in private, instead of the shameful and public death on the cross? Why was he sentenced to death for crimes he did not commit? First, Athanasius argues that, because wicked men were limited only to understanding things they could see and touch, Christ came in the body not just for a few moments but for many years. He did many things publicly, for all to see. Second, Jesus died a death that was inflicted upon him, not from, say, an illness as he was lying in his bed. The manner of his death shows that it was different, not one that came from natural corruption, but one he freely chose in order to accomplish victory and to prepare for the resurrection. A public and indisputable death was required to ensure that we would believe he was actually dead and prove he was resurrected. By choosing the worst and most severe kind of death, with all its shame and dishonour, he showed that his power over death was not limited to a pleasant death, but covered even the very worst kind of death. Third, he died on the cross so that he might become a curse, as Paul argues in Galatians. Fourth, he died on the cross with outstretched arms to show his ransom for both Jew on the one hand and gentile on the other. Fifth, he was lifted up in the air to defeat the prince of the power of the air, the devil. Sixth, he was in the grave for three days for good reason. An immediate resurrection would raise questions as to whether he had really died. Three days would give enough time to display his glory in that his body would not have been corrupted by decay. Any longer and people might begin to forget, and doubt whether it was the same body.

In Chapters 6 through 8, Athanasius turns to answering some objections from the Jews and the gentiles, responding to their accusation that the incarnation and the cross are an unfitting thing for God to do. Regarding the Jews, he argues in detail that the Old Testament teaches these things in certain verses and when it is considered as a whole. The prophets – especially Isaiah –, Moses, and the Psalms all foretold Christ's incarnation and death. Regarding the gentiles, his arguments are more philosophical. He appeals to an idea already held by Pagan philosophers – that the Word, or Logos, of God is active in the world. Yet if they are willing to admit this, there is no problem in the Word's activity in the world, including the taking on of a human nature. Others complain that the Word would have taken on a more noble part of creation than mere man, something like stars or fire. Athanasius responds that the Lord did not come to make a display, but to actually heal and save men, who were the ones in creation that sinned. Athanasius thinks that the Pagan world turning from worshipping idols to worshipping Christ is a demonstration that he is the incarnate Word.

In the final chapter, Athanasius concludes with the second coming of Christ, in which he will return in glory to judge the earth, deliver the righteous, and punish the wicked.

CRITICISMS

Perhaps the most serious criticism of *On the Incarnation* comes from Athanasius' treatment of the humanity of Christ. Does his Christology allow for Jesus to be fully human, or did he merely just appear to be human? He speaks about Christ having a human body, and mentions a few times that Christ has a human nature, but he seems to say nothing about Christ having a human mind, will, or soul. Athanasius might be accused of saying that the divine Christ *replaced* the human mind of Jesus, and in that case, how was he fully human? In his later writings, he may have addressed this question in more detail. In places it seems he says that the Word was incarnate with a body and a soul, but even this leaves his meaning unclear. Yet even if he did say this in a few places, the human mind/soul of Jesus does not do much work in his system and seems theologically unimportant to him. However, it is unfair to be overly critical about his ambiguity, working as he was in an historical context before the Council of Chalcedon. The Christian tradition after him demanded more clarity on some of these matters, but we do well to read Athanasius in his own time.

A second criticism is that too little is said about the Holy Spirit in this book. Has Athanasius not given due attention to the Trinity? Well, he does give more attention to the Holy Spirit in later works, and this is perhaps understandable given that this book is about the incarnation.

BASIL OF CAESAREA

ON THE HOLY SPIRIT

INTRODUCTION

Basil of Caesarea, styled 'the Great', was Bishop of Caesarea in what is now Turkey in the middle years of the fourth century. He was deeply involved in the controversies over the doctrine of the Trinity* that were then raging, and led the way towards their final resolution at the Council of Constantinople**. He is often named alongside two fellow bishops, Gregory of Nyssa (who was Basil's younger brother) and Gregory of Nazianzus; the three together are often called 'the Cappadocian Fathers' (all three served in the Roman province of Cappadocia), and they developed together an account of Trinitarian doctrine that was found convincing enough to finally settle the arguments that had consumed the churches through the fourth century.

Basil was the oldest of the three, and he laid the foundations that the other two would build upon. As Basil entered church leadership, the confusing arguments of the first half of the century were coalescing into a simple point: is the Son God just as truly as the Father is God, or not? Part of the problem was an argument which ran something like this: to be God is to have no beginning; but the Son has a beginning ('begotten of the Father'), therefore the Son is different from God. Early in his career, Basil seemed to find this argument convincing (in a letter, *Epistle* 361), and it was being pressed by Basil's key opponent, Eunomius. However, Basil later developed an account in which he distinguished between the divine essence, shared by Father and Son, and the personal existence of Father and Son. The essence of God is uncreated; the life of God is the Father's (eternal) begetting of the Son.

At the heart of this argument was an idea sometimes called 'the doctrine of inseparable operations'. This begins with biblical data: according to New Testament texts, the Son does things, or shares with the Father in the doing of things, which in the Old Testament are unambiguously the work of God. (One example would be the descriptions of the Son's role in the creation of all things in Col. 1:16ff and Heb. 1.) This suggests that the word 'God' is properly used of the Son as well as of the Father, or of the Father and the Son together.

Working from a series of points like this and building on similar arguments made by Athanasius** and Hilary of Poitiers, amongst others, Basil began to claim that to be God was to do the work of God. Father and Son together do the work of God; therefore, Father and Son together are God.

What, however, of the Holy Spirit? Basil certainly wanted to say the Spirit was a third personal existence of God, but this view was challenged by a group called the 'Pneumatomachoi' (Greek for 'those who fight against the Spirit') or the 'Macedonians', after an early leader of the group, Macedonius, Bishop of Constantinople. In response, in 375, Basil wrote his celebrated treatise *On the Holy Spirit*, in which he extended the arguments he had made about the Son to the Spirit.

SYNOPSIS

Basil begins with a suggestion that the problem has come to pastoral prominence in his church as a result of liturgical diversity. Should the doxology end 'glory to the Father with the Son, together with the Holy Spirit' or 'Glory to the Father through the Son in the Holy Spirit' (3)? Basil regards this as a matter of indifference, but others have accused him of introducing new doctrines into the liturgy: the former phrasing asserts the equality of the three persons, the latter a hierarchy, with the Father above the Son and the Spirit. This reminds Basil of his debate with Eunomius (he actually quotes Aetius, Eunomius' teacher), which had turned on the claim that different words name things that are different in nature (4).

Basil's first argument is to look at the use of pronouns in Scripture; there is no biblical ordering, nor are certain terms reserved to certain persons. Then, he rehearses the standard arguments for the deity of the Son before turning to the matter at hand, the status of the Holy Spirit. His claim is blunt and straightforward: 'The Lord has delivered to us a necessary and saving dogma: the Holy Spirit is to be ranked with the Father' (24).

How does he argue this? Throughout, he assumes an important point: the question of rank is a straightforward either/or matter; there are no middle terms. We cannot argue that the Spirit (or the Son) is nearly God or very similar to the Father. As Basil has it, 'either He is a creature, and therefore a slave, or He is above creation and shares the Kingship' (51). For Basil, the gulf between the Creator and the creation is so huge that any gradations of honour in creation are utterly irrelevant, like claiming that standing on a couple of sheets of paper puts you nearer to the moon than your neighbour. The slug and the archangel are creatures, and so slaves; if the Holy Spirit is incomparably the highest and most glorious creature made by God, he is still a creature, and so just a slave. If the Holy Spirit is eternal and shares in the work of creation with Father and Son, He is God, of equal rank with the Father.

With this assumption in place, Basil offers six arguments for ranking the Holy Spirit as the Creator, not a creature. First, according to Scripture the Spirit does the work of God; second, the Spirit is named alongside the Father and the Son, particularly in the baptismal formula of Mt. 28. The third argument is a little more complicated: Basil develops the linkage of Mt. 28 by noticing that sometimes the angels are named alongside the Son; he claims that this is different than the linking of the Spirit to the Father and the Son in that it is passing and occasional, whereas the Spirit is always and inseparably united to the Father and the Son. This is evidence of the divide between creatures and the Creator: 'One does not speak of the Spirit and of angels as if they were equals; the Spirit is the Lord of life and the angels are our helpers, our fellow servants, faithful witnesses of the truth' (29). Fourth, the Spirit gives the divine blessings of salvation, particularly adoption, and only one who is God can cause another to be adopted as a child of God. Fifth, the work of Father, Son, and Spirit is presented as inseparable in Scripture; sixth, the Spirit shares in titles that are given only to God: he is holy, good, called 'Advocate' just as the Son is (Jn 14:16), and so on.

In analysing Basil's various arguments, it is important to notice how significant the defence of the full deity of the Son is: Father, Son, and Spirit are named together in Scripture; if we accept that Father and Son are equal in rank, this act of naming must imply the same to be true of the Spirit. If, however, we do not assume the full deity of the Son, the list could be in rank order, as in 'gold, silver, bronze' at the Olympic Games.

In fact, Basil is happy with a certain sort of rank order: the Father is properly named first, the Son second, and the Spirit third; this relates both to their personal existence – the Son is begotten of the Father; the Spirit proceeds from the Father – and to their roles in the divine work, as we shall see. There must not be any 'rank' in terms of levels of deity, however: the Father is no more truly God than the Son is truly God.

On the divine work, Basil develops and deepens the doctrine of inseparable operations discussed above. The particular work of the Spirit is in making perfect all that has been begun by the Father and carried forward by the Son. Basil offers two fairly lengthy examples: the creation of the angels and the gift of salvation. He discusses the angels in Chapter 38; his crucial point is that holiness properly belongs to the Spirit alone, and if the angels are holy, it is only because they are made holy by the Holy Spirit. To establish this point, he considers the way the triune God works in creation: the Father is the first cause of all created things; the Son creates them; and the Spirit perfects them. The angels, then, are created because the Father wills them to be. The Son brings them into being, and the Spirit perfects them by enabling them to persevere in holiness.

Salvation is discussed similarly in Chapters 39 and 40. Again, the main point is not the inseparability of the operations; rather it is the intimate role of the Spirit in the divine work of salvation. So Basil traces the work of the Spirit in leading, guiding, empowering, and inspiring Old Testament prophets and leaders; then he traces the work of the Spirit in the life of Christ, from his anointing with the

Spirit at his baptism. Jesus is led by the Spirit to face temptation, casts out demons by the power of the Spirit, and bestowed the Holy Spirit on his followers – and so on the whole church (Jn 20:21-23). He begins this list, however, with a reference to the order of Trinitarian operations: salvation is the will of the Father accomplished by the Son – and ends it with an assertion that the final perfection of the saints at the general resurrection will be the work of the Spirit, whose proper work it is to make holy. The 'Father initiates, Son works, Spirit completes' pattern is visible again.

Basil turns from establishing that the Spirit is to be numbered alongside the Father and the Son to giving an account of how we may speak of Father, Son, and Holy Spirit whilst still confessing only one God. He explores the general meaning of collective nouns, noting that they get more specific by a process of division: 'human' is more specific than 'living being'; 'man' more specific than 'human'; 'Peter, James, and John' the most specific. This sort of logic cannot possibly work with God, however, and particularly it cannot be what his opponents want to affirm. If 'Father', 'Son', and 'Spirit' were each particulars of a genus 'God', then two conclusions follow which they would want to deny: first, the Father is less than wholly God (just as Peter's existence does not exhaust humanity), and second, Father, Son, and Spirit would each be equally God, but then there would be three gods (just as Peter, James, and John are three humans).

Basil lists and discards various approaches of this form before insisting that the ineffable divine nature is beyond number. 'We worship God from God,' Basil says, 'confessing the uniqueness of the persons, whilst maintaining the unity of the monarchy' (45). 'Monarchy' here refers to the uniqueness of the divine rule: there is one God in the sense that there is One who reigns over the created order; there is one power and one glory and one majesty of the One who reigns. That One is properly named three times over, however, as Father, Son, and Holy Spirit.

Basil finally returns to the consideration of prepositions with which he started. He points out all the different uses of the words 'in' and 'with', and lists which of them are appropriate (in his view) to the Spirit and which are not. He also lists several writers who have spoken of the Spirit using these words previously in order to demonstrate that his view is not novel. In closing, he claims that there are many teachings – including several liturgical rules – which are not in written Scripture, but have been passed down in unwritten tradition; he also bewails the current confusion in the churches, using a memorable extended parable of a sea battle in the dark.

CRITICISMS

On the Holy Spirit is a brief text, and very much an occasional one. Basil is writing to combat a particular local error, and his arguments are shaped by that purpose, at times addressing very eccentric counter-arguments that, at this distance, seem merely senseless, and ignoring other points. There are arguments that most modern readers will find very unconvincing – perhaps particularly the appeal to an unwritten tradition, originating with the apostles, that defines various liturgical practices as necessary for the life of the church. Appeals to tradition may be made in theology, of course, but we know enough of the historical development of liturgies to find this particular appeal fairly unconvincing.

The text also comes, as the final image of the confused sea battle poignantly illustrates, from a very particular moment in the history of the development of doctrine. The doctrine of the Trinity was far from settled; Basil writes as if the Eunomian debates were over, but in fact they were not. Eunomius would reply to Basil's criticisms at about the time of Basil's death, and Gregory of Nyssa would be left to respond. Questions concerning the status of the Spirit were still very live, as is clear from Basil's text, and the right way to speak of the unity of the three persons without denying their particular existence was still largely to be settled. One – powerful – example in the text is the fact that Basil nowhere says straightforwardly that the Holy Spirit is God – he says it of the Son and insists that the Spirit is of the same rank as the Son, but there is still a hesitancy there.

That said, in this text Basil offers a brief and fairly simple account of the crucial points that would become orthodox Trinitarian doctrine. He insists on the real existence and equal rank of the three persons and on the undivided monarchy and glory of the one God; he also develops and affirms clearly the doctrine of inseparable operations, giving it shape and substance with his account of the one single work being intended by the Father, carried through by the Son, and perfected by the Spirit.

The point missing from the final synthesis that would be enshrined at the Council of Constantinople is a precise definition of the differences between the three persons. This would be the work of Gregory of Nazianzus, on the one hand using the language of 'relation' to describe how Father, Son, and Spirit are differentiated from each other, and on the other specifying that all language applied to God is common to the three persons except the language defining the relationships. Basil was certainly moving in this direction with his powerful insistences that God's glory and majesty are undivided, but the point is not precisely specified in this text as it would be in Gregory of Nazianzus' work.

5

CREEDS AND CONCILIAR DOCUMENTS

INTRODUCTION

The ecumenical creeds and the decrees of the early ecumenical councils of the church are central documents for Christian theology, held to be authoritative by most Christian traditions and referred to, or commented upon, very regularly by later generations of theologians.

There are three creeds (from Latin *credo*, 'I believe') usually called 'ecumenical': the Apostles' Creed, the Nicene Creed, and the Athanasian Creed. Confusingly, none of them were written by the people the titles might suggest. The Apostles' Creed is so-called because of a fourth-century legend that the twelve apostles wrote a creed by contributing one line each; what we call the 'Apostles' Creed' reached its final form around the year 600, probably somewhere in France. It became the standard creed of the Western church, and so became identified with the legendary creed written by the apostles.

In fact, its origins are in the old creed of the Roman church, taught to candidates for baptism and recited by them as part of the service. We can trace a Roman creed in a form fairly similar to the Apostles' Creed back into the third century, at least, although it seems likely that it was one of several creeds used in Rome at that time. The Apostles' Creed in its final form was championed by Charlemagne, the great eighth-century Frankish emperor who united Western Europe for the first time since the collapse of the Roman Empire. His influence ensured its widespread adoption.

The Nicene Creed is not the creed written at the Council of Nicaea (325), which we still have and which is different at several points. The Nicene Creed is more properly known as 'the Nicaeno-Constantinopolitan Creed,' a name which suggests the standard story of its origin: the Council of Constantinople (381) adapted the old creed of Nicaea to bring a final end to the debates of the fourth century.

There are two problems with this story, however: first, the Nicene Creed does not look like an edited version of the creed of Nicaea; and second, the Acts of the Council of Constantinople make no mention of a creed being written there. The creed was read and recited at the Council of Chalcedon (454) and asserted there to be written by the Council of Constantinople; it seems possible that it was written for Constantinople and not needed, but that, at the time of Chalcedon, the Emperor, then living in Constantinople, was keen to have a local creed accepted as one of the central documents of the church.

The Athanasian Creed, finally, has nothing to do with Athanasius**. Instead, its origins are again in Western Europe, probably around 500. It appears to be composed of two earlier documents brought together.

These three creeds are still set in liturgies to be recited regularly (although it is fair to say that the Athanasian Creed has fallen out of use in many places), and are referenced in the foundational documents of many Christian denominations. They may be said to define the basic beliefs of Christianity.

Seven councils are generally regarded as ecumenical, that is, belonging to the whole of the church before it was divided. Of these, the first four are generally acknowledged to be the most important: Nicaea (325); Constantinople (381); Ephesus (431); and Chalcedon (454). At each of these councils, bishops and other leaders from across the Christian world gathered primarily to make doctrinal decisions. They also considered pastoral and administrative issues. Nicaea and Constantinople were concerned doctrinally with controversy over the Trinity*; Ephesus and Chalcedon with Christology*.

The councils, then, are the places where the shapes of central Christian doctrines are defined. In each case, they are defined in opposition to one or another view that had arisen within the church and that was causing controversy. The conciliar documents, then, must be read in this context. That said, they treat central topics of Christian theology, and the errors they are trying to refute might be considered to be perennial: errors that must repeatedly be guarded against. They thus take their place as classic and influential – and, for many Christian traditions, authoritative – documents in Christian theology.

SYNOPSIS

We will work through the various documents in chronological order, as far as that can be determined.

1. THE COUNCIL OF NICAEA (325)

Nicaea was called in response to the Arian* crisis, and it ended with the condemnation of Arius and two others, who were exiled. A creed was written, which asserted that the Father and the Son are homoousios* ('of the same substance') and that in God there is only one hypostasis* (i.e. one actual existence). At the same time, it addressed a schism in the church, settled a question concerning the date of Easter, and passed various rules about how bishops were to be ordained, when it was permissible to kneel to pray in church, and why it was forbidden for people to castrate themselves!

Theologically, Nicaea sought to end the Arian problem by defining the proper relationship between Father and Son. Although Arius' claim concerning the Son having a beginning in time was clearly rejected, no clear account of the relationship of the Father and the Son was offered which could command the assent of the wider church. The language used, indeed, was potentially unhelpful ('homoousios' was not a well-defined word, and its only previous theological use had been by an acknowledged heretic, Paul of Samosata), and so the controversy was not settled. Arius and others soon returned from exile; while the debate had moved on from Arius' own ideas, by the middle of the century, those who stressed the difference between Father and Son were in the ascendency and had the support of successive emperors.

2. THE COUNCIL OF CONSTANTINOPLE (381)

Constantinople was a second attempt to end the Trinitarian controversies. The arguments had moved on, and a creative theological proposal for understanding how Father, Son, and Holy Spirit could be one God had been worked out by three bishops in what is now Turkey: Basil of Caesarea**, Gregory of Nazianzus (who chaired the Council of Constantinople for a time), and Gregory of Nyssa (known collectively as 'the Cappadocian Fathers'). They drew a distinction between 'ousia' ('essence') and 'hypostasis' ('person'/ 'particular existence') and suggested the right way to think about the Trinity is to speak of one divine ousia (echoing Nicaea's 'homoousios' language) but three hypostases: one God exists three times over, so to speak. The only distinctions between the three hypostases are their relationships of origin: Son and Spirit find their origin in the Father in different ways, and that makes the three different existences of the same God.

This was affirmed, along with extensive condemnations of various erroneous Trinitarian ideas, at Constantinople (a Christological heresy* was also condemned). The Council also passed various canons concerning the rights and responsibilities of bishops, particularly affirming that the Bishop of Constantinople is second in rank to the Bishop of Rome 'since Constantinople is the new Rome' (Canon 3).

3. THE NICENE (NICAENO-CONSTANTINOPOLITAN) CREED (381?)

The Nicene Creed has four sections, addressing belief in Father, Son, Spirit, and the church. In the first section, God the Father is asserted to be 'almighty' and the creator of all things. The longest section – over half the creed – concerns belief in God the Son. It may be divided into two parts: a series of phrases insisting on the shared deity of Father and Son ('God of God, Light of Light ... of one essence with the Father') and an account of the incarnation, passion, resurrection, and future return of Christ. The Holy Spirit is asserted to be the 'giver of life' who proceeds from the Father; the Spirit is equally worshipped, and so equally divine.

The fourth section might be seen as a continuation of the third: the life of the church is the work of the Spirit. The wording of the creed, however, suggests a distinct fourth clause, albeit set apart from the first three. The church is 'one, holy, catholic, and apostolic'; there is one baptism, 'for the remission of sins', and the creed ends with the people reciting it looking forward to the resurrection of the dead and eternal life.

The Western, Latin version of the creed differs from the Eastern, Greek version in two significant ways. First, it is singular, not plural: it asserts 'I believe' not 'we believe'. Second, it asserts that the Holy Spirit 'proceeds from the Father and the Son', whereas the Eastern version teaches procession 'from the Father'. The addition of 'and the Son' (in Latin, '*filioque*', so often known as 'the filioque clause') became common fairly early in areas of the West; its insertion into the formal Eucharistic liturgy of the Roman church in 1014 was one of the factors that led to the 'great schism' between the Roman Catholic and Eastern Orthodox Churches in 1054.

4. THE COUNCIL OF EPHESUS (431)

Constantinople essentially settled the Trinitarian question; the next area of controversy was Christological: having found an adequate way of speaking of Father, Son, and Spirit as one God, the question becomes, how can we speak of Jesus Christ as both truly God and truly human? The origins of the Council are in a dispute between Cyril, Patriarch of Alexandria, and Nestorius, Patriarch of Constantinople. Nestorius had objected to a priest calling the Virgin Mary 'the Mother of God', suggesting instead 'Mother of Christ', since God cannot have a mother; this enraged Cyril.

Behind the immediate debate was a history of different approaches to the question of how best to speak of the union of deity and humanity in the incarnation. Cyril belonged to a tradition which placed great emphasis on the unity of the mediator, and Nestorius belonged to a tradition which stressed the need to maintain the distinction between deity and humanity. Nestorius thought that speaking of the 'mother of God' was wrong: Mary gave birth to the human person that was united with God the Son in the incarnation; Cyril responded that denying that the one Mary bore is properly called 'God' is denying the incarnation itself. Equally, Cyril wanted to speak of one nature ('phusis') of the incarnate one to emphasize unity, but Nestorius thought that this was unacceptable: the divine nature and the human nature each had to remain whole and unmixed.

The Council supported Cyril's position and condemned Nestorius. As with Nicaea, however, the decision was not adequate to end the controversy. This was partly because an opposing council had been convened, and so there was uncertainty over which truly represented the mind of the church, but it was mostly, as at Nicaea, because the Council was clear about what it opposed, but could offer no coherent account of how to think rightly about the union of divine and human in the incarnation. Nestorius' way was not the right answer, but what was the right answer was left undetermined. In particular, Cyril's language of 'one nature' was difficult, and Cyril himself soon stopped using it, at least in formal theological declarations.

5. THE COUNCIL OF CHALCEDON (454)

Others remained committed to 'one nature' language, however, and a new dispute soon arose, centred on a monk named Eutyches. Eutyches pushed the old 'one nature' language and tried to explain it. He proposed that in the event of incarnation the divine nature and the human nature fused and became one new nature. To some, this sounded like he was teaching that Jesus was neither truly human nor truly divine, but some third sort of thing, hovering between humanity and deity. The dispute escalated, and another council was called to settle it.

Chalcedon tried to find a way of talking about the incarnation that avoided the errors of both Eutyches and Nestorius. The Council re-affirmed the creeds of Nicaea and Constantinople, affirmed three letters of Cyril (who had since died) as being adequate expressions of orthodoxy, and also affirmed a short book by Pope Leo, written in response to (what he had heard of) Eutyches, called the *Tome*.

The Council's definition proposes a doctrine known as 'hypostatic union'. Hypostasis means, as it did at Constantinople, something like 'particular existence'; the unity of the mediator is ensured by there being only one being, one particular existence, one hypostasis. However, that one hypostasis instantiates two natures, divine and human, united in his existence. The two natures are not mixed or mingled, but they cannot be separated, since there is only one mediator.

6. THE ATHANASIAN CREED

The Athanasian Creed is composed of two parts, one asserting the doctrine of the Trinity and one asserting the truth of the incarnation. The language in both cases is careful and technical, and represents the developed doctrine of the councils. It is poetic in form, probably composed to be sung or chanted in worship. It seemingly delights in stressing the apparent logical tensions of the received faith: '... the Father is almighty, the Son is almighty, the Spirit is almighty – and yet they are not three almighty beings, but one almighty being ...'; 'Just as we are compelled by Christian truth to acknowledge each person by himself to be God and Lord, so we are forbidden by the catholic religion to say that there are three Gods or three Lords'. One notable feature of the Creed is the so-called 'damnatory clauses': four times the creed asserts that anyone who does not believe what it teaches cannot attain salvation.

7. THE APOSTLES' CREED

The Apostles' Creed is the shortest, and least controversial, of the documents we are looking at here, which is no doubt due to its origins in an ancient baptismal creed, rather than in response to a particular controversy. Like the Nicene Creed, it first asserts belief in God the Father as omnipotent creator and then in Jesus Christ, affirming the incarnation and a simple narrative of suffering, death, descent into hell, resurrection, and coming judgement. Belief in the Holy Spirit is simply asserted, and then we have the church, the communion of saints, the forgiveness of sins, bodily resurrection, and coming eternal life.

CRITICISMS

1. THE CONCILIAR DOCUMENTS

It is important to read the canons and decrees of the various councils in their full context and to realize that the famous theological definitions are not great moments of definition, but one part of the church's continuing attempt to regulate its own life. Speaking rightly about the Trinity and ordaining bishops properly are treated alongside each other as both being problems that threatened the peace of the church. The conciliar decrees are, first, local and time-bound responses to particular difficulties. That they have also been received by many churches as definitive and irreversible decisions concerning true doctrine should not lead us to forget the first point.

We might ask whether the councils adequately solved the questions of Trinity and Christology; the question is a fair one, and there is a body of scholarship today that would express doubts, particularly concerning the Chalcedonian definition. Against that, we might set the very wide, and lasting, agreement that these answers are good ones; this history should lead us to conclude at least that, even if somehow wrong, the conciliar doctrines are extremely plausible.

More serious, perhaps, is the criticism that the conciliar decisions are framed using concepts that no longer have any meaning. We do not typically analyse problems in terms of 'essence', 'particular existence', 'nature', and the like. Schleiermacher** claimed that all the old doctrines needed translating into new concepts, and the old concepts then discarded; the claim might not be accepted, but it points towards a real issue which any reader of the documents will be faced with.

2. THE APOSTLES' AND NICENE CREEDS

The Apostles' and Nicene Creeds are the most familiar documents we consider in this book, being recited daily or weekly in Christian worship around the world to this day. We have noted the dispute over the filioque clause; in recent decades, there have been creative ecumenical proposals to heal this ancient breach. Beyond this point, there can be little doubt that the two creeds have functioned successfully for centuries as summaries of Christian belief and that they continue to do so today.

That said, there are some serious lines of criticism, mostly concerning what is included and what is left unstated. On the first, the question of the virgin birth (asserted by both creeds) has been raised – not, necessarily, with the suggestion that it is wrong, that Jesus was not born of a virgin, but with the suggestion that the question is not as important as the creed makes it: true or not, is it really so central a matter of faith? The line 'he [Jesus] descended into hell' in the Apostles' Creed is more controversial: even its meaning is uncertain (the medieval church tended to picture a 'harrowing of hell', in which Jesus between his death and resurrection entered hell and rescued the souls of the righteous Israelites. Calvin**, by contrast, taught that the phrase meant that Jesus suffered all the pains of hell on the cross).

The most significant recent line of criticism, however, has been what has been left out. Both creeds move directly from Jesus' birth to his suffering and death, with no mention at all of the earthly ministry of Jesus; is this really adequate?

3. THE ATHANASIAN CREED

The Athanasian Creed is passing out of fashion; officially, it is to be recited on the four great holy days in the Western liturgy, but it is fair to say that most churches choose not to. The creed's delight in apparent paradox, and its length and complexity, make it an unattractive document; the doctrine it summarizes is a developed Western form (it includes the filioque, for example) that would not be found palatable in the Eastern churches, and so its claim to be 'ecumenical' must be regarded as dubious. Most seriously, the damnatory clauses seem impossibly strict, given the level of abstractness of the doctrine presented in the creed: will all who do not believe precisely this really be excluded from salvation?

6

AUGUSTINE OF HIPPO
ON THE TRINITY

INTRODUCTION

Augustine is the greatest theologian of the first millennium of the church's history, perhaps the greatest of all history. His influence on almost every area of theology in the Western, Latin-speaking church is incalculable. The Reformation*, to take only one example, has been described as the triumph of Augustine's doctrine of grace over Augustine's doctrine of the church. Such sound bites oversimplify, but they also indicate something of his influence. Had we not taken the decision to restrict ourselves to one work by any author, we might have reasonably treated four, perhaps five, of Augustine's works as amongst the thirty greatest classics of Christian theology.

Augustine was born in 354 in Tagaste, a town in North Africa near what is now the border between Tunisia and Algeria. His mother Monica was Christian and raised him in the faith. However – on his own account in an autobiographical work, the *Confessions* – he wandered from faith during his twenties, led by self-interest (he was forging an impressive career as a teacher of rhetoric, a career which took him to the heart of the Empire in Rome and then Milan) and by a fascination with a non-Christian sect called the 'Manichees'. Augustine came under the influence of Ambrose, the great Bishop of Milan, and received baptism from him in 387. He returned to Tagaste, but a few years later was ordained in Hippo in 391, becoming Bishop of Hippo remarkably quickly. He served as Bishop until his death in 430.

Augustine had begun writing Christian theology almost as soon as he was converted, and his output was voluminous by any standard. He wrote, and published, sermons; much of his writing was occasional, responding to the queries of others in letters or addressing doctrinal problems that threatened the diocese (i.e. the Donatist controversy) or that at least seemed to in Augustine's mind (i.e. the Pelagian controversy).

His anti-Pelagian writings, collected, deserve the status of classic, but he left three less controversial works which are generally considered the peak of his output. His *Confessions* invented the genre of spiritual autobiography, narrating his own early life and conversion as a lesson in God's saving grace. His *City of God*, written 413–426, is a masterful account of God's providence at work in the world, occasioned by the accusation that Rome's abandoning of its old gods had led to the city being invaded and sacked by the Goths. *On the Trinity* (*Trin.*) was written 399–419.

Augustine knew all about the arguments that had been raging in the Eastern church over the Trinity and about the settlement reached at Constantinople**. Much of the argument had concerned the interpretation of biblical texts: there were texts that seemed to support the full equality of the Father and the Son ('I and the Father are one') and texts which seemed to suggest that the Son is subordinate to the Father ('The Father is greater than I'). Much of the intellectual effort of fourth-century Trinitarianism was an attempt to find ways of speaking about Father and Son which allowed a greater and greater set of texts to be understood fairly naturally. Although he knew the debate was largely settled, Augustine thought he had some better exegetical positions to offer, and so began to write on the Trinity. His aim, initially, was to help believers to understand how the church's doctrine made sense of the texts. As the book is written, however, this expands into a more devotional aim to encourage spiritual growth by contemplation of the Trinity.

Towards the end of his life, Augustine wrote an interesting book called *Reconsiderations*, in which he surveyed his writing career and

noted places where he was unhappy with what he had said, either
because he had changed his mind (rarely!) or because readers had
convinced him that this phrase or that was difficult or obscure.
When he turns to *Trin.*, he notes that he had been writing the
book on-and-off for many years, but that someone stole and started
circulating an early and partial draft, which encouraged him to
finish it quickly so as to get the 'authorized version' out.

SYNOPSIS

Trin. is divided into fifteen books. The first four deal with exegetical questions; Books 5–7 address the proper language to be used
when talking about God the Holy Trinity; and the final eight
books are an extended meditation on a series of possible created
analogies of the Trinity.

Book 1 begins with Augustine stressing that he is seeking to
explore the church's faith, not question it. He suggests that it is
necessary to believe in order to understand, and so *Trin.* will be an
exercise in trying to understand what he has already confessed to
believing. His exposition of the Trinity begins with one of his main
points: divine works in creation are inseparably the work of Father,
Son, and Spirit together. This teaching has become a problem for
some, who hear that the Spirit (alone?) descended in tongues of fire
or that the Son became incarnate. Again, he notes that some
struggle with the question of the origin of the Spirit: how is
procession* different from generation*?

In response, Augustine states the received doctrine and then turns
to some of his exegetical moves. The first set of texts he looks at
concern statements that apparently show the Son to be subordinate
to the Father. Augustine borrows a distinction, from Hilary of
Poitiers, that some texts speak of the Son 'in the form of God',
whereas others speak of him 'in the form of a servant' (the phrasing
is borrowed from Phil. 2, of course). The subordinationist texts,
then, do not teach that the Son is beneath the Father, but that the
incarnate Son relates to the Father as both the divine Son, who is
equal to the Father in every way, and a human being, who relates
to the Father as a creature to its creator.

Books 2, 3, and 4 address the question of sending: Augustine
appears to have encountered a claim that the one who is sent by

another is necessarily lower in honour or status than the one who sends. Given the gospel history, that the Father sends the Son and that the Father and Son send the Spirit, this demonstrates a hierarchy and lack of equality in the Trinity.

Augustine's response is first to complicate the claim: the Son and the Spirit are both omnipresent, so to talk of their being 'sent' is difficult: they are, necessarily, 'sent' to where they already are. What can 'sending' mean in this case? Augustine suggests that the answer is bodily appearance: the sending of the Son is the incarnation, and the sending of the Spirit is the appearance of the Spirit as a dove at the baptism of Jesus and as tongues of fire at the Pentecost.

The identification of the sending of the Son with the event of incarnation is important: Bible (Lk. 1:35) and Creed** both assert the involvement of the Spirit in the incarnation, so Augustine can claim that, just as the Spirit is sent by Father and Son, so the Son is sent by Father and Spirit. If this is true, then the original claim, that one who is sent is necessarily lower in rank than the one doing the sending, must be false: if it were true, the Son would be below the Spirit, and the Spirit would also be below the Son, which is absurd.

This argument is a fine example of the ways in which the exegetical* debates over the Trinity in the fourth century proceeded. Texts are inevitably interpreted according to existing presuppositions, and the arguments were less to do with what particular texts meant than with what assumptions allowed the greatest number of texts to be understood. Augustine addresses head on a claim that sending establishes a hierarchy; his disproof of this claim is to show that, if it is accepted, the biblical texts cannot be read in a coherent way. If the claim is true, the Bible cannot be true, so the claim must be false.

Book 5 turns to another standard fourth-century argument concerning the Trinity. Greek philosophy worked with categories of 'substance' (what a thing is) and 'accidents' (the properties attached to a thing that are not necessary to it being what it is). So, I am sitting at a wooden desk; its substance is its 'deskness' so to speak; that it happens to be made of wood is an accident: it could still be a desk and be made of metal, for example.

This sort of analysis was standard, but it raised a problem for the doctrine of the Trinity: for various reasons, all sides agreed that there is nothing accidental in God. If this is true, the difference between Father and Son must, apparently, be a difference of substance, and so the standard orthodox claim, made at Nicaea** and confirmed at Constantinople**, that Father, Son, and Spirit are 'homoousios' (of the same substance) cannot be true.

There were two standard Greek responses to this, which Augustine is well aware of. One of them, however, is not very helpful for him: the Greek distinction between 'ousia' ('substance') and 'hypostasis' ('particular existence') did not translate well into Latin (where the traditional language had been 'substance' and 'person') and had problems anyway because it seemed to make God one example of a larger class ('substances'), which can never be true (because then the class would be greater than God, which is impossible). The other response he finds more helpful: Gregory of Nazianzus had suggested that the distinction between Father and Son was not substantial or accidental, but relational. Augustine devotes a substantial portion of Book 5 to working through the logic of this and to arguing that, philosophically, it is a robust and biblically interesting suggestion. On the one hand, it is possible to speak of three existences of one God differentiated by relationships; on the other, many of the biblical names for the three persons are in fact relational names: most obviously, 'Father' and 'Son'. (He has more trouble with 'Holy Spirit,' but suggests that the Spirit is called 'Gift' in Scripture, and this is a relational term.)

Books 6 and 7 look at another standard line of argument in the fourth-century tradition, which Augustine approaches through a biblical text, 1 Cor. 1:24, which speaks of the Son as 'the power of God and the wisdom of God'. Texts like this had been embraced early on in the Trinitarian debates as proof of the eternity of the Son: God is never without power/wisdom, so God is never without the Son. Augustine accepts the conclusion, of course, but finds the argument troubling: it seems to suggest that the Father is not 'wisdom' and, indeed, that the Son is not God.

Augustine's response is first to insist that all divine titles, except the personal names (Father, Son, and Holy Spirit), properly name all three persons or, better still, name the deity which the three persons are. He points to another strand of the fourth-century argument, which found its way into the Nicene Creed**, language of 'God from God, light from light': Father and Son (and Spirit) alike are 'light' – and indeed 'power', 'wisdom', and every other name. How, then, to read a text like 1 Cor. 1:24? Augustine suggests that Scripture is in the habit of ascribing certain titles that properly belong inseparably to the Trinity to the Son or the Spirit in order to emphasize the unity of the Son and the Spirit with the Father. Paul's point in 1 Cor. 1 is to highlight the fact that the Son is only able to save us because he possesses the fullness of deity, just as the Father does.

Books 8–15 mark a shift in approach. Augustine begins with the biblical claim that human beings are made 'in the image of God' (Gen. 1:26); on this basis, Augustine suggests that we ought to be able to discern some sort of echo of the Trinitarian life in humanity. Where might we look? Augustine begins with the claim, 'God is love': in the experience of human love, we find one who loves, one who is loved, and the love they share. However, this is not a good image of God: God's love is supremely self-love; this seems to leave us with only two terms, however: the lover and the love.

Augustine invites us to consider more closely what is going on here: the mind can only love itself if it knows itself, so that we might think of the mind, its self-knowledge, and its love for itself as a Trinitarian image. Through Books 9–11, he offers a developing series of such triads, which differ and develop in ways that are perhaps of more interest to the student of ancient psychology than to the theologian.

In Book 12, Augustine introduces a further reflection: the image of God in humanity was defaced by the fall*, and this needs to be taken into account. Through Books 12–14, he offers an extended, and somewhat allegorical, reading of Genesis 3 to describe and explore the defacement of the image. He then turns to redemption: God restores the image in us through Christ and through the work of the Spirit. Augustine believes that we are renewed through the practice of contemplation of God in prayer, and so suggests that we should think of the image of God within us as more like the image in a mirror – there when we look, but disappearing when we turn away – than the image of a painting.

The last book might be read as a confession of failure, but is perhaps better read as a sober awareness of limits. Augustine acknowledges that there will always be more dissimilarity than similarity between God and creatures, but he hopes that, by offering plausible, if limited, analogies, some may have been helped to imagine how the doctrine of the Trinity might be believable.

CRITICISMS

There has been a fashion recently to read Augustine as offering a fundamentally different account of the Trinity than the fourth-century Greek theologians. On this account, the Greeks began by asking how three divine persons might be one and found the answer in an account of unifying personal relations. Augustine, by contrast, began by wondering how one divine being could be named three times over and came up with an answer that depended on subtle philosophical distinctions. This criticism seems to us to be fundamentally misdirected, but it is common enough that it needs to be noted.

As noted above, Augustine's long digression into different possible psychological images for the Trinity is not the most helpful or accessible part of the book for a modern reader; the general point about seeking images for the Trinity in human life is a good one, but the development − however helpful it may have been at the time − seems now opaque and laboured.

These things said, *Trin.* is unquestionably a masterpiece. Much of the problem with reading it (and perhaps the reason for mis-understandings such as the one we began our criticisms with) is that there are so many arguments offered and so many lines pursued; Augustine is often consciously intervening in a debate of the day, but he does not pause to tell us this or to summarize his account of the debate thus far. His arguments, when understood, provide a satisfying, biblically grounded, and philosophically coherent account of the Trinity. Augustine's account defined the doctrine of the Trinity for the Western church for a millennium or more.

7

ANSELM
WHY THE GOD-MAN?

INTRODUCTION

Anselm, c. 1033–1109, was a monk who became Archbishop of Canterbury. Although most famous for his ontological argument* for God's existence and his satisfaction account of the atonement*, Anselm's theological contribution extends much further. His thoughts on the atonement have been very influential – on those who follow him and on those who seek to distance themselves from him as much as possible. *Cur Deus Homo*, translated as *Why the God-Man?*, is a significant work in theology, dealing with sin, the incarnation*, and the atonement*. Anselm felt he was forced to complete this work too quickly, but nonetheless it remains worthy of attention even today, despite some weak areas and despite some difficulties arising from its distance from us in history.

In *Why the God-Man?*, Anselm has in view critics who believe in God, in his goodness, love, mercy, and justice, as well as in man's sinfulness and debt to God – however, they do not believe that God had to become incarnate and take care of the debt, and they doubt that God did these things in the historical person of Jesus. So he argues *remoto Christi* – that apart from anything we might know about Christ, he believes he can show that his opponents' own commitments require them to accept that there must be an incarnation and atonement. It's not that the Christian faith can be proven from the discoveries of reason, apart from revelation (as some accuse Anselm of doing), but that, given some accepted premises, certain details of the Christian faith are implied thereby. Anselm tries to really understand the *why*, namely, *why* incarnation and atonement, and *why* they are as they are.

Generally, the theological question of atonement is this: despite sin, how can humans be made right with God? Anselm's important work is an attempt to explain how atonement is only available through Christ, whereas up to that point such a careful and intentional account was largely absent. The argument, in short, is this: only a person who is both God and man – a God-Man – could ever save humanity because humans owe the debt to God for sin, but only God could ever make such recompense.

Before going any further, we should say a few words of explanation about some of the key terms Anselm uses. Society in his time was a complex hierarchy of obligations and debts, and this feudalism is often seen as the source of his terms like 'satisfaction', 'debt', and 'honour'. The more lowly owed a certain debt or obligation to those over them, and to violate this obligation offended their honour; recompense was then required to bring satisfaction to the honour of the one offended, and only then could things get back to the way they were before. However, to interpret *Why the God-Man?* as a superficial translation of this societal reality into the theological realm would be irresponsible (although it is all too common). Certainly, society at this time influenced his thinking in some way, but it seems much more likely that he adopted these terms and concepts only to change their meaning subtly when applied to things like the seriousness of sin against God and God as the greatest conceivable being*. We will now look at some of these terms in more detail.

'Debt' is the same Latin word in Anselm's writing as is used in the Lord's Prayer ('forgive us our debts') in the Latin Bible he read. For Anselm, creatures have certain responsibilities to God their Creator that cannot be ignored if they are to fulfill the purpose he gave them and thus be happy. Failure to meet any of these responsibilities creates a debt that the creatures then owe God above and beyond the responsibilities they already owe God by being his creatures. Debt is very much an idea that is internal to the creature; this is very different than the way debt worked in feudal society. 'Honour' is a term that in the Bible is often linked with 'glory', and it is better to think that Anselm, a monk who read Scripture regularly, took his meaning there more so than from society around him. Against a mere feudal meaning of the term, for Anselm, showing God honour was not about placating someone who, in the system, has been upset by some violated law; rather, it is for the creature to give proper respect and worship to the Creator, whom the creature has let down by failing to do and be what a creature should. 'Satisfaction' is achieved when one has done enough, which would be determined by the context in question. So Anselm's theological satisfaction would be different than satisfaction in the feudal system – for Anselm, the 'doing enough' in order to satisfy was not just whatever would pacify the one offended; rather, it is what is required to objectively make things right. When we add God into the equation, Anselm will argue that man can never make things right on his own.

For Anselm, there is an order and a beauty in creation that God has put there, and, being who he is, he will always act to restore this order and beauty if it should be compromised. This idea does some important work in Anselm's thinking because it is simply unreasonable – illogical – for God to do something that is not consistent with his nature and being, that is in his words 'unfitting'. The doctrine of God* that Anselm works with is important for us to understand. God is just, merciful, and all-powerful, and, particularly, God exists *a se**. This aseity* is very important. For Anselm, sin does not harm God because he does not depend in any way on creatures for his existence or for any of his attributes. Sin lessens the honour done to God by creation, but not God's actual dignity itself. Sin threatens the right ordering of creation.

A brief note on the use of the word 'man' – throughout this chapter, it should be understood to mean 'mankind' or 'humanity', just as Anselm would have used the term. It does not refer to the male gender, 'man', over against the female gender, 'woman'.

SYNOPSIS

In *Why the God-Man?*, Anselm argues that man has a debt to God – to obey his will – and that sin is the non-payment of this debt. Sin brings a disruption of the order and beauty of the universe, and it brings physical and spiritual death, which otherwise would not come to humanity. Sin does not make man the property of the Devil: man is still God's (Anselm rejects what was up to that point a long-standing view in the church). Adam, who fell into sin by his own free will, is man's representative, and therefore the whole of mankind shares in his guilt. In a famous statement, Anselm says that God must either demand satisfaction or punishment. (If this seems harsh and unmerciful, that's because Anselm is talking *remoto Christi*; note that later on, this is the same God who makes himself the satisfaction.)

Satisfaction is the making of amends for the harm done in addition to the regular responsibilities and obligations owed to God of obedience to his will. Both of these need to be fulfilled for sin to be put right before God. Satisfaction is not quite punishment in place of someone else; for Anselm, it is restitution and compensation for the offence and it must be of the measure required by the gravity of the offence. No one can make this satisfaction, for any good deeds and obedience are already owed to God and thus they cannot make amends for the harm previously done. Further, since even one little sin is against God's will, every sin is exceedingly grave. This is because sin is a violation of God's requirement of total obedience from his creatures, and these are the requirements of *God* – a person of the highest dignity. Any offence against the commands of an infinite God is an infinite one, and it is better for everything which is not God to be completely annihilated than for even the slightest sin to be committed. The price of satisfaction is just too high – man cannot pay it.

For Anselm, punishment is the only alternative to satisfaction. There is no third option: God cannot just pretend as if sin never happened. This would do the unthinkable: put God's 'stamp of approval' on sin and violate the moral order of the universe. A just God will, by definition, punish sin unless satisfaction is made. For God's forgiveness to be possible, satisfaction must be made.

Anselm stresses that it is unfitting for God not to save man. There are two reasons that God's salvation must be given to humanity. First, God created rational beings so that they should obey him and so that they should give him honour and make themselves blessed; this purpose cannot go unfulfilled or be thwarted. Second, there is a perfect, and therefore fixed, number of beings that achieve happiness in contemplating God, and humans, along with some angels, make up that number (and there is a gap in that number from the fallen angels that needs to be filled by some humans). This second reason seems strange to us today, but thinking like this was common in Anselm's time.

Since salvation must come, logically speaking, it must either come through Christ or through some other way. But, Anselm argues, it is not possible for salvation to come through some other way, so therefore it must be through Christ and his death.

Before moving on, we should note something important. Anselm considers the objection that salvation is not from God's free grace because God seems to save humanity out of necessity: if he did not do as much, his purposes for mankind would be thwarted. If God must save at least some humans, how is salvation gracious, and how is it a free choice of God? Anselm says that, first, God is obligated to save man because he initially decided to create man and bring him to perfection, and this first act God did graciously and freely. Second, Anselm says that God is only obligated by himself, that is, by his nature and attributes. God does not save unwillingly, as if forced or required to do so by something outside him, but willingly submits to the obligations that come from his own self and from his intentions in initially creating man. And this salvation, which has no external compulsion, is gracious. In fact, for Anselm, the 'necessity' that comes from God's acting with the integrity of his own nature and attributes is really not necessity at all because God completely self-determines his activity in agreement with consistency, truth, and righteousness (amongst other virtues) — and these all stem from God's own being.

Why can salvation only be accomplished through Christ? Satisfaction is only accomplished if there is a person who can, of his own self, pay to God for human sins with something greater than everything other than God. Yet this person must also himself be greater than everything that is not God. (Anselm has argued that even one tiny act contrary to God's will is not worth doing, even if that one tiny act would prevent all of creation from disappearing into nonexistence. So the payment and the payer must be greater than all of creation in order to make up for sin.) The only candidate, then, is God himself. However, a human being must make the recompense because humanity owes the debt. Therefore, only a God-Man could do what needs to be done.

How can a God–Man exist, with human nature and divine nature being so different? One nature cannot turn into the other, and they cannot be combined to create a third nature. The two natures must be conjoined in such a way that there is just one person who is both perfect God and perfect human, so the one who owes the debt will also be the one who can pay the debt. Fulfilling the details of the Council of Chalcedon,** Anselm says that both natures must be preserved intact.

The human nature of the God-Man must be sinless if he is to make satisfaction because he cannot owe recompense himself to God. Anselm says that it is a divine mystery how God takes on a human nature that truly belongs to sinful humanity, but is not itself sinful. Nonetheless, it had to be this way because a divine person cannot be sinful. Christ could not have sinned, but only because he could not have willed to sin, for he is God.

How does God will that the God-Man die – and a horrible death no less? If God can do all things, why could he not save humanity some other way? If he cannot save any other way, then how is he all-powerful; if he can but does not, then how is he good and wise? Anselm says that God did not will or allow Christ to die against his will, but that Christ did so freely. His own will was to be faithful to truth and to who God is. Christ was freely faithful to this general demand that God gives every rational being. In the particular circumstances he found himself in, this meant choosing his own death. God did not directly ask that of Christ, says Anselm. Anselm says it would be wrong for God to force an innocent man to die for the wicked, so it can only be that Christ was not forced to die, but did so freely. The Father knows that salvation requires man to offer something as valuable as the death of Christ; the only other option is that man is not saved. Christ knows that leaving man unsaved is not really an option for God, so he wills his own death. So in a sense the Father did will the death of the Son because it was the only way to bring about what the Father directly willed. Since Christ's will is the same as God's will, and since God does not will anything because of any external factors, but only according to his self and nature, the God-Man was not forced to die. It was possible that he would have kept his life, if he so willed, but being who he is, he would not so will.

It is only sinners who are obligated to die; since Christ was sinless, his death was not something owed, but was rather something he was in a position to freely give. The death of Christ was of such an infinite value because it was not already owed to God. It is not a necessary consequence of sin (Christ did not sin) because Christ gave it freely and because it is God himself who is being offered. It is valuable because Christ freely gave something extra, something he did not owe, and the merit of him doing so is what secures satisfaction. It is vicarious or representative satisfaction because the God-Man substitutes himself for man in making satisfaction.

How is Christ's death so valuable that it can make satisfaction? Since even one sin (knowingly) done to hurt the God-Man exceeds the sum of all other sins, the giving of his life, which is such a good thing and is much better and more lovely than the sins of the world, is enough to pay the debt owed for all the sins of the whole world.

The God-Man needs to be given his reward from God for laying down his life. But since he does not need forgiveness, God cannot offer that for the reward. Because the God-Man is God and thus does not need anything, there seems to be a reward that cannot rightly be given. So God gives the reward over to mankind so that satisfaction can be made, the debt of sin can be repaid, and mankind can be saved. (We must note that Anselm here is talking about corporate entities, not individuals, so his theology does not necessarily entail universal salvation, although it could lend itself to it.)

We should also note that Anselm speaks of the death of Christ as being an example of the type of righteousness that man should follow. The significance of the atonement for Anselm is not just vertical, but horizontal too. But only those who have received the vertical benefits of the atonement can follow the horizontal example.

Ultimately, the answer as to why God became man is because *God willed to do so. Why the God-Man?* is not designed to show why God had to will it, but rather to show that God's willing the incarnation can be investigated from certain givens, such as God's character and being, God's purpose for man, man's sin, and the need for satisfaction to be made.

CRITICISMS

In the introduction, we considered how Anselm drew from the feudal system of his day. Repeatedly Anselm is accused of being too 'feudal'. Many criticisms have come from this, but most do not seem to be fair critiques of *Why the God-Man?* However, some criticisms have more teeth, and a few are worth mentioning.

One criticism comes from Anselm's famous statement that sin requires either punishment or satisfaction: how does punishment restore God's lost honour? Consider this analogy: a thief steals some expensive whisky and drinks it all, but then gets caught. He's too poor to even repay the cost of the whisky, much less make restitution for the loss of honour to the storeowner. He is thus thrown in jail – but this does not 'make good' on the storeowner, who is still dishonoured and who still has not recovered the cost of the whisky. With God, how is it that man's punishment restores the loss to God's honour caused by sin? Anselm first says that it is impossible for an unchangeable God to actually lose any honour himself, as far as God is concerned. However, the honour that creation gives to God can be lost. He then says that in punishment God extracts the honour due him by taking from man his eternal happiness. But elsewhere Anselm says the sinner has nothing that can make repayment to God, so it seems Anselm might have a problem. Further, it is against man's will that he is punished and that he gives God any honour back – in fact, since he does not submit and obey willingly in Anselm's picture, it is not clear how to avoid a picture in which the dishonour seems to continue.

Another criticism is that, in Anselm's scheme, the death of Christ is apparently disconnected from his life and ministry. Some accuse Anselm of saying that Christ only needed to die; the rest is nice but not necessary. However, Anselm says that Christ offers both his life and his death, in one self-offering. The problem seems to arise from some of the limitations Anselm has placed on himself in *Why the God-Man?* and because of the narrow scope of the work.

In addition to this problem, it is said that Anselm's argument requires that death be a result of sin and that if humans had never sinned, they would not experience physical or spiritual death. Many modern thinkers do not see death this way, but perhaps this criticism is requiring Anselm to be in a time different than his own. Also, some linking of sin and death certainly seems biblical, as the apostle Paul is emphatic about that point – perhaps Anselm is on more solid ground than one might think.

A final criticism is that Anselm's view of sin is sometimes accused of being too impersonal. Objectors say that for Anselm, sin is merely a breach of the law, an upsetting of societal harmony. Further, 'debt' is too commercial, and the personal elements are lost. In defence of Anselm, this criticism is weakened when we read him more closely because his view of sin is actually very personal; sin is, first and foremost, a religious reality. It depends on the Creator/creature relationship; robbing God of his honour is to say we wrong an infinitely great *person*. Also, Anselm's use of 'debt' is primarily religious and moral, not just commercial.

8

THOMAS AQUINAS
SUMMA THEOLOGIAE

INTRODUCTION

Thomas Aquinas (1225–1274) was born near Aquino (a town south of Rome) and educated in a monastic school. At the age of 14, he was sent to the University of Naples, which at the time was the only European university teaching Aristotle's natural philosophy. (Most of Aristotle's works had been lost to the Latin-speaking West after the decline of the Roman Empire; they were, however, known and studied in Islamic North Africa. The contact between Africa and Europe occasioned by the Moorish invasion of Spain led to the works being re-introduced to Europe together with the tradition of commentary developed by Jewish and Islamic scholars.) This early encounter with Aristotle would shape Aquinas' intellectual career.

At Naples, he also encountered the Dominicans, then a very new and somewhat disreputable order. He applied to join the order in 1244, a move which horrified his family (who at one point imprisoned him to prevent this). The Dominicans sent him to study in Paris and Cologne, and then to teach in Paris; between 1259 and 1269 he travelled with the papal court before returning to Paris, again to teach.

His literary output was prodigious, stretching to approaching ten million words of Latin. He wrote commentaries on the Bible and on many of Aristotle's works, and left records of hundreds of formal disputations, as well as other more varied works. There is no doubt, however, that the *Summa Theologiae* (*ST*) has been the work by which he has chiefly been remembered: indeed, it is arguable that it is only in the last few decades that a broad view of his thought, not distorted by an exclusive focus on the *ST*, has emerged.

The *ST* was intended to be a simple textbook of theology intended for priests who would not go on to higher study. Its form is unusual for the contemporary reader: Aquinas expounds doctrine through a series of 'questions', each divided into sub-questions called 'articles'. For each article, Aquinas first gives a series of arguments for supposing one side to be correct, the 'objections', before offering one reason for upholding the other side, the '*sed contra*' (Latin, 'but against this'). Then Aquinas offers his own view in the 'response', which generally agrees with the '*sed contra*' position. This is finally followed by a series of responses to each of the initial objections.

Aquinas is very capable of offering incisive philosophical argument, but he more often cites authorities: a verse of Scripture, or a quotation from the church fathers, or a line from Aristotle (who he simply refers to as 'the Philosopher'). Aquinas expects his readers to assume, as he does, that if the Bible or a church father said something, then it must be right. (He will rarely disagree with Aristotle.) His responses to objections, then, are never of the form 'Augustine (e.g.) was wrong'; instead, he strives to show how the quotation from Augustine did not mean what it seemed to mean or how it is not in fact relevant to the question. The authorities are assumed to be always right.

In a sense, then, the *ST* is a massive exercise in harmonization: all the apparent disagreement over issues in the church can be shown, in fact, to be agreement if only one is attentive to the detail of the question.

SYNOPSIS

The *ST* is divided into three parts, which are usually known as the *prima pars* (Ia), the *secunda pars* (IIa), and the *tertia pars* (IIIa) – these are the Latin terms for 'first, second, and third part'. The second and third parts are subdivided. The second part is subdivided into the *prima secundae* (Ia IIae) and the *secunda secundae* (IIa IIae) – the 'first part of the second part' and the 'second part of the second part'. Finally, Aquinas stopped writing before he completed the *tertia pars*, and the closing sections are composed by his students from his lectures; these sections are usually known as the *supplement*.

The *prima pars* covers the doctrines of God, creation, and providence. The *secunda pars* covers ethics. The *tertia pars* covers the incarnation, the sacraments, and eschatology*. This arrangement is unusual, and was unusual in Aquinas' day, when Peter Lombard's *Sentences*, which took their structure from the Apostles' Creed, were the model for most writers (including Aquinas himself in other books). It is also worth noticing that over half the book is concerned with what we would now call 'ethics', not doctrine. There is a logical progression of going out and return: God creates the world and supremely human beings who fall from grace and so are alienated from God. Through Christ and the appropriation of his grace through the sacraments, human beings – and with them all creation – may be reunited with God in the end. This does not explain the extended focus on ethics, however.

When Aquinas wrote, one of the chief duties of a priest was the hearing of confession and the ascribing of appropriate penance. To help priests in this duty, confessional manuals that listed and evaluated the relative severity of different sins circulated. There is little doubt that the structure of the ethical parts of the *ST* is an attempt to elevate the discourse around sin and virtue. Aquinas begins his ethics with a theoretical discussion of the nature of sin and virtue (the whole of the *prima secundae*) before offering any consideration of actual acts (which comes in the treatment of the virtues in the *secunda secundae*). Aquinas then sandwiches this extended discussion of virtue between an account of God and creation, and an account of incarnation and salvation, giving theological context, as well as a theoretical ethical basis, to the material that priests were typically interested in.

The *prima pars* begins with a single question 'on sacred doctrine', which is nonetheless vital in that it defines the genre and basis of all that follows. Aquinas is not doing philosophy, he is doing theology, a discipline that is built on revelation, and so the question ends with an article on the Bible, in which Aquinas briefly sketches his principles for finding truth in Scripture.

After this, Aquinas turns to the doctrine of God. We can know that God exists, but we cannot know comprehensively who/what God is. We can, however, speak – haltingly and analogically – about God. We can also speak about what God does. God is triune, and Aquinas offers a careful account of what can be said properly about the divine Trinity.

Aquinas treats creation first as an act of God and then from the perspective of the creatures, looking at angels (spiritual creatures), material creatures (through a commentary on the six days of Genesis 1), and humanity, in which the spiritual and material realms meet. The *prima pars* ends with a discussion of providence*, God's government of the creation. Here, and in the original treatment of creation, Aquinas considers the origin and continuation of evil in the world. He argues (as Augustine** had) that every evil is only the absence of some good and that the cause of evil is therefore always the lack of something else.

The *prima secundae* begins with a consideration of human destiny: all human beings are created to find their true fulfillment only in knowing and loving God. The rest of the volume is given to an extensive and penetrating ethical analysis of human life: how and why do human beings act? How are we acted upon by our passions/ emotions? In all of this, where do we find an account of good and evil?

Somewhere near the heart of Aquinas' analysis is the concept of 'habit'. His ethical analysis will identify virtues and vices as 'habits' – patterns of behaviour that are inscribed on our nature – although they are patterns that can be re-inscribed by deliberate practice or by grace. Aquinas' great insight is that ethical questions are not primarily about the rightness or wrongness of a particular act – although he will come to that – but about the shape of our decision-making. Do we tend to embody love and justice in our actions and decisions, or not?

Salvation, for Aquinas, necessarily involves becoming holy: having evil habits (vices) replaced with good habits (virtues). He defines 'justification' as the process of becoming just, not as a legal declaration of forgiveness. This is only possible by grace and by the gifts of the Holy Spirit; however, at this point, Aquinas does not speak further of how grace might be attained or received.

The *secunda secundae* turns to what is normally considered the stuff of ethics: what is right and what is wrong. Aquinas constructs it as an analysis of the seven virtues (three 'theological' virtues: faith, hope, and charity, and four 'cardinal' virtues: prudence, justice, fortitude, and temperance). Under each virtue, Aquinas first gives a definition of the virtue and also lists and defines its opposing vices; beyond this, there is some variety in the treatments, but Aquinas' concern is to give a clear understanding of the habits of life that are holy and of how they will be lived out and shown in one who possesses them.

The *secunda secundae* ends with a section on 'acts which pertain to certain people', an opaque title which covers the particular ethical demands made on two groups of people: those who have received miraculous gifts from God (the ability to speak in tongues, to prophesy, or to perform miracles) and those who have taken vows in the religious orders and/or who have been ordained into the church's ministry.

The *tertia pars* turns back to the question of how grace and justification may be obtained. Having described perfection, and shown the evil of habits of vice, Aquinas is now ready to show his reader the way to attain perfection. It begins with the incarnation, since the fundamental cause of all human salvation is God's entering into human life in Jesus Christ. Aquinas gives a careful account of the classical doctrine of the hypostatic union, drawing in particular on John of Damascus. In the person of the mediator, human and divine nature, each complete and perfect, are united without being confused.

Aquinas then considers what must be said about Jesus, given the truth of the incarnation. How does one speak of his knowledge or priesthood, for instance? His answers are again traditional and unoriginal, but worked through extremely carefully. It is proper to speak of Christ as equal to the Father, since in his divine nature he is the divine Son incarnate; it is also proper to speak of Christ's subjection to God, since in his human nature he is a creature, called as all creatures are to pray, worship, and serve the Creator.

After this, Aquinas turns to the life of Christ, which he explores from birth – indeed, from before birth, since the section begins with some discussion of Mary's receiving the news and the gift of Jesus – to death, resurrection, and ascension. Aquinas is concerned with two things in this working through of the narrative: to speak with theological accuracy of what happened and how (what happened to Jesus when the Spirit descended on him at his baptism? How did Jesus perform miracles?), and to draw out the consequences, for our salvation, of all that Jesus did and suffered.

With Christ's heavenly reign at the right hand of the Father, Aquinas has brought his account to the present moment, the time of the church, and so his treatment turns to the life of the church. His interest is particularly in how human beings can become holy, so he deals with the life of the church through the seven sacraments*, through which (on Aquinas' account) grace is received: baptism; confirmation; eucharist; penance; the 'last rites'; ordination; and marriage. (Aquinas stopped writing in the middle of his discussion on penance, and the material after that is found in the *supplement*.)

The most famous of these discussions is the treatment of the eucharist. There had been an ongoing debate concerning the meaning of Christ's words, 'this bread is my body ... this cup is the new covenant in my blood', spoken (according to the biblical records) at the last supper and repeated by the priest celebrating the eucharist week by week. A ninth-century debate between Radbert and Ratram had offered some surprisingly literal understandings, which nonetheless struggled to explain how, if there was a real work of transformation of bread into Christ's body and wine into Christ's blood, the elements still tasted and felt like bread and wine.

Aquinas found a helpful way through such problems in the Aristotelian philosophy he learnt. Aristotle distinguished between 'substance' and 'accidents': the substance of a thing is what makes it what it is; its accidents are properties (including look, feel, taste, and smell) that adhere to it. Meat looks, feels, tastes, and smells different if it is fresh or cooked, dried or rotten; however, it always remains meat. The substance is constant; the accidents change. Given this account of the way things are, Aquinas can propose that the miracle of the eucharist is a real change of substance with no corresponding change of accidents. The bread ceases to be bread and becomes the body of Christ; however, it retains the accidents of looking, feeling, tasting, and smelling like bread. This understanding of the eucharist, known as 'transubstantiation', was novel when Aquinas proposed it, but later became Roman Catholic orthodoxy.

For Aquinas, however, it is the grace conveyed by the sacrament that is most important. The eucharist conveys grace, offers spiritual refreshment and nourishment, fits us for heaven, brings forgiveness of sins, and is a sacrifice offered for others, not just those who receive. In different ways, Aquinas wants to say the same of all the sacraments: they are vehicles of grace which, in different and complementary ways, fit the recipient for heaven by making him/her holy.

The *supplement* completes the discussion of the sacraments and then turns to the coming resurrection and final judgement. After death, souls are conscious and enjoy a foretaste of their final destiny in heaven or hell, or are further prepared for heaven in purgatory. In the end, all people will rise to be judged by Christ and will survive eternally either in a state of unimaginable bliss or in a state of unimaginable horror.

CRITICISMS

Aquinas' method of asking questions and offering distinctions takes some getting used to; many of his arguments are obscure to the modern reader and depend on mastering an extensive set of technical terms that he deploys with some freedom – and often without definition. Of course, some of these problems would have been significantly eased for Aquinas' first readers, and it is hardly a criticism that he wrote in the language – and employed the assumptions – of his own day.

That said, the variety of later interpretations of Aquinas' thought has been astonishing. In part, this is no doubt because of his status as the premier theological interpreter of the Catholic faith, which meant that Roman Catholic theologians can be eager to read their own programmes into Aquinas. In part, however, it is because the complexity and subtlety of his thought can lead interpreters astray.

Why is Aquinas' thought so complex? As noted above, his programme is based in part on the assumption that none of his authorities are ever wrong, and it is this that sometimes leads him into astonishingly subtle distinctions or extremely abstruse arguments. He is often seeking to reconcile doctrines that are simply opposed to one another. We might – perhaps should – praise the generosity of Aquinas' method; there is something admirable about the determination never to criticize or condemn. We have, however, to acknowledge that, at times, it makes his thought more convoluted and obscure than it needed to be.

As noted above, Aquinas departed from the traditional ordering of an account of doctrine around the Apostles' Creed; this has both positive and negative effects on his account of doctrine here. Positively, he is able to locate his ethical reflections within a broader theological narrative, which seems a significant gain. Negatively, however, there are some surprising omissions. There is no section on the work of the Holy Spirit in salvation. There are three questions on the gifts, blessings, and fruit of the Holy Spirit in the *prima secundae* (qq. 68–70), but, for instance, nothing at all on the coming of the Spirit at the Pentecost (other than the reference to the gift of tongues at the end of the *prima secundae*). The doctrine of the church offered by Aquinas here is so focused on the sacraments that he has nothing to say (in this book) about preaching, evangelism, or worship (other than in the context of sacrament).

These criticisms might be lessened (although not eradicated because the Pentecost looks to be a difficult omission on any telling) by reflecting further on the nature of the *ST*; it is not a body of doctrine in the manner of a modern systematic theology textbook; its interest is far more practical than that. The extensive focus on ethics at the heart of the work demonstrates that it is perhaps better seen as a manual on Christian living, a guide to attaining heaven. Of course, if we look at it like this, the complexity and exactitude of the doctrine taught will surprise us, but Aquinas believed that right doctrine was central to salvation.

JULIAN OF NORWICH
REVELATIONS OF DIVINE LOVE

INTRODUCTION

We know little of the life of Julian of Norwich. She was probably
born in 1342. On May 13, 1373, she received a series of visions of
Christ, which she called 'revelations' or 'showings', and which she
wrote about, completing her writing in 1393. By 1394, she was
living as an 'Anchoress' – a solitary life in a cell attached to a
church, in her case the Church of St Julian in Norwich. Another
mystical writer, Margery Kempe, visited her there because she was
well known to be an expert in spiritual guidance. Isabel Ufforde,
the Countess of Suffolk, left Julian twenty shillings in her will in
1416, which suggests she was still alive at that time. Robert Baxter
left three shillings and fourpence to 'the anchorite in the
Churchyard of St Julian's' in his will of 1429, which might suggest
Julian was still alive at that time – but it is also possible that she had
died and that another anchorite had taken her cell.

Julian repeatedly tells us that she was illiterate at the time she
received her visions, but this, in fact, seems unlikely (perhaps
she meant that she was untrained in literary style); she seems to
have read Latin fluently and to have known the Vulgate (the Latin
Bible), many of the classic spiritual writings of the Christian tradition, and even the works of some medieval theologians (some of

her distinctive ideas seem to be derived from William of St Thierry, who died in 1148).

There are two different texts of the *Revelations of Divine Love (Revelations)*, known as the 'short text' and the 'long text', respectively. Comparing them suggests that the short text was written first and the long text subsequently. The long text tells us it was finished in 1393. There are various minor differences between the two texts, but essentially they give similar descriptions of the visions she received. The long text shows wider and more mature reflection on the meaning of the visions; the synopsis below is based on the long text. The text is divided into short chapters, and references below are by chapter number; translations are our own.

Julian's *Revelations* remained relatively unknown until the twentieth century. The first printed edition came out in 1670, followed fairly rapidly by a French translation which was more known than the English original. In the twentieth century, there was an explosion of interest in Julian, and several modernized versions of the *Revelations* appeared. Several of her themes – particularly, perhaps, her reflections on God as Mother – resonate strongly with contemporary concerns, and she is widely read and well known today.

SYNOPSIS

After a brief list of the sixteen revelations (1), Julian explains that she had prayed in her youth for a recollection of Christ's passion; that God would send her a life-threatening sickness when she was 30; and for three 'wounds' – of sorrow for sin, of compassion, and of longing for God. She explains the second prayer as a desire to face the reality of death in order to live better afterwards (2). God granted her prayers, and she recounts the illness she suffered, how she was at the point of death, and how she had received the last rites of the church before a miraculous sudden recovery. Immediately, her visions began.

She records that a priest was holding a crucifix in front of her to prepare her for death and that her first vision was of blood flowing from the crown of thorns on the crucifix. As she saw this, she had a series of impressions which form the theme of her later visions: the love of the Trinity; the power of Christ's passion; the devotion of the Virgin Mary to Christ; and the love of Christ holding the world in being.

The second revelation is of the suffering of Christ, which Julian sees in the face of the crucifix, which changes colour and becomes encrusted with blood. Julian understood this disfigurement to be an image of how our sin and shame was borne by Christ, and turns to meditate on the love of God that led to human salvation. The third revelation begins, 'I saw God in an instant' (11), a sight which leads Julian to think about sin and God doing all things well – a thought she will return to. In the fourth revelation, she sees Christ's body bleeding from the wounds of the whip, with an emphasis on the quantity of the blood. From this she understands the generosity of God's gift of redemption.

Julian's fifth and sixth revelations are brief words: 'With this the Fiend is overcome' (13) and 'I thank you for your service, and especially for your youth' (14). Her reflections on the first are about the overcoming of the devil, achieved in the passion of Christ and to be made complete at the final judgement. The second word leads Julian to contemplate the joys of heaven, where God hosts a joy-filled feast for all who are saved.

The seventh revelation is emotional feeling rather than sight or words. Julian describes a feeling of utter security and peace, and then a feeling of dissatisfaction with her own life, both extraordinarily strong; she suggests that she alternated perhaps twenty times between these two emotional states (15). There was no natural cause for these changes – she comments that they happened so quickly that she had no time to do anything which might have caused them. From this, she understands that God's ways with the human soul will involve both the gift of consolation and the experience of desolation, and that these will sometimes come because God knows that one or the other will be good for us at a given moment.

Julian's discussion of her eighth revelation is longer than those that have come before it, filling chapters 16–21. The revelation itself is another vision of, she says, 'a part of [Christ's] passion when he was close to death'(16). She describes in detail changes of appearance in Christ's face and body, and the 'dry, hard, wind and remarkable cold' of the day he died. Dryness is the overwhelming image of the vision: Christ's body gradually becoming desiccated as he died. Julian unsurprisingly thinks of Christ's words, recorded in the New Testament, 'I thirst' (17). She interprets this both as a bodily thirst and as a spiritual thirst, which she promises to discuss later.

The description of Christ's suffering in 16–17 is detailed and graphic; Julian's vision turns next to the suffering of his mother and his friends: 'those who were his friends suffered pain because of their love', she explains (18). Julian identifies herself with this suffering friendship, suggesting that she was invited to turn away from the sight of Christ's suffering and to look to heaven instead, but that her response was that Jesus alone would be her heaven, in all his pain and disgrace (19).

Chapter 20 re-affirms the extent of Christ's suffering, suggesting that the fact of incarnation gave him a capacity to suffer more than any other human person could (this was a common theological idea in the middle ages). Julian then turns to the reason for his suffering: he suffered 'for the sin of every person that will be saved', and in compassion he mourned every person's sorrow or distress. The vision ended with Julian expecting to see Christ die; instead, she saw his face become cheerful, which made her rejoice. From this, she understood that the end of our suffering, as of Christ's, is salvation and so heaven, and so we should bear suffering with cheerfulness.

The ninth revelation (22–23) is a brief conversation between Christ and Julian. 'Are you happy that I suffered for you?', he asked; 'Yes, good Lord, thank you …', she replied; then – the substance of the revelation – Jesus said to her, 'If you are pleased, I am pleased; it is joy, bliss, an endless satisfaction to me that I suffered for you; if I could suffer more, I would' (22). Immediately, her thoughts were lifted to heaven. She interprets Jesus' words to her as a cipher for the Trinity: 'By "joy", I understood the pleasure of the Father; by "bliss", the worship given to the Son; and by "endless satisfaction", the Holy Spirit. The Father is pleased; the Son is worshipped; the Holy Spirit is satisfied' (23). Terrible as the sufferings of Jesus were, they were a part of the perfect plan of salvation conceived by the triune God, and so they should be seen as something good and right.

The next three revelations are dealt with quite briefly. Julian saw another vision, her tenth revelation. Still cheerful, Jesus looked at the wound in his side; Julian's thoughts are drawn through the wound to look into the heart of Christ, 'a beautiful and delightful place, large enough for all redeemed humanity to rest in peace and love' (24). She heard Jesus speak again, testifying to his joy and to his love. Julian's gaze was again redirected, and in her eleventh revelation, she had a vision of the Virgin Mary standing at the side of the cross. She saw Christ's love for Mary and heard Christ promise that she would be loved as Mary was loved. Finally, in her twelfth revelation, she saw Jesus again, now glorified, speaking and proclaiming that he is highest of all, the content of all true Christian faith ('I am the one that Holy Church preaches and teaches' (26)), and the one who Julian loves, serves, and now sees in her visions.

The next revelation is discussed at much greater length than any of the others. Comparing the short and long texts, we can see that in part this is because Julian's reflections over the years enabled her to understand more of the questions raised here. Her thirteenth revelation began with the realization that sin alone prevented her, or anyone, from coming to God. As she contemplated the word 'sin', God gave her a brief sight of 'all that is not good' (27), and Jesus spoke to her in perhaps the most famous line of the book: 'Sin is necessary – but all shall be well, and all shall be well, and all manner of things shall be well!' (27). Julian is concerned to stress that she did not see sin itself because 'sin' has no real existence (this is one of the more obvious echoes of fairly sophisticated theology in the book).

How will 'all manner of things be well'? Julian cites Anselm's** account of the atonement: Adam's sin is the worst thing that has ever happened or will ever happen in the world, but the satisfaction made by Christ is incomparably more pleasing to God than Adam's sin was displeasing. God has made the greatest evil well, so we may trust that every evil will be made well (29). This part of God's counsel, that concerns the salvation of all 'people of good will', is revealed plainly by God to the church; God's purposes beyond this known salvation are not revealed, and our role is simply not to speculate or be concerned – but to trust that all things will be made well (30). Julian is particularly concerned about the fate of fallen angels and those people who die outside the faith of the church, or in mortal sin. The Church taught that they shall be condemned to 'hell without end'; how, then, 'shall all be well'? Julian will not doubt the faith of the church, nor what she has seen revealed, and so she announces her willingness to accept that what she could not reconcile in her mind would nonetheless be reconciled perfectly by God.

This coming fulfillment of all things will be the final satisfying of the spiritual thirst of Christ, which Julian had written about in Chapter 17. In Chapter 31, Julian works this out with attention to the categories of technical Christology. Jesus Christ is both divine and human; in his divine nature, his glory and joy is never less than perfect, and he cannot suffer; in his human nature, he suffered for our salvation, and his joy is still less than complete as he waits for the coming fulfillment.

Julian's discussion turns from sin and evil in general to her own actions and motives: all our actions are sinful without God's grace, but God will work good for us, in us, and through us, and our sin will not hinder that. Julian was shown that she herself would fall into sin, but given the promise that God would keep her safe for salvation. In exploring this, she first mentions one of her distinctive teachings: 'in every soul that shall be saved is a Godly will that never assented to sin, and never will' (37). This sits alongside a 'beastly will' which wills only evil. Her next daring move is to suggest that even the sins of Christians will be turned into occasions for joy, insofar as they have been repented of and sorrowed for on earth.

The fourteenth revelation begins with the statement, 'After this, our Lord showed concerning prayer' (41). The revelation is again a word from God: 'I am the basis of your asking: first, I desire that you have something; then, I make you desire it; then I make you ask for it, and you do ask for it. How, then, will you not receive what you ask for?' (41). She offers a Trinitarian understanding of prayer: it 'is a true, gracious, lasting desire of the soul, joined and united to our Lord's will by the sweet inward work of the Holy Spirit' (41). The Spirit causes us to desire what Christ desires for us, and so to turn to the Father in prayer. Christ hears our prayers first, she suggests, and offers them on to the Father. Thankfulness is also a part of prayer. It begins in a constant, quiet enjoyment of and gratitude for all God's blessings, which will inevitably spill out into words from time to time.

In Chapters 44–63, Julian offers reflection on what she has learnt in the fourteen revelations. She discusses God's love, our sinfulness, and the work of redemption. Her two most distinctive doctrines are developed in this section: the 'Godly will' in Chapter 53 and the motherhood of God in Chapters 58–63. The doctrine of the 'Godly will' appears as a part of the answer to Julian's question, how can God love us even though we are sinners? Julian stresses God's good desire in creating humanity, particularly the always-intended incarnation of the Son and the human soul as something immediately created by God. This creates a certain unity between the human soul and God, in which the soul is always kept safe and in which sinful desire is impossible.

The doctrine of divine motherhood begins to be developed in Chapter 58, with an account of echoes of the Trinity in human life that is reminiscent of Augustine**. Our life is threefold: beginning, growth, and fulfillment. Each stage reflects a different aspect of divine goodness to us: our created nature, God's mercy, and God's grace. Each of these gifts may be appropriated to a different person of the Trinity: the power of the Father makes us; the wisdom of the Son nurtures and cares for us; and the love of the Spirit brings us to completion. Reflecting like this, Julian speaks of the Son as 'God our Mother', whose maternal care and motherly mercy lead us and guide us through our earthly journey. In the chapters that follow, she works this identification out at length, stressing and developing the maternal aspects of Christ's care for his people.

Julian's fifteenth revelation was verbal once again and consisted of a promise that she would be saved and enter heaven when she died. She develops this, not as a special gift to herself, but as an account of the love God shows for all who serve him and the sure promise that all may believe. The sixteenth revelation was a vision of her own soul as a capacious city where Christ reigns. This again is true of all true believers, and because Christ reigns at the heart of their souls, they may take with complete seriousness the promise that, whatever comes, they will not be overcome. The closing chapters of the book are spiritual guidance on how to live in the light of these great promises.

CRITICISMS

Julian's *Revelations* is a very different book from many of the texts we consider here; it is unquestionably a significant work of theology, but it is also a record of mystical visions and an account of the well-lived spiritual life. The reader has to decide what to make of the visions Julian records: for her, they were gifts from God, opening up knowledge of divine purposes and of Christ's feelings towards his people; the reader who finds such an account implausible, and assumes that what we have are delusions brought about by her illness, will evaluate the book very differently from the reader who believes Julian's own understanding.

Again, readers may have different views on the appropriateness of combining theology and practical piety in quite such direct ways; this was normal in Julian's own time, but it is far less so now. We might find in Julian a challenge to think harder about how intellectual discussion and spiritual formation interact, or we might find her unhelpfully unacademic on this point.

The writing of the book is often beautiful and profoundly moving. The main themes, a serene confidence in God's love and an understanding of the purpose of the sufferings of Christ, are in the mainstream of Christian theology. Her account of God as mother has attracted much attention in recent times, but in fact is not uncommon in medieval devotional literature – although Julian might offer the fullest development of any writer. The idea of the 'Godly will' is perhaps more difficult, but we see in Julian a classical mystical view of the fundamental unity of the human soul with God, which will always lead to some sort of account of an inviolate aspect of human nature. Julian's version is perhaps more realistic about the problem of sinfulness than those of many other writers in this tradition, however.

MARTIN LUTHER
COMMENTARY ON GALATIANS

INTRODUCTION

There is a common idea in our world that if a person does enough good deeds in his/her life, he/she will earn his/her way into salvation and heaven. Martin Luther would have none of this. For him, not only is this thinking wrong, it is dead wrong and is the opposite of the Christian gospel.

Martin Luther (1483–1546) was a German professor of theology and a foundational figure in the Protestant Reformation. He was raised a Roman Catholic. His father pushed him to become a lawyer, and after receiving his master's degree, he enrolled in law school, but dropped out very quickly. In 1505, he was nearly struck by lightning and, being afraid of death and God's judgement, he promised in that moment to become a monk. Against his father's wishes, he became a monk – and an extremely devoted monk at that. He became a priest and then a theology professor in Wittenberg, where he spent the rest of his career.

Luther became increasingly critical of what he considered to be abuses of the Roman Catholic Church. This led him to write and publicize his *Ninety-Five Theses* in 1517, an act that became a catalyst for the Reformation. Originally desiring to correct errors in the Catholic Church, Luther eventually abandoned this effort as doomed and became a highly influential figure in the Reformation movement.

Luther's *Commentary on Galatians* is the product of lecturing on the book multiple times. The book we have today consists of the lectures he gave on Galatians in 1531. It played a significant role in the Reformation, summarizing key doctrinal points such as justification*. Luther said this was his favourite among the books he wrote. Luther saw himself fighting a similar battle to Paul's in the Book of Galatians – Luther fighting 'Papists and Anabaptists', Paul fighting the false apostles in the Galatian church, but in both cases, the fundamental issue was the right understanding of the gospel. In this book he is famously harsh towards his opponents, but we must interpret this in light of his historical setting and of how he considered these issues to be a matter of gospel truth. For him, the issue was one of doctrine, and if his opponents would repent of their errors, he would happily welcome them; he even hoped that such a thing would happen. He says that if the Pope were to concede the doctrine of justification by faith alone, 'we would carry him in our arms, we would kiss his feet'.

Since this book is a commentary on the biblical book of Galatians, a brief summary of Galatians is in order. Paul spends the first part of his letter defending his apostleship and condemning the false apostles who had taught the Galatians that they needed to be circumcised on top of having faith in Christ in order to be saved. Theirs was a false gospel because it adds a feature of the Mosaic Law to faith, but justification is by faith, not works. The Law cannot save, only condemn. Yet good works do have a place in the Christian life: after we are justified before God, we are to love one another.

Since Luther's work is a biblical commentary that progresses through each verse of Galatians in order, our summary presentation of this work will not follow Luther's standard commentary structure. Instead, we will organize our presentation around several of Martin Luther's key theological concepts.

SYNOPSIS

THE LAW

By 'the Law' Luther usually means the Mosaic Law – the whole of it, not just the civil or ceremonial parts. However, he uses the word 'law' occasionally to refer to any law that is used in attempting to build an idea of a works-righteousness. The Mosaic Law is good and holy. The problem is that the Law is weak, unable to justify. It was given to keep the Israelites together as a nation, so Christ might come from that nation in due time.

The Law needs to be kept in full if it is to make us righteous before God. If a person makes one minor mistake or one violation, then he/she is entirely guilty. The Law requires perfect obedience. No one can live up to the Law. The Law condemns. To completely keep the Law is to live up to every external command and also do so with completely pure motives, with a pure heart – no one can do that. Since we all break the Law and sin, we are put in a state where we are completely unable to do anything pleasing to God.

The Law has two purposes: first, to restrain wicked people from being even worse and harming society even more, and second, to reveal sin. This second point was a major emphasis for Luther. He says that the monster of self-righteousness needs a big axe – the Law. In vivid imagery, he says that the Law works on this stiff-necked beast until the conscience is scared stiff. The Law terrorizes the conscience; it reveals God's judgement and wrath because we all break it. We need the Law to help us recognize our sin for what it is and our need for salvation, but it cannot do anything beyond that. The Law is an usher to lead to the way of grace. It drives us to despair. Luther says we should let it drive us a bit further, into the arms of Jesus; he says that hunger is the best cook. The Law prepares a person to look for the promises of God that are fulfilled in Christ.

Even without the Mosaic Law, deep down every person knows that there is a God who created the universe. Every person knows that this God is just and holy, and that he will punish the wicked. However, knowledge that we are guilty comes from a special revelation from God – the Law. Likewise, knowledge of how we can be saved comes from a special revelation from God summed up in the person of Jesus Christ. The difference between this general knowledge and special knowledge is like knowing what a certain man looks like and being able to recognize him, but not knowing what this man thinks about you and what he wants for you. The Law is the first step in moving from merely recognizing God to being reconciled with him.

WORKS-RIGHTEOUSNESS

Martin Luther tried as hard as anyone could to be righteous before God by doing good works. He physically beat himself when he sinned. He went to the extremes of sacrifices and self-denial, even for a monk. He spent years trying to earn God's grace, eventually concluding that all his efforts were a waste.

Luther realized that sin cannot be removed by good works, no matter how good the person. Sin cannot be removed from our lives by our righteous deeds, and even further, the penalty that we all deserve for our sins cannot be removed by them either. Good works are powerless to save. They cannot be added at all to the gospel as part of being justified before God.

If we could remove our sins by our own good works, then there would be no reason for the incarnation or the atonement – which were very costly to God. If we could earn grace and mercy through doing good things, then Christ is not really necessary and we no longer really need to be Christians. For Luther, to seek a works-righteousness in any form is to reject the grace of God.

Luther regards those people who call themselves 'righteous' but teach a works-righteousness to be the enemy, much worse than those who live in obvious sin. He says he would take a drunkard or a prostitute over the Pope any day because at least the obvious sinner is not denying the gospel.

THE GOSPEL

The false apostles had taught the Galatians that, in addition to believing in Christ, one needed to be circumcised in order to be saved. A person needs to observe this aspect of the Law after having Christian faith in order to be saved, they said. Luther took up Paul's harsh condemnation of these false apostles, saying that it is the gospel plus *nothing* that saves us. We cannot add anything to the gospel without undercutting it. It is by faith *alone* that we are saved. If we add good works to the gospel, we destroy it – if we add observing traditions or ceremonies or circumcision or anything else, we no longer have the gospel. Luther notes that this true gospel is hard to grasp and easy to lose: it is very easy to slip back into a works-righteousness mentality.

Luther has a strong distinction between the Law and the gospel in this thinking. He says that the one who gets this distinction right is a true theologian. Law and gospel are to be kept far apart in our minds, yet both are necessary for preaching that leads to salvation. The Law is preached to show people their sin and their inability to save themselves through anything they could do. The Law shows that the wrath of God is upon them. They are then ready to hear the gospel preached to them, that by faith in Christ alone they can be justified before God and thus saved.

JUSTIFICATION

This idea of justification is a matter of life and death. Take this away, or change it even slightly, or add something to it, and you have lost the true gospel. Justification has to do with our being considered righteous by God. We are justified by faith in Christ and by faith alone, which is a gift from God which he accepts for perfect righteousness. Luther says that in justification, God 'winks' at our sins and covers them up (not 'winking' at our sins and merely pretending as if they never happened, but covering them in Christ – an important difference). Christ's righteousness is transfused to us through having faith in Christ.

Luther insists that justification is the centre of all of the Christian faith. We do not speculate about the nature of God, but only begin from what we see in Christ, and Christ came to win our justification. For Luther, justification is the centrepiece and starting place for all theology; it is the foundational doctrine of the Christian faith: if we get this doctrine right, all the others are confirmed. For example, he says that justification entails a correct Christology.

Not only is justification the centre of Christianity, it is unique to true Christianity. Luther says that other faiths such as Roman Catholicism and Islam only provide a justification by works. When it comes down to it, only the true Christian faith can provide actual justification – one that is achieved by Christ alone, which we receive by faith alone. This is the unique feature of the genuine Christian faith that imitators and other contenders cannot match.

FAITH

Luther says that faith is entirely a gift from God. It is something no one earns or deserves; it is something no one achieves for themselves. All glory in our salvation, then, goes to God. Even before the Law was given, God justified people by faith: Abraham is the prime example. Abraham believed God, and it was credited to him as righteousness. In order to be justified before God and spared from his wrath, we must have faith like Abraham's.

Justification is by faith in Jesus Christ alone without any deeds of the Law. Faith does not justify us because it is pure or perfect or a good work. Faith brings our justification because it apprehends Jesus Christ. True faith will always have Christ as the object of faith – Christ is present in faith itself. Faith is credited to us as righteousness. When we have faith, the righteousness of Christ is imputed to us.

DOUBLE IMPUTATION

The notion of double imputation is very important in Luther's theology. First, the believer's sin has been imposed upon Christ, on the cross. Second, Christ's righteousness is credited to us as if it were our own. He himself is our righteousness, which we have through being united with him through faith. Christ changes places with us: he takes on our sin and we take on his holiness. Our sin and guilt are imputed to him and his righteousness is imputed to us.

PENAL SUBSTITUTION

To explain a bit more about the believer's sin being imputed to Christ, we must discuss Luther's doctrine of penal substitution. Luther follows the thinking of Anselm** and takes it further. We offend God when we sin, and this offence is so severe that God cannot just pardon it. Yet we cannot give adequate satisfaction for our sins. Christ had to come between us and God as our mediator. He did so in the way described in Col. 2:14, by taking the penalty of the Law and nailing it to the cross. Christ makes satisfaction to God for us in that he suffers the penalty due to us by taking on our sin. Christ is personally innocent and in no way deserved the punishment of his death. Yet because he took our place, he was punished and made to be the curse of the Law. Christ took our sins upon himself and died for them. Taking on the sins of the whole world, Christ was no longer an innocent person: he was charged with our sins, which were imputed to him. This is why Christ experienced death, which is the penalty for sin – because in his death, he took our place. It was as if he had committed all those sins himself. Christ voluntarily put himself under the full force of the Law for us. It accused and condemned him because our guilt was on him, condemning him to death. Yet because Christ was God, he proved victorious over sin, death, the wrath of God, and hell.

GOOD WORKS AFTER JUSTIFICATION

Luther recognizes that his theology would be accused of leading to apathy and licentiousness. If good works play no role in our justification, why would anyone be good? If there is no law to force us into doing good deeds, but we are completely justified before God anyway, why would Christians do anything good?

Luther was insistent that we can only talk about Christians doing good works *after* we really understand justification by faith alone. We cannot confuse them in any way and we must take care to properly understand justification first. Once we do, we see that good works are the embellishment of faith, a faith which is completely the gift and the work of God. True faith is a faith that leads to good works done in Christian love. This is not to say that good works are a part of faith itself, but rather that if one's faith is sincere and true, it will bring about justification, which should lead to good works. Once a person is justified, he/she will be productive in doing good, just like a good tree produces good fruit. The Holy Spirit is what makes us good trees, and the Holy Spirit in us produces the good works called 'the fruits of the Spirit'. Good works do not cause righteousness, but when we are declared righteous by being justified, we then produce good works.

Only acts done by a Christian can be truly good and acceptable to God. This is because only a Christian can do acts in faith, with a spirit of gratefulness to Christ. Any 'good' works that lack this Christian motivation are actually rubbish in God's eyes. Only once we are justified by faith can we genuinely please God, and when we do please God with our good works that spring from the Spirit in us, he grants us rewards in his grace. The believer does good works not at all to earn any favour with God. He/she does it for two reasons: first, for the glory of God, and second, for the benefit of other people.

CHRISTIAN LIBERTY

A Christian is above the law and above sin. The Law has no claim on him/her, and neither do his/her sin and guilt – he/she is free. Christian liberty is a conscience that knows it is free from the wrath of God. This then means that the Christian is free from obedience to the Law, is free from the sting of death, is free from sin, and is free from the power of the devil. This freedom is true freedom – not what people usually mean when talking about 'free will'.

This liberty is only because of Christ, who justifies us before God and who sits at the right hand of the Father and intercedes for us. We have liberty not to abuse it, not to do whatever we want, but to use our liberty to serve each other out of love. If someone abuses his/her liberty and fails to do good works, he/she is not actually free. If he/she bears no fruit at all, that is indication that he/she is not really a true believer.

A true Christian will not need any law to constrain his/her behaviour. A true Christian will obey the Law willingly and freely. This is true freedom.

CRITICISMS

The first criticism we will address deals with Luther's idea that justification is being righteous in the eyes of God. How is this justification not just a legal fiction? The question is an important one, but Luther does have an answer. He says justification has a paradox in it: we are at the same time completely righteous before God and still not entirely free of all the sin in our lives. Our righteousness is not just a certificate we have been given with no bearing in reality. Justification is more than just a declaration – it comes through union with Christ. This union, admittedly, is a bit of a mystery. We are declared righteous because we are one with Christ. How are we one? What does that mean? This is to press the mystery too far – that we do not know the detailed mechanics of this union does not make it any less real.

The second criticism is hotly debated in theology today and it comes from a movement called the 'New Perspective on Paul' (NPP). Notable figures in this movement include E.P. Sanders, James Dunn, and N.T. Wright. It is largely a movement from New Testament Studies, focusing on the Jewish background to Paul's letters, especially Romans and Galatians. Is Judaism legalistic? The NPP claims that the Reformers saw it this way, but they mis-interpreted Paul. Works-righteousness of the individual is not what Paul is combating. The NPP says that he was fighting a 'national righteousness' that the Jews of Paul's day had in viewing themselves as God's chosen people.

The gospel is not justification by faith alone, the NPP says. The gospel is the proclamation of Jesus as Lord, in his death, resurrec-tion, and exaltation. Justification is not the centre of Paul's thought, but rather an implication of it. Justification is not so much about our legal standing before God, but about being inside the New Covenant. The NPP denies that there is an imputation of Christ's righteousness onto believers.

However, it is possible that the NPP has not quite given Luther the most charitable reading. Luther's theology of salvation is bigger than his commentary on Galatians, and there is a richer, fuller doctrine of salvation in his wider work. The prominence Luther gives to justification is part of a polemic shaped by his time and context; perhaps he would be more nuanced if he were writing today.

11

JOHN CALVIN

INSTITUTES OF THE CHRISTIAN RELIGION

INTRODUCTION

John Calvin (1509–1564) must be judged the greatest theologian of
the Protestant Reformation, if judgement is made on grounds of
intellect alone. We do not have good details of his early life:
he studied in Paris and converted to the Protestant cause in 1533.
The following year he left his native France for Switzerland, where
he eventually became a minister of the city church of Geneva, a
post he held until his death. His main task was the exposition of
Scripture; he produced commentaries on much of the Bible and
preached regularly. He was also endlessly involved in the various
theological controversies of the day, however, and produced a series
of polemical works on various issues. He is chiefly remembered,
however, for the *Institutes of the Christian Religion* (*Inst.*).

Calvin first wrote *Inst.* in Latin in 1536, a mere three years after
his Protestant conversion; he significantly expanded the book in
1539, expanded it further in 1543, made minor changes in 1550, and
then produced another massive expansion in 1559. Alongside these
Latin editions were French editions, usually translations of the Latin
and appearing a year or two afterwards. We will describe the 1559
Latin edition, which is usually accepted as the standard one.

Calvin's literary output was prodigious; as already noted, his core
task was commenting and preaching on the Bible. Alongside this sit

numerous interventions in theological controversies – some public, some more private – in letters and the like, and some works written to strengthen and encourage the churches, particularly those in Geneva and in his native France. The relationship between these various works is important to understanding Calvin's thought and is also somewhat controversial. The crucial question concerns the relationship of *Inst.* to the biblical commentaries.

An older tradition of scholarship reads *Inst.* as the centre of Calvin's writing, with the commentaries being, in a sense, the mining of raw materials to construct the system of theology contained in *Inst.* This, however, ignores both the facts of Calvin's career and his stated purpose in writing his theological textbook, which was to provide a companion to illuminate or expand discussions in the commentaries. So, where a topic was disputed, rather than rehearse the entire argument each time it came up in the biblical text, Calvin dealt with the controversy in *Inst.*, allowing him to treat biblical material more simply and straightforwardly. Equally, he wrote his theology to provide a guide to the themes that would come up again and again in the biblical commentary, and to offer an account of how they were related to each other.

For all its fame – and indeed for all its brilliance – then, we should read *Inst.* as a preparation and guide to reading Calvin's extensive writings on the Bible. Indeed, he would insist that the focus should be on the text of Scripture, not on a system of theology. Is the fame of *Inst.* misplaced, then? We will return to that question in the criticisms section below; for now, we will outline the book itself.

Inst. is divided into four books, each divided in turn into around twenty chapters. Each chapter is further divided into several sections. References to *Inst.* are typically given in the form 1.13.5 for 'Book I, Chapter 13, Section 5'. (Roman numerals are sometimes used for the first two numbers, hence: I.xiii.5.)

SYNOPSIS

The first book is entitled 'The Knowledge of God the Creator'. It begins with the famous line, 'Nearly all wisdom we possess ... consists of two parts: the knowledge of God and of ourselves' (1.1.1); this division structures the rest of the book. True knowledge of

God will inevitably involve love for God, commitment, and piety. In the beginning, before the fall*, human beings were given innate knowledge of God, and in a sense this remains: there is an awareness of the divine within every human mind. However, this innate knowledge is lost or distorted because of the fall: either we no longer know what should always have been obvious, or we twist truth out of shape. The same is true of revelation of God in creation: no reasonable mind could doubt the proofs there offered, but our fallen minds are no longer adequately reasonable, and so we do not see the truth that shines so brightly.

How, then, can we know God? Calvin points to the Bible. This is the only place that, in our current condition, we find true knowledge of God. In Scripture, God speaks, and in Scripture, God is revealed to be both creator and redeemer – the subjects of this book of *Inst.* and the next. Scripture speaks to us because it is the word of God; without it, we inevitably fall into error. In saying this, Calvin was not disagreeing with anything any Christian tradition of his day would have claimed, but the place of the Bible was a significant point of dispute in the Reformation: the Roman Catholic Church taught that the Bible was true and authoritative, but also taught that the recognition of its authority, and the interpretation of its truth, were properly functions of the church. On this basis, Reformers could not challenge the teaching of the church on the basis of the Bible.

Calvin opposed this conclusion by insisting that the Bible justified the church, not *vice-versa*. Ephesians asserts that the church is 'built upon the foundation of the prophets and apostles' (Eph. 2:20), proving for Calvin that authority flows from Bible to church, not the other way around. But how do we recognize the authority of the Bible if we do not rely on the teaching of the church? Calvin asserts that the Holy Spirit testifies directly to the authentic word of God in Scripture. Firm evidence to support the testimony of the Spirit is available in the excellence and agreement of the biblical texts, but the believer's faith rests on the Spirit's witness, not on any external support.

Knowledge of God involves, first, knowledge of God's character, which means God's attributes or perfections. God is absolutely good, just, wise, and loving, and this sets the true God apart from all the imagined gods in the world. God cannot be illustrated or portrayed, and so the Old Testament ban on images must be upheld, a thought that leads into a consideration of idolatry: only the true God is to be worshipped and served. The true God is identified as Father, Son, and Holy Spirit, three persons in one God.

What of the knowledge of ourselves, of humanity? Calvin discusses creation only briefly (I.14) and then focuses on the creation of humanity. The book ends with a discussion of providence, God's care for God's people in the face of a harsh and seemingly uncaring world.

The second book focuses on – the title is lengthy – 'The Knowledge of God the Redeemer in Christ, first disclosed to the fathers under the law, and then to us in the Gospel'. The theme of redemption, of course, demands an account of why humanity needed redeeming, and so Calvin discusses the fall* of humanity. Calvin's interest in the fall is particularly in its effects, rather than its origin or causes: he takes it for granted that human beings are fallen – arguing that any real self-knowledge will convince us of this fact – and asks what this means for our lives and capacities today. His answer, it has to be said, is not encouraging.

First, the fall of humanity means that all human beings now labour under the curse of 'original sin'. The sin of our first parents taints the whole human race, not just because we imitate that sin, but because we are implicated in it. Gifts entrusted to Adam on the basis of his obedience have been lost, and so now we live a vitiated, partly-human life, distorted and depraved. In our fallen state, we are unable to will anything good – not because our will is bound, but because our desires are disordered. God's redemption is a re-ordering of our desires, so that we can – we must – desire the good.

Calvin is very interested in faithful Jews before the coming of Jesus. On his view, the promises they had received from God were sufficient that they could know and trust in Jesus, even if they did not know his name, prior to his incarnation. The Old Testament law contained the gospel promise for those who were prepared to listen. We cannot, of course, fulfil the Law given in the Old Testament, but that very fact helps all who take the Law seriously to realize their need for a saviour and to look to God for someone who will save them from the curse of the Law.

How can Christ redeem us? For Calvin, the answer begins with incarnation: only one who was both genuinely God and genuinely human could fulfil the office. The Divine Son became human for no other reason than to redeem fallen humanity. He inherited and fulfilled three offices from the history of God's people, Israel: he was prophet, priest, and king. As prophet, he fulfilled the ancient prophecies, taught the truth, and lived out God's law perfectly. As king, he rules over the church and protects all its members; as priest, he lives in perfect obedience to God, offers his own life as a sacrifice for sin, and, after rising from the dead and ascending into heaven, prays endlessly for his people.

Book 3 is entitled, 'The way in which we receive the grace of Christ; what benefits come to us from it; and what effects follow'. It is by some distance the longest of the four books, nearly twice as long as any of the others, and deals with how the theological realities of the first two books become transformative for the individual human being. The core idea here is, unsurprisingly, 'faith', and it is worked out in several different ways.

First, the basis of faith is the secret working of the Holy Spirit in the believer's heart. Only as the Spirit makes us alive and gives us eyes to see the truth can we have any real faith. Second, Calvin offers an extensive definition of 'faith' itself as the crucial concept in his development: faith is faith in Christ, not 'faith in faith' or anything else; it is based upon a firm acceptance of the truth of Scripture, an acceptance that may reasonably be described as 'certainty'. Notwithstanding this 'certainty,' there is ongoing struggle in the believer's faith against doubt and against despair. The Bible is the key support and aid in this struggle.

Faith grasps hold of Jesus Christ and the promises he makes, and so leads to salvation. The first act of one who truly believes is repentance, a serious confession of all known sin and an ardent desire to live according to Christ's law ever afterwards. Roman rites concerning the need for auricular confession, or the existence of purgatory* as a place of repentance after death, are ignored or dismissed here: for Calvin, the moment for repentance is always now. Nonetheless, Calvin does not suppose that the one saved is freed from all sin immediately in the sense of seeing it as abhorrent and so to be avoided; instead, justification – the freedom of guilt from sin – is instantaneous; sanctification – the freedom from all that causes guilt – is far more gradual and lifelong.

Believers in Christ are free and are particularly free to pray. Prayer increases our love for God, cleanses our hearts, and teaches us to be thankful and to reflect on God's goodness. True prayer is honest, and so extempore, and is directed to God alone. Directing prayer to, or requesting prayer from, the Saints, the faithful departed, is inappropriate because we do not know that the Saints can hear us, nor do we know that they know what is best for us in God's good providence; further, the Bible commands us to pray to God alone. Seeking the help of the Saints appears to be a violation of this rule. How should we pray? We are taught by the Lord's Prayer. We pray that God's name may be glorified; we pray that we can redirect our desires to godly ends; we pray for our bodily needs – daily bread – and for our spiritual needs – we pray that we might know God's forgiveness for our failures and that we might be protected from those situations which might tempt us to fail in the future.

On Calvin's account, the security of believers in Christ is founded only on God's election*. God eternally predestines some to eternal life, others to destruction. Election is an actual choice that God makes, not merely divine foreknowledge of our choices; nonetheless, God's choices are just, and those who are reprobate* are dealt with rightly on the basis of their rebellion against God. Those who are elect will be called by God, ordinarily through hearing the Bible preached. The book ends with a chapter on the final, bodily resurrection.

Book 4 is simply called 'Of the Holy Catholic Church'. Unsurprisingly, this is the most consistently controversial part of *Inst.*, given that most of the Reformation debates were about church government and practices. Calvin identifies the true church as the community where the Bible is preached faithfully and the (two) sacraments are properly celebrated. The officers of the church are properly pastors and deacons; they are to be chosen by election of the people. Calvin offers a historical account of how he believes this biblical and original church order changed into the reign of bishops, and finally of the Pope. He discusses at length what power is properly possessed by the church in terms of determining doctrine and disciplining offenders. The church is not infallible, not even when gathered in a council*; the church has no power to invent laws and bind the consciences of Christians with them; proper church discipline consists in nothing more, and nothing less, than the excommunication of offenders.

The discussion then turns to the sacraments. Calvin discusses baptism and defends the baptism of infants of Christian parents (the Anabaptist belief that only believers able to give an adequate account of their own faith should be baptized had recently arisen in Switzerland). Next he turns to the eucharist. Luther and Zwingli, two earlier Reformers, had disagreed over the eucharist, and Calvin had made a significant effort to try and find a doctrine which would be acceptable to both camps; the history of these debates is visible in his lengthy treatment in *Inst.* He teaches that the believer feeds, genuinely but spiritually, on Christ when he/she receives the eucharistic elements. He, of course, criticizes what he sees to be the abuses of the Roman mass, particularly the idea that the eucharist is a sacrifice which may be offered to God in exchange for some gift or blessing.

Inst. ends with an account of the role and purpose of civil government. Civil government is established by God for the protection of people; it has power to enforce laws and to engage in warfare under certain ethical rules.

CRITICISMS

Inst. covers the whole of Christian theology, engages deeply in several controversies, and is still a (fairly) manageable size and extremely readable. Its clarity and compactness of treatment are both testimony to Calvin's literary skill. The treatment of theology in the book might be seen as distorted by the extended controversial sections, but as we saw above, Calvin's purpose in writing this book is precisely to collect up his controversial material so it does not keep re-appearing in his commentaries.

Calvin is famous for his doctrine of predestination; that is here, but it is far from being the heart of the system; further, Calvin does not say very much on the topic that would be denied by others of his day, either Lutheran or Roman Catholic. Predestination is dealt with much more briefly than controversies over church officers or the eucharist (for example), and it serves a mainly pastoral purpose: faced at the end of his discussion of salvation with the question 'Can a believer be sure he will remain faithful?', Calvin suggests that his faith, and his salvation, are at root God's decision and gift, and so are therefore secure. This pastoral purpose, however, gives a certain sort of prominence to the doctrine: it ceases to be a merely intellectual belief and becomes an idea which people will be pointed to when in emotional need. This might explain the importance it has achieved as a 'Calvinist' doctrine in popular memory in spite of how briefly Calvin in fact discusses it.

The methodological reflections above might lead us to think that it is Calvin's commentaries that should be considered the 'classic' and not *Inst.*, which was merely a primer and handbook for the reader of the commentaries. There is no doubt that Calvin's collection of commentaries is a remarkable achievement; biblical commentary is a more historically-located form of writing than doctrinal theology, however. As we discover new historical facts, get better editions of the original texts, and make advances (often through archaeological work) in our understanding of the ancient languages, the commentator is able to offer better insights; Historical commentaries are therefore generally regarded as superseded by more modern ones. Doctrinal texts are more resistant to such historical relativization, and so it is perhaps right that, despite its merely supportive intention, *Inst.* is the text of Calvin's that has lasted.

12

THE CANONS AND DECREES OF THE COUNCIL OF TRENT

INTRODUCTION

The Council of Trent (1545–1563) produced one of the best presentations of the theology of the Roman Catholic Church to date and set the course for the Roman Catholic Church up to and even through Vatican II in the twentieth century. Trent was unique among other Catholic conciliar decisions in that it contained substantial and detailed exposition of many key doctrines. It was the last church council for centuries, followed by the Vatican Council of 1870 which affirmed the infallibility of the Pope. Despite being called an ecumenical council, the Eastern church was never invited; Protestant rulers and theologians were invited, but they declined because they would not be allowed a voice in discussion or a role in decisions. This was to be, from the beginning, a thoroughly Roman Catholic event. It completed the theological system of medieval Catholicism and ensured in its response that the Protestant objections would not be a movement of internal reform, but would lead to schism.

The Council involved many gatherings – twenty-five public sessions and many more committees – over an eighteen-year period, and its decrees were signed by 255 members, two-thirds of whom were Italian. The sections related to doctrine are divided up into decrees, which contain further statements offering support for them, and canons, which condemn opposing views with the formula, 'If anyone says such-and-such, let him be an anathema'. It should be noted straight away that – as we shall see – the Protestant doctrines said to bring anathema are usually exaggerations and caricatures mixed in with heresies the Protestants would also condemn.

The Emperor wanted to discuss the reform of the Catholic Church and its practices; the Pope was more interested in doctrinal discussion and clarification. Trent handled both of these in parallel. The corrections to church practice are broad and were, unfortunately, quite necessary, as most serious and pious Catholics recognized. These will not receive much attention in this chapter, although they constitute much of the actual content of Trent. Reforms included rules for bishops and priests being appointed: how they were to govern, their owning of property, how nuns should be treated, the prohibition of selling indulgences, and many others. The Counter-Reformation launched by the Council of Trent brought long-overdue corrections to abuses and injustices in the Catholic Church, and the focus was on ensuring honourable conduct and piety in priests and bishops, a clarifying and firming of the structure of the church to curtail abuses, and a renewed focus on the care for souls.

What doctrinal issues are addressed? This work carves out what is distinctive about Catholic theology, addressing in detail items such as the relation of Scripture and tradition, justification, and the seven sacraments of Catholicism, while saying little to nothing about matters broadly agreed upon in Christian thought, such as the deity of Christ and the Trinity.

A main goal of the document is to distinguish Catholic teaching from that of the Reformers; it is not an attempt to address intra-Catholic debates.

SYNOPSIS

The Canons and Decrees of the Council of Trent cover a number of theological topics. We shall summarize those treatments, paying particular attention to the distinct contributions this work makes to theology from the Catholic perspective.

Trent decrees that Scripture and tradition are to be received as equally authoritative as two parallel streams of authority. Regarding Scripture, several books are included in Scripture that do not appear in the Protestant Bible (Tobit, Judith, 1 and 2 Maccabees, etc. None of these has content that changes Christian theology dramatically, although a passage in 2 Maccabees is used to support the doctrine of purgatory). Regarding tradition, the authority in the tradition goes back to Christ himself, who speaks (through the Spirit) through the continuous succession of the Catholic Church and its tradition. The interpretative authority of Scripture is in the Catholic Church alone, who judges its true sense and interpretation. This is very much in contradistinction to the Protestant approach, where Scripture is the ultimate authority, where tradition is a second-order authority that, unlike Scripture, is fallible, and where the final locus of interpretative judgement is in the individual believer, not in any institutional church.

Trent affirms an Augustinian view of original sin and the fall: Adam sinned, lost his original righteousness, and in so doing injured all his posterity by making them sinners. This original sin inherited from Adam is only taken away by the merit of Jesus Christ, which is applied by the proper administering of baptism in the Catholic Church. Infants are to be baptized, and baptism (of infants or adults) effects the forgiveness of sins and regeneration. Thus Trent affirms baptismal regeneration.

The section in Trent on justification* is one of the most sustained and lengthy theological treatments of all the topics in the document, and it deals with a key issue that divided – and still divides – Catholics and Protestants. Since this is the case, it will receive the most detailed treatment in this chapter, beginning with the historical context.

The conversation on justification in the middle ages is essentially Augustinian, trying to develop his thought in a way relevant for the day. Justification became the most appropriate way in the Western church to talk about God's saving work in mankind. Salvation was discussed in moral and legal language, following the influence of Anselm. The views on justification in the middle ages are diverse, but share some commonality: 'justification' refers to the process of being made righteous – not just to some aspect at the beginning of salvation, but also to its continuation and final completion.

Christians are made righteous through a fundamental change in their nature and being, not merely a change in status. Justification was understood in such a way that a separation of justification and sanctification was not viable.

The Reformation brought with it a different approach to justification. Protestants saw justification as a forensic notion, where God's justifying righteousness is alien and external to the person being saved. God, in an act of legal declaration, considers a believer to be in righteous standing before him; this is conceptually distinct from the internal act of regeneration which leads to sanctification. In most of Protestantism, the two are strongly linked, but are nevertheless distinct.

The Council of Trent represents the Catholic response to these (and other) Reformation movements. It is forced to focus on 'justification' in a way it might not otherwise have done – it is a polemical document, and the emphasis on the concept of justification (as they understood it) did not endure in Catholic theology the way it did in Protestantism. In other words, Trent defined 'justification' in contrast to the Protestant movement and was, in that way, not approaching the issue on its own terms. Further, there were various views within Catholic thought on justification that were mutually exclusive, not to mention the presence of precursors to Luther's views on justification in the Catholic Church, and even the presence of some at Trent who sympathized with him. Despite this diversity of opinion, Trent ultimately rejected the Protestant perspective.

Trent attempted to address several questions about justification raised by the Protestant challenge. Is justification just the forgiveness of sins, or must it include sanctification within humans? How should the relationship between faith and good works be understood? What roles does the human will play in justification? How does justification relate to baptism and penance? Can a believer be certain of his/her justification? What is the human contribution, if any, to justification?

Trent's answers to these questions can be seen by a rough sketch of its Catholic understanding of justification. Justification is being made righteous before God. God effects actual righteousness (not merely forensic righteousness) in a believer through Christ on the basis of Christ's righteousness. Christ's righteousness is not imputed to the believer, but rather the believer is made righteous by God on the merit of Christ's righteousness. In this understanding of justification, good works are a necessary *part* of a believer's justification, not merely the *result* of it.

In Trent's decree on justification, three different senses of the term 'justification' are adopted. The first nine chapters discuss what we might call the 'initiation of justification' or 'first justification' in the sense of moving from a state of unbelief and sin to one of faith and grace. The next four chapters address 'second justification', the increase in righteousness of believers. The last three chapters deal with losing justification and how to regain it through penance. We will explain each of these in detail.

Trent has much to say on the initiation of justification. No force of nature and no obedience to the Law can justify a fallen sinner. God sent Christ to accomplish this, and he died for all. Yet justification only comes to those who are born again in Christ, to those who are regenerated. Justification is a person transferring from a state of being born in sin to a state of grace. The beginning of justification comes from the prevenient grace of God, a grace that 'goes before' and assists a person to assent and co-operate with that prevenient grace. God touches a person's heart, but the person is able, through prevenient grace, to accept or reject that grace, and a person is called to do so and dispose himself/herself towards justification. While the Reformers insisted that a person is spiritually dead and can only choose sin until God regenerates him/her and then he/she chooses God, Trent seems to say that God has given enough grace to allow sinners to choose 'to convert themselves to their own justification'. It is specified that this choosing is without any merit that a person contributes. This preparation for initial justification culminates in the sacrament of baptism.

Trent clearly specifies that justification is not merely the forgiveness of sins, but also the inner sanctification and renewal of a person. The ultimate purpose of justification is God's glory and receiving everlasting life. The efficient cause of justification is God in his grace; the meritorious cause is Jesus Christ; the instrumental cause is the sacrament of baptism; the sole formal cause is the justice of God in making us just. We are justified by faith because faith is the beginning of human salvation, but we are not justified by faith alone. Also, no one can know with a high degree of certainty whether this grace of God has been received.

Trent then turns to discuss what we have labelled 'second justification', what the Reformers commonly called 'sanctification'. This is an active obligation of duty that comes from the initial justification. Justification is increased day by day through the process of faith co-operating with good works. The commandments are to be observed and a holy life is to be lived in this growth in justification, and those who persevere to the end will be saved. Human efforts are a co-operation with grace that do receive merit, increase justification, and in the end merit the reward of eternal life.

Losing justification becomes the final topic of this section. The distinction is introduced between venial sins, which do not threaten justification, and mortal sins, which amount to a forsaking of God and a total loss of justification if they are not dealt with properly through penance (note that no other sacraments are mentioned at this point). Mortal sins cause us to fall from grace, but justification can be restored through the sacrament of penance. One must confess one's sins to a priest in a prescribed manner, receive absolution, and make satisfaction through fasts, alms, prayers, and other pious activities. This satisfaction is not to avoid eternal punishment, which is avoided through the forgiveness that comes through the sacrament of confession, but to mitigate temporal punishment. Any mortal sin brings the total loss of the grace of justification and must be handled through penance. Mortal sins are, in this sense, deadly sins – fornication, adultery, drunkenness, etc.

The canons on justification provide several examples of misunderstandings of Protestant doctrine; it seems in some ways Catholics and Protestants were talking past each other. Protestants insist that the distinction between external justification and intrinsic sanctification is conceptual and never actual; they are distinct but never divided. For Calvin, both are aspects of our union with Christ. One cannot be justified but then fail to be sanctified. However, Trent seems to think Protestants *did* believe they could be divided, that justification amounts to little more than a 'legal fiction' in the Reformer's hands. Crudely, what Catholics understood by 'justification' the Reformers understood as 'justification' and 'sanctification' together. This speaks to the Protestant distinction of 'justification by faith alone'. By this phrase Protestants meant that good works do not contribute to justification (which, in their view, comes at the initiation of the Christian life). Under the

Catholic formulation of justification, Reformed doctrine seemed to entail that good works are depreciated for the Christian, whereas under the Reformed formulation of justification, Catholic doctrine seemed to entail a salvation by works.

The Council of Trent explains the seven sacraments of the Catholic Church: baptism, confirmation, the eucharist, penance, extreme unction, ordination, and matrimony. These sacraments are said to have all been instituted by Jesus Christ, and they can only be administered by someone authorized by the Catholic Church to do so – usually a priest. Ordination to the priesthood and matrimony are for those who are called to them, but the other five (or at least the desire for them, in extreme situations where they cannot be attained to) are required for salvation. However, they are not all equal in standing. The sacraments actually contain the grace of God that they signify; they are not merely outward signs.

Baptism with water is required for salvation, and at baptism a person is regenerated – it is no mere outward sign. Since infants and little children are to be baptized, he/she is too considered to be regenerated. Confirmation is a ceremony that culminates a process where a person previously baptized – usually as an infant – is, when they are of appropriate age, presented to the church as having personal faith and receives his/her first communion. The sacrament of the eucharist contains the real presence of Jesus Christ. It is a visible sacrifice that represents (in the strongest sense of the word) the bloody sacrifice of Christ on the cross – it *is* a sacrifice, not just a commemoration of the cross. The bread and wine, once consecrated, truly, really, and substantially contain the Lord Jesus Christ under the form of those elements (and each element entirely contains him, so the bread is given to the layperson, but the wine can be restricted to the priest without any loss of efficacy). This is called 'transubstantiation', and those who say that Christ is only spiritually present in the elements (i.e. many Protestants) are an anathema. Penance was touched upon above, under justification: the sacrament of penance is required for salvation as a means of sanctification. Jesus gave the apostles the power of forgiving and retaining sins, and as the successors to the apostles, the Catholic Church exercises that power through contrition, confession, and satisfaction. Contrition is genuine remorse and sorrow for one's sins and an intent to turn away from them. Confession is the telling of all of one's mortal sins to a priest for forgiveness from God. The priest absolves these sins and offers a means of satisfaction to the sinner so that temporal judgement might be avoided. If baptism is entrance into the church, penance is what it is to be under the church. Extreme unction is the completion of penance and of the entire Christian life, and is administered just before a person's death. It removes any last sins or remains of sins in anticipation of departure from this life. Ordination is the ceremony in which a person joins the priesthood of the Catholic Church or ascends up the ranks in the institutional hierarchy of the Church. The priesthood is a special role, and Trent denies the Protestant notion, supported by the New Testament, that all Christians are priests. Finally, matrimony is a sacrament involving one man and one woman (polygamy is expressly prohibited) being united in marriage. The matrimonial bond cannot be broken because of heresy, 'irksome cohabitation', or the absence of one party, but matrimony can be dissolved on account of adultery. Clerics are not allowed to marry, and while both are permissible, it is better to be celibate than to marry.

Other sundry issues addressed in Trent are worth mentioning. The mass should be celebrated in Latin, as had been the medieval church's practice, but effort should be made to regularly explain the meaning of what is being said in the native language. Purgatory is affirmed – a place where, after death, souls go to be finally purged of all sin and guilt in anticipation of heaven – but the more difficult questions with this doctrine are to be excluded from 'popular discourses before the uneducated multitude'. Relics, saints, and sacred images are to be venerated and used in worship, but are not to be worshipped themselves, and abuses along these lines must be completely abolished.

CRITICISMS

By excluding Protestants from the conversation and by failing to achieve a fair and thorough understanding of what beliefs Protestants actually held, the Council of Trent somewhat misses the intended target and repeatedly condemns a Protestant theology that never actually existed. This period in church history was tumultuous to say the least, and major changes to theology, practice, and church structure were underway, so the impetus to shore up

Catholicism and stem abuses is understandable. Nevertheless, it is unfortunate that such an influential document contains mis-understandings that helped to cement one of the biggest schisms in church history.

For the Roman Catholic Church, Trent is the point of definition of most of the controversial doctrines – these positions were held before, but not dogmatically defined before Trent. For example, this is the first time the number of sacraments is dogmatically stated as seven. The significance of this lies in the fact that this is a polemical document built around a felt need to rebuff opposing positions. Yet these opposing positions appear not to be carefully studied and understood. This is an unfortunate way to go about defining dogma.

13

THE ANGLICAN FORMULARIES

THE BOOK OF COMMON PRAYER, THE THIRTY-NINE ARTICLES, AND THE HOMILIES

INTRODUCTION

The Anglican Formularies are a somewhat diverse body of writings formed over several decades, even centuries. The authors varied, although Thomas Cranmer's voice, if not pen, lies behind much of this literature. *The Thirty Nine Articles* (*The Articles*) were originally written by Cranmer in 1552 and underwent an extensive revision in 1563 (in Latin – the English version was published in 1571) under the direction of Matthew Parker, whose revisions still fundamentally retained Cranmer's voice. Closely related to *The Articles* are *The Homilies*, which are two books containing authorized sermons intended, in part, to explain *The Articles*. The first book was edited by Cranmer and published in 1547, and the second was published in 1563 – receiving some additional sermons in 1571 – by John Jewel, who wrote all but two of them. The *Book of Common Prayer* is a compilation of prayer books which contain liturgy for worship services. A 1549 edition was revised by Cranmer in 1552, which was then modified in 1604 under the orders of James I. The official *Book of Common Prayer* used today was formed by a major revision in 1662.

It is impossible to understand these works apart from the history that produced them, so it is necessary to briefly set them in historical context. Generally, the Reformation in Britain was both a church and a state movement. It was guided by both bishops and statesmen, unlike on the continent, where scholars and theologians led the way. The movement in Britain was also less original, happy to follow the theological lead of figures like Calvin, but it also showed more organization and stability than its continental counterparts.

Initially, Henry VIII declared himself the ultimate governor of the church. This removal of the Pope's leadership was fundamentally and famously driven by unworthy motives (the Pope refused to legitimate his divorce and remarriage; in response, Henry declared himself supreme head of the church in England in 1534), but it enabled the religious reformation that would soon follow. After Henry's son Edward took the throne, Reformation doctrine and worship practices spread, bringing the conflict between semi-Catholic and Puritan sympathies to a head. Mary Tudor took the throne after Edward's short reign, and her attempts to reinstate Catholicism led to bloodshed and persecution of Protestants. Her reign was also short, and the turmoil she brought birthed the Reformed Church of England. Queen Elizabeth oversaw this process having a purely political agenda; yet despite this, Reformation thought flourished in Britain.

The shape of the Reformed Church in England was, and arguably still is, formed by two centres of gravity – Roman Catholic on one end and Lutheran and Calvinistic on the other; later, a tradition of celebrating Anglicanism as a 'middle way' between the two would be developed. *The Book of Common Prayer* might be seen as Catholic with a few modifications; *The Articles* and *The Homilies* are moderately Calvinistic. There is a tendency towards church hierarchy and sacramentalism, which can in part be explained by the political and social role the church played in England: many groups with different emphases and views are held together in one tent, a tent supported by the poles of the episcopacy and the liturgy. In another context, these groups could easily become separate denominations.

The English Reformers were themselves bishops in the Roman Catholic Church, and after the break, they retained an episcopal hierarchy they saw to be in line with the ancient church and suitable for England, but not necessary for the identity of the true church (in other words, they rejected the Roman Catholic notion that the church as an institution *was* the church). This system of church government was later strengthened and sanctioned in 1662. A key factor in understanding the Anglican Church is that it grew as a national church rather than a church centered on the theology of a figure such as Calvin, Luther, or Zwingli.

The historical context that birthed these works helps us understand their own history and merits mentioning. There are actually two versions of *The Thirty-Nine Articles*, one in Latin published in 1563 and one in English published in 1571. The latter, however, is not simply a translation of the former. They are slightly different and considered mutually explanatory; both are equal in authority. The *Articles* contain the basic tenets of the Reformation at their foundation: justification by faith alone, *sola scriptura*, etc. Yet they are more moderate and broader than their continental counterparts (see Westminster Standards**). Also, *The Articles* function differently than a creed and a confession for Anglicanism; they have less centrality and a slightly different purpose, they are to be read in conjunction with *The Book of Common Prayer*, and they are attempting to be broader and more comprehensive of the Christian faith.

The Thirty-Nine Articles will be covered in more detail in the synopsis section, but first we will describe *The Book of Common Prayer* and *The Homilies*. *The Book of Common Prayer* in its final form appeared in 1662 at the restoration of the monarchy. It is in many ways an imposition of the High Church and Arminianism* upon what was something like a Presbyterian Church of England. The 1662 edition is a push towards Roman Catholicism; crudely put, the words spoken tend to be Reformed, but the actions enjoined tend to be quite Catholic. The language is beautiful and poetic; the theology is sometimes liable to be incoherent. It follows the liturgical church calendar throughout the year and includes prescribed readings of Scripture that yearly cover most of the Old Testament once and most of the New Testament twice. Morning and evening prayer times are structured. Readings and songs are prescribed for daily services and for holy days. It contains prayers and thanksgivings for a variety of occasions, including weddings and funerals, prayers for rain and for fair weather, prayers in times of war, prayers to be used at sea, etc. It also contains detailed instructions for Communion, including prayers, exhortations, and prescribed actions, including a prayer of consecration of the elements. It contains likewise instructions for infant baptism (both in public and in private), baptism of those who 'are of riper years', confirmation, funerals, a ceremony for a woman after childbirth, etc.

The Homilies provided a model of topical preaching and also taught Reformation doctrine and explained theological points in detail – in this way interpreting *The Articles*. Topics addressed include: reading Scripture, the sufficiency of Scripture, the fallen and sinful state of man, justification by faith alone, the role of good works, Christian love and loving one's neighbour, apostasy, the resurrection, and others. It also contains sermons that are more practical, devotional, and exhortative, addressing sexual immorality, fighting and strife in and out of the church, idolatry, cleaning and repairing the church building, the place and time of prayer, marriage, and much more.

It would not be unfair to say that Anglicanism is more shaped by liturgy and tradition than rigorous logic in theology. The English Reformers were trying to reform the historic church rather than create a new one, and along these lines they kept ritual and episcopate leadership. In many ways, it is a compromise – a 'middle way' – between Catholicism and Protestantism.

SYNOPSIS

For the reasons mentioned above, our synopsis will focus on the theology of *The Thirty-Nine Articles*, particularly on the unique contributions of Anglicanism. There is a sense of moving from broad to narrow as *The Articles* progress, from the Trinity to relationships between church and civil authorities. It is somewhat unique in beginning with the Trinity and the incarnation, not, as other documents do, with Scripture, or methodology, or the creation-fall-incarnation-salvation progression. In this way, it tends to follow reality rather than our path of knowing or our experience. Further, by beginning with the Trinity and then immediately discussing the incarnation, it links faith in the Trinity to faith in Christ. The first five articles stand in a broad Christian faith, and apart from one exceptional clause in Article V, Christians East and West from most all traditions can affirm them.

The Articles then turn to Scripture and become much more about epistemology. Scripture contains the authoritative record of testimony of God's redemptive work, with the incarnation at the centre, and has all things necessary for salvation. In good Protestant fashion, it also rejects any alternative or additional tradition as authoritative. The Nicene Creed, the Athanasian Creed, and the Apostles' Creed are considered to be authoritative because these can be proven by Scripture.

With Article IX, the issue of sin is addressed. *The Articles* are Augustinian on anthropology, sin, grace, and free will. Yet there is nothing mentioned about the nature of man; nothing about the *imago dei*. With sin, we are corrupt by nature and we are guilty before God – original corruption and original guilt. In Article X, free will is treated theologically and denied apart from grace: man is spiritually dead, and we have no power to do anything good or pleasing to God apart from the grace of God.

After the topic of sin comes salvation in Christ in Articles XI–XVIII. Salvation is in Christ alone, and only by his name are we saved. We are counted righteous before God by Christ's merit, not our own, and this we receive by faith. Good works follow after justification from a lively faith, not as a means of justification before God. Any good works that do not spring from faith in Christ are not truly good and do not please God. Our salvation can be accomplished by Christ because he was like us in every way – except he did not sin. Once we are justified, and have received baptism, it is still possible to fall away for a period. On falling from grace, *The Articles* say that this is not a full and final apostasy but a temporary backsliding that might happen to the elect (who, by implication, will return to and persevere in the faith). Article XVII offers a nuanced yet ultimately Calvinistic take on predestination. Our salvation is based on God's predestination to save 'those whom he hath chosen in Christ out of mankind'. He has willed that the elect would be called by the Spirit, that they would obey that calling by grace, that they would be freely justified, that they be adopted as sons of God, that they would be made into the image of Christ, that they live the life of faith and good works, and that they would receive everlasting happiness. The stance taken is Reformed, and Calvin's influence is evident; however, *The Articles* focus on election to life of the saints and on the blessings Christians receive while directly avoiding addressing the issue of predestination and damnation (although the implications can be readily drawn).

Article XIX begins the topic of the church, which in broad terms is the theme of the remaining twenty articles. Strangely, *The Articles* specifically talks about the visible church and the requirements for it – preaching of the Word, right ministering of the sacraments – but says nothing on the invisible church. This leaves some important theological points unspoken: that there is a universal church of all true believers and that it is possible to be a part of the visible church (be a regularly attending member) but not genuinely a believer. Perhaps Cranmer wanted to focus on Christ in answering this question about a person's salvation, rather than on the church as an institution. Yet the lack of a theological treatment of the church is certainly noticeable and is liable to an individualistic understanding of the gospel and a de-emphasis on the community of believers. Anglicanism avoided this liability through its emphasis on formal liturgy and on the visible church (a solution that has its own pitfalls, as we shall see).

The Articles are loosely structured by the church's two areas of authority (from XX): first, to decree rites and ceremonies, and second, to speak to controversies of faith. The first is about making (often arbitrary) decisions about non-essential matters in the Christian faith, such as allowing priests to marry or the role of the church and the state. The second is about the authority the church has in proclaiming the gospel. This authority is exercised with fallibility, as the last sentence of XIX shows, but it is an authority that the institutional church holds because the institutional church is an expression of the church. The church, in short, has authority in expositing the gospel, as entrusted to it by the apostles, to the world.

The Articles deals with this second category first, handling the teaching authority of the church in XX–XXIV. On controversies of faith, the declarations of councils (or any other teaching) only have authority if their pronouncements can be taken out of Scripture (XXI). As we have mentioned, *The Articles* deem that the products of Nicaea and Chalcedon (in the form of the Athanasian Creed) pass this test. Things like purgatory, veneration of relics, and prayer to saints do not (XXII). Since the identifying marks of the church are preaching of the Word and the ministering of the sacraments, these tasks are prohibited unless one is an ordained minister in the church (XXIII). Also, the teaching must be in a language known to the people in the congregation (XXIV).

In Anglican thought, the sacraments are somewhere between these two categories of the church's authority – thus *The Articles* covers them next in XXV–XXXI. Here, Anglicans have paid particular attention and poured more effort into controversy than the other Reformation traditions. In line with Protestant commitments, the sacraments are limited to baptism and the Lord's supper, specifically excluding the additional five from the Roman Catholic tradition (XXV). We will briefly look at baptism before considering the Lord's supper in detail.

Baptism is a sign of Christian profession, but it is also a sign of regeneration by which a person is grafted into the church (XXVII). Baptism of young children and infants is commended, and Article XXVII seems to teach general baptismal regeneration (see also *The Book of Common Prayer* on the administration of public baptism of infants, where, after the water baptism, the priest is instructed to say, 'Seeing now, dearly beloved brethren, that this child is regenerate ...' and '... that it has pleased thee to regenerate this infant with thy Holy Spirit ...'). It appears that baptismal regeneration is kept from Roman Catholicism, but Anglicanism insists that it is not the ritual itself that does the work and that baptism does not remove original sin and guilt. The theological contradiction is difficult to deny. Some Anglicans take the words spoken in baptism in a hypothetical or hopeful sense, rather than in a literal one. Others make a distinction between baptismal regeneration, which is becoming a part of the visible church, and spiritual regeneration, which is linked with personal conversion. Some others make a distinction between the regenerate and the elect.

The Lord's supper is addressed in the next three articles, XXVIII–XXXI. Today, some in the Anglican Church – High Church Anglicans and Anglo-Catholics – have views on the Lord's supper that might appear similar to a version of transubstantiation. Some others adopt views similar to consubstantiation, while still others hold views like that of Calvin and the Reformed tradition. This last group seems to have the best claim to standing in accord with *The Thirty-Nine Articles* and *The Homilies*, which explicitly deny transubstantiation (XXVIII). Yet this is not entirely decisive because in Anglicanism, a dynamic occurs that is sometimes called 'the law of prayer is the law of belief'. The liturgy and ritual prescribed in *The Book of Common Prayer* may be in tension with *The Articles'* expression of views similar to those of Calvin on the Lord's supper, and if this tension is more than an illusion, then the High Church Anglicans may have grounds for their views.

The once-for-all nature of the sacrifice of Christ is insisted upon by the Reformers, and England was no exception (XXXI). The medieval Roman Catholic doctrine seemed to involve a recreation of the sacrifice of Christ, threatening to undercut the sufficiency and uniqueness of his passion. No grace can be added beyond that which is found in Christ's sacrifice, and it cannot be repeated.

The Anglican tradition accepted negations such as these about the sacraments and the boundaries they constitute and affirmed that Christ is present to us in them in a special way, but details about how this might be are not made entirely clear. It is clear that the wicked 'carnally and visibly' partake in the Lord's supper but in so doing do not partake in Christ or his presence – rather, they merely consume the sign to their own condemnation. Regarding the faithful, it is the union of the faithful with Jesus Christ that is the grounds for the grace of God received in the sacraments. In Anglicanism, the sacraments are taken to be objective; they are 'certain sure witnesses and effectual signs of grace and God's good will towards us, by which he doth work invisibly in us ...' (XXV). Yet this objectivity, more strongly stated than in other Reformation traditions, is qualified subjectively: it must be received by faith and in a right manner, and only believers actually partake of Christ.

After dealing with the essentials on controversies in the faith, non-essential issues regarding the authority of the church to decree rites and ceremonies are addressed. The parameters are that the church cannot ordain anything that is contrary to Scripture, that in its decrees it cannot emphasize one idea in Scripture to the neglect or contradiction of another, and that it cannot enforce anything additional beyond what is required in Scripture to be believed as a requirement for salvation. It is important to see in *The Articles* that the church's obligation to Scripture is shaped by negative boundaries. This creates space for the church to exercise authority to attempt to better understand the apostolic faith (e.g. the Trinity) and to draw out the implications of the faith for other matters (e.g. stem cell research).

Articles XXII–XXVI deal with various matters of church order. The Anglican Church has the authority to make, develop, and change these traditions as it sees fit (by implication, so do other church structures). However, any individual who openly and intentionally breaks these established traditions and ceremonies is to be rebuked (unless he/she is doing so because he/she does violate God's Word). The individual is to follow the traditions and ceremonies established by a 'particular or national Church', which has authority over these matters for the purpose of edification of the church. Unlike most other Protestant traditions, the church's freedom over tradition is corporate, not individual, and the individual's freedom is only limited as is necessary to protect the individual's conscience and faith. In other words, the freedom of the church from tradition belongs to the church rather than to the individual believer.

Finally, Articles XXXVII–XXXIX deal with the civil magistrates. The context that produced the articles did not have the distinction between church and society that we have in our modern world. This distinction was not held when this document was written, and the lines between sacred and secular, church and state, were not what they are today. The idea of a king seemed reasonable to them, finding a pattern from which to draw in the Davidic kings of Israel. The king could oversee and direct church matters and practices that varied from culture to culture, but could not speak to those which stood on some fundamental theological principle.

CRITICISMS

Perhaps the most significant criticism of the Anglican Formularies is that they tend to seek uniformity rather than unity. Many diverse groups are held together by a shared liturgy and church affiliations based on a national identity; unity is not necessarily the result of this arrangement.

Another criticism is that emphasizing ordained priests as part of the essential order of the church seems to undercut the idea that every member of the church participates in the church's authority in proclaiming the gospel and that every member of the church is gifted by the Holy Spirit.

14

THE WESTMINSTER STANDARDS

THE WESTMINSTER CONFESSION, THE SHORTER CATECHISM, THE LARGER CATECHISM, AND THE BOOK OF COMMON ORDER

INTRODUCTION

The Westminster Standards are considered to be some of the premiere theological works to emerge from the Reformed tradition. They were written by the Westminster Assembly, which met in Westminster Abbey, London in the middle of the seventeenth century.

The Westminster Assembly must be seen in the context of the Puritan story. Puritanism was a movement aimed at purifying the church and the state on the basis of the Word of God alone. It was a radical renewal movement in the Church of England that attempted revolution from within. Standing in the tradition of Calvin, the Puritans emphasized the greatness of God alone and the primacy of Scripture. It was surrounded by turmoil and bloodshed in the conflict between Protestant and Roman Catholic sympathies in England, but eventually birthed a degree of religious liberty and legal protection beginning with the Act of Toleration of 1689.

The Westminster Standards came from this context. The Puritans in English Parliament fought to order this assembly, and after repeatedly being blocked by King Charles, was ordered without his consent in 1643. They appointed 30 laymen and 121 clergymen/theologians to restructure the Church of England. It was to be a reforming and renewing force, bringing the liturgy, church government, and even its doctrine into greater purity according to Scripture. The intention was to move England's church closer to the Church of Scotland and the continental Reformed churches. It initially set out to revise *The Thirty-Nine Articles*** (see Chapter 13), desiring to make them more explicitly Calvinist, but those present became convinced that something more radical was necessary.

The Assembly met over a period of five years, holding over 1,150 sessions. For several years, it met every weekday for several hours each day, with even more time reserved in the afternoon for committees. During this period, the commissioned task was completed; afterwards it dwindled into an irregular and poorly-attended affair until it disappeared along with the Long Parliament that gave it existence. We must recognize that Parliament retained final authority over the work of the Assembly; *The Westminster Confession* was presented to it as 'humble advice'. Yet this parliament was thoroughly Puritan in character and did not interfere with the Assembly, only asking it to add scriptural proofs to its statements.

The Assembly was comprised of Englishmen and Scotsmen. Parliament nominated all the members, save for those from Scotland, which it approved. Those selected were noted theologians who were also faithful and pious churchmen. It was an attempt to bring together the major parties of the English Church. Representatives from the Church of Scotland did not participate initially, but joined soon enough to have substantial influence on the results. Delegates from the North American colonies were invited, but were largely prevented from attending by their suspicions of English authority.

Despite a diversity of representatives, there was a great deal of agreement in doctrine. All were Calvinists. However, regarding church government, there was much disagreement that consumed much of the debate. The different perspectives included Episcopalians, Presbyterians, Congregationalists, and Erastians. The key point of disagreement between them was the role that the state should play in church affairs and the degree of centralized authority in church organization. The Episcopalians wanted a hierarchical structure in which the bishop held authority over local congregations and tended to desire strong ties between church and state. The Presbyterians, the majority party, influenced by Puritan thought as they were, wanted an assembly-based structure where elders rule in the local congregation, groups of local congregations are ruled in a more limited way by a higher-level presbytery, presbyteries are grouped in synods, and national synods convene for a general assembly. They were agreeable to a close connection between church and state. The Congregationalists wanted each local church to be autonomous and independent, governed by its own members, and they wanted to dissolve the ties between church and state. Finally, the Erastians saw the state as supreme in church affairs. In the end, the Scottish Presbyterian perspective prevailed, only to soon be dropped in England in 1660.

The Westminster Confession (*The Confession*) is a scholarly and mature form of Calvinistic theology. Many of its ideas are indebted to the thought found in continental creeds and confessions. The conflict between Calvinism and Arminianism in Holland, which led to the Synod of Dort, had great impact on England and on those in the Westminster Assembly. The form of the *Confession*, however, was closer to *The Thirty-Nine Articles* than to these continental forerunners. In fact, *The Confession* has echoes of the earlier and more Calvinistic version of *The Articles* that took hold in Ireland.

The Confession states doctrines with unusual care, clarity, logical precision, and caution, showing a theology whose doctrines are richly interrelated and form a coherent whole. Yet mysteries are respected as such, and *The Confession* refrains from attempting to solve things like divine sovereignty and human freedom. The theology of *The Confession* proclaims the glory and supremacy of God. It also places the highest value on Scripture, offering carefully selected scriptural proofs for nearly every statement in the *Confession* and the Catechisms.

A few other works were produced by the Assembly besides *The Confession*. The Westminster Catechisms are intended to be simple questions and answers designed to educate laypeople in doctrine. They reinforce the teachings found in *The Confession*, with the matters of church polity and discipline being omitted. *The Shorter Catechism* has 107 questions and was used for children and new converts; *The Larger Catechism* adds further questions, bringing the total to 196, and expands those found in the shorter version. The questions are organized in a logical scheme by topic, dealing with God and creation, mankind and sin, Christ and redemption, the

Ten Commandments, the sacraments, and the Lord's Prayer. The first question of *The Larger Catechism* famously reads, 'Q: What is the chief and highest end of man? A: Man's chief and highest end is to glorify God, and fully to enjoy him forever'.

The Book of Common Order is a collection of liturgies for public worship. It contains prayers and instructions for diverse situations, including visitation of the ill, burials, marriage, baptism, etc. It also contains metrical versions of the Psalms for use in worship services. Since these works reflect the theology of *The Confession* and implement it into a body of liturgy, our focus for this chapter will be on *The Confession* itself.

The products of the Westminster Assembly are unique is several ways. First, the Standards attempt to cover the whole of theology, addressing a breadth of issues (unlike its counterparts such as the Synod of Dort, which focused on the debate between Calvinists and Arminians). Second, *The Confession* failed in the country in which it was written and for which it was written, but it succeeded in Scotland and America. This product of English Puritanism gained no long-term traction in England, but became an enduring standard of doctrine for Presbyterianism. Third, these documents have had a lasting influence. No other confessions or standards have had such vitality and enjoyed such enduring influence on Reformed Protestantism as those from Westminster.

SYNOPSIS

The *Westminster Confession* covers many other topics. For example, it contains careful statements about God's attributes, the Trinity, and about the person and work of Christ. These parts of *The Confession* stand in agreement with Nicaea and Chalcedon (see Chapter 5). Rather than attempt to summarize all of it, we will focus in on some of its distinguishing contributions.

The Confession starts with the doctrine of Scripture, like the continental confessions but unlike *The Thirty-Nine Articles* (see Chapter 13). It very nicely sums up Protestant commitments about the Bible. Scripture is divinely inspired, although the relationship between God and human authors is hardly addressed. It has authority over the Christian life and faith. It is the infallible rule of faith and practice. It is sufficient, meaning that it is above church tradition and above natural reason. A bit more discussion on these points should prove helpful.

The authority of Scripture is from God alone, not from any church authority. *The Confession* says we do recognize that the church has testified to Scripture as the Word of God and that the Bible itself gives evidence that it is such, but ultimately we are persuaded and assured of this by the Holy Spirit's work in our hearts.

The necessity of Scripture is taught. There is enough knowledge of God in creation for us to be without excuse, but there is not enough in nature to give the knowledge of God required for salvation. For that, God has revealed himself in a special way at various times and places, now found in Scripture. Thus the Bible is necessary for salvation.

Everything we need for our salvation, life and faith, and glorifying God is found in Scripture, either stated directly or available by deduction. Some things are clearer than others, and faithful readers of Scripture may disagree on some things. Still, a sufficient understanding of what needs to be 'known, believed, and observed for salvation' is available from Scripture to the learned and unlearned alike. This idea is called the 'perspicuity of Scripture': that the basics required for salvation are clear enough for anyone to find them (through reading the Bible and also through having it explained by pastors and teachers). However, to come to an understanding of these things that leads to our salvation, we need the Holy Spirit to work in us.

The discussion of the doctrine of predestination is noteworthy. This is a distinguishing doctrine of Calvin and the other Reformers. Debate about this issue in Christian theology has endured from the beginning and at times it has proved extremely divisive. It is the object of ire by many who reject Reformed theology, but held dearly, with reverence and humility, by those who affirm it. *The Confession* says this doctrine is mysterious and must be handled with care; it must be used with the purpose that Christians might have assurance about their own salvation. The impression from *The Confession* is that the doctrine is not for those outside the faith, who should be called to repent and obey the gospel, but is for those who have already done so.

Predestination is a part of God's eternal decree, so *The Confession* begins its treatment there. From eternity past God has freely ordained all things on the basis of his will. God did not decide things based upon a look into the future, although he knows what would happen in every possibility. No, God has decreed every detail of everything that comes to pass based on his own wise and holy will. In short, God's decision on what will be and what will happen comes from himself, not from anyone or anything else. Yet his eternal decree does not make him the author of sin and it does not remove free will or secondary causes (*The Confession*'s theology is not fatalistic, and although it does not attempt to explain how divine sovereignty and human freedom are compatible, it affirms that they are).

God does not merely decree what will happen, he also upholds and directs all things in accordance with his decree, using means and secondary causes as he sees fit. This is called 'providence'. For Westminster, God's providence covers everything, including the fall (and all other sins). God did not give 'bare permission' for sin, but puts even sin and evil in his plan so as to accomplish his will. Even so, sinfulness attaches only to the creature, not God. With God's providence, a person's will is free in that it could be good or evil – there's nothing inherent or necessary in the creature that it be one way or the other. Adam and Eve had the freedom to will and do good, but in the fall, humans lost the ability to will anything that is truly good accompanying salvation. Rather, all are dead in sin. Only God can act to even begin to deliver someone out of this state, and he only does so for the elect (those chosen for salvation).

A part of this view of God's sovereignty is the difficult entailment that some men and angels are predestined for everlasting life, others for everlasting death. *The Confession* states that this is more than just God ordaining two indefinite groups, but that this election is particular and unchangeable – certain ones to life, certain ones to death. However, for Westminster, the decision does not work the same way for both. Those elected to life are chosen freely by God, in Christ, for everlasting glory. This decision is based on God's free grace and love, not on anything in the creature: not on foresight of faith, good deeds, perseverance in the faith, or anything else. God has chosen the ends – that the elect be glorified in everlasting life – and also the means, the redemption found in Christ. Only the elect are effectively called by God through the Spirit to faith and experience salvation (justification, adoption, sanctification), unfailingly kept by

God's power until the end. For the elect, God's decision is active. For the rest of mankind, God's decision is one of inaction – he, for reasons unknown to us, in his sovereignty, withholds his mercy from some who have fallen in Adam, leaving them to receive punishment for their sin, to the glory of his justice. God's pre-destination to salvation or eternal punishment logically assumes that a fall has happened (called the 'infralapsarian view'), rather than first choosing some for life and some for disgrace and then deciding on sin and the fall to achieve that decision (called the 'supralapsarian view').

Election is only the beginning of the story of salvation, and *The Confession* skillfully states the Reformed understanding. Those (and only those) whom God has predestined for everlasting life receive an effectual call. This is an inward call, not just the external call to repent found in the preaching of the gospel. God, working through his Word and his Spirit, calls a person from sin and death to grace and salvation, effectually drawing him/her to Jesus Christ. He brings him/her to a state of spiritual vitality (regeneration) and works in such a way that whoever receives this call *will* answer it, freely embracing the grace offered. All recipients of this call are justified, meaning that their sins are forgiven and they are con-sidered righteous before God. There is a double imputation that comes with having faith: the debt and guilt of the elect is imputed to Christ – who, through his obedience and death, fully satisfied the Father's justice on their behalf – and Christ's obedience and right-eousness is imputed onto the elect. This comes by faith alone, which is a gift from God. All those who are justified are adopted as children of God and can call him Father. They are also sanctified really and personally through the Word and the Spirit dwelling in them. Their actual condition is gradually made more holy and less sinful, and although their lives will be marked by increasing holi-ness, the process is never completed in this life, but only in death and glorification. By the work of the Spirit, sanctification produces good works, which are the evidence of a true and lively faith, but which do not contribute in any way to justification.

Another somewhat unique contribution of *The Confession* is its theology of covenants (note that this is not a theology of the covenants between God and man explicitly found in Scripture, per se). It distinguishes two covenants between God and man: the covenant of works, which requires perfect and personal obedience, and the covenant of grace, which requires faith in Christ for salvation. The covenant of works was made with Adam, but his disobedience (and our connection with him) has made this merely theoretical for us all. So a second covenant was made, the covenant of grace. This covenant is administered in two ways, through law and through gospel. First, law: under the Old Testament arrangement, it came through promises, prophecies, sacrifices, circumcision, the Passover lamb, and other things given to the Jews. These all pointed to Christ and were enough for faith and salvation of the elect living at that time through the work of the Spirit. Second, gospel: in the time of the gospel, the covenant comes through the preaching of the Word and the sacraments (baptism and the Lord's supper). These are not two covenants of grace, only two different ways of administering the one.

Other doctrines are worth noting, if only more briefly. *The Confession* makes a distinction between the visible and invisible church, where the invisible is all the elect from all times and places and the visible is all who profess Christian faith (and their children). At different times, the visible church has been more or less pure, and even the purest visible church has both mixture and error to some degree.

Calvin's view of the sacraments is repeated in *The Confession*. The sacraments are baptism and the Lord's supper, and there is a 'spiritual relation' between the sign (water, bread, and wine) and that which is signified. Through the work of the Spirit, grace is exhibited to worthy receivers. Baptism is a sign and seal of the covenant of grace and of salvation. *The Confession* allows sprinkling of water for the act, and infants who have at least one believing parent are to be baptized. The Lord's supper is not a real sacrifice (*contra* Roman Catholicism), but a commemoration of the cross. Yet it is more than a mere memorial (*contra* Anabaptist and Zwinglian views), for in this meal, worthy recipients receive spiritual nourishment. The body of Christ is not in, with, or under the elements (*contra* Lutheran views), but Christ is spiritually present to the faith of believers as the elements are to the outward senses.

The Confession contains the Puritan theory of the Christian Sabbath which was not found in the work of the Reformers. It involved a strict observance of the Lord's Day (Sunday) based on the fourth commandment, other Old Testament laws, and as a divine law of nature worked into the very nature of man. The Jewish Sabbath became the powerful template for the Christian Sunday. Work and leisure activities were to be rigorously avoided, and worship services attended.

CRITICISMS

The first criticism has largely stuck: Westminster did not allow for enough religious freedoms or for a freedom of conscience in society. It assumes a Christian government and the union of church and state established by Constantine in the fourth century. This entails a duty for the state to protect and support the church. The Assembly itself was called for a purpose along these lines. Religious tolerance in society was fought for by some in the Assembly, and although they did not prevail then, they might claim vindication in light of the history that unfolded soon after. In fact, many since have either modified or moderately interpreted these parts of *The Confession* to make them compatible with religious freedom without substantially changing the character of its theology.

The second criticism, often made by Arminians, is that predestination is unfair and that holding the views Westminster does about the divine decree and providence makes God the author of evil, despite any denials of such. This is a serious accusation, and the Westminster divines would admit they have left much unexplained as to how their view protects human freedom and does not implicate God in evil. However, they would likely not be distraught that certain popular notions of human freedom are incompatible with their theology, and would defend their high view of God's sovereignty from Scripture.

Third, related to the previous criticism, Westminster does not spell out what is meant by several scriptural passages stating that God wants all to be saved or that Christ died for all. Here, *The Confession* is ambiguous, and given the clear difficulty on these issues raised by the doctrine of predestination, the lack of clarity seems problematic.

15

JONATHAN EDWARDS
THE RELIGIOUS AFFECTIONS

INTRODUCTION

The British colonization of the east coast of North America coincided with religious persecution in England. As a result, parts of New England became a haven for 'Puritans', English Protestants who could not accept (what they saw as) the compromises of the Church of England. Because of this history, the religious tradition of New England was held on to jealously: it was an ingrained part of its identity.

Jonathan Edwards (1703–1758) was schooled in a New England Puritan tradition that was already looking old-fashioned; he discovered the philosophy of John Locke as a relatively young man, and gave his life to reforming New England orthodoxy. He did not intend to change any doctrine – far from it; he was self-consciously conservative – but he recognized that doctrines needed restatement and new defences in the new philosophical climate that was coming. He saw the Enlightenment on the horizon and tried to respond.

At the same time, Edwards was pastor of a local church in Northampton, Massachusetts. In the mid-1730s, he saw a remarkable, extended period of heightened interest in religion, with people responding in remarkably emotional ways to sermons, with many people professing conversion. Edwards' experiences here were the beginning of a widespread movement in the American colonies that became known as the 'Great Awakening'; with a parallel movement in the British Isles, the 'Evangelical Revival', this gave birth to the modern Evangelical movement, which remains an extremely significant strand of Christianity in the world today.

The emotionalism of the 'new lights' (as supporters of the Awakening came to be known) drew much criticism; Edwards published works narrating his own experiences and observations, and defending the Awakening. As time went on, his position became more nuanced, and he began to criticize those who placed too much stress on a visible emotional response, as well as those who rejected any emotional display as being inappropriate in church. *The Religious Affections*, published in 1746, was his last and longest discussion of the Awakening and remains a classic text of religious psychology, analysing with insight and discrimination the meaning – or lack of meaning – of various human responses to the work of God's Spirit.

SYNOPSIS

The Religious Affections is a long book, but it is cast in standard Puritan sermon form: there is a biblical text and some discussion of the meaning and context of the text, resulting in the statement of a 'doctrine' – a brief summary of an idea that then provides the theme for the rest of the discussion. The doctrine is then developed in various ways – it might be defended, explained, or compared with other biblical ideas, for example. Finally, the doctrine is applied in several ways, perhaps to various different groups (young people; parents; older people; farmers; etc.).

The Religious Affections is divided into three parts. The first contains the text, the doctrine, and the development of the doctrine. The second and third are (very extensive) applications of the doctrine. Edwards takes 1 Pet. 1:8 as his text: 'Whom having not seen, ye love; in whom, though now ye see *him* not, yet believing, ye rejoice with joy unspeakable and full of glory' (KJV, the translation that Edwards used). He argues that this text describes the heart of true religion and that it suggests two parts to this: true religion is, essentially, love to Jesus Christ and joy in Jesus Christ.

Love and joy are both emotions, and so Edwards states his doctrine: 'True religion, in great part, consists in holy affections'. He defines 'affections' as 'the more vigorous and sensible [i.e. "felt"] exercises of the inclination and will of the soul'. Edwards, like others of his day, thought human beings had two mental faculties: the mind/understanding, which sees, knows, and interprets; and the heart/will, which desires, dislikes, approves, and rejects. Edwards asks the question, is religion mostly a matter of knowledge or of desire? His answer is that (notice the 'in great part' in the doctrine) religion is mostly a matter of desire or emotion – the love and joy mentioned in his text.

Edwards defends this doctrine in various ways. First, he offers long lists of biblical texts which stress love, joy, hatred of sin, longing for God, and so on. Second, he suggests that it is a matter of common human experience that our actions generally follow our affections – usually, we do the things we want to do and avoid the things we hate. As a result, if we are to live out our religious faith, it has to be rooted deeply in our emotions. Third, he notes that there are many people who understand the doctrinal content of Christian faith very well, but who are not committed to Christian living (this point was probably truer in Puritan New England than it would be today); this demonstrates that true religion is not essentially about grasping doctrines. Fourth, he looks at the biblical discussions of various emotions and particularly singles out love as the central piece of Christian practice. Fifth, he examines the piety of the great saints of the Bible, and particularly of Jesus himself, and suggests that in each case affections are central to what is going on. There are more strands of proof than just these, but these give an indication of the argument: the Bible, our own experience, and a proper understanding of doctrine all combine to suggest that true piety is in our hearts, not just in our minds.

Having argued this, however, Edwards offers a warning: we should not be quick to judge ourselves or others on the basis of our perceived level of emotional commitment to the faith at a given moment. We have many affections that are not spiritual – an able preacher can easily whip up the emotions of a crowd, for instance. Our state of health, or our tiredness, affects our emotions significantly on a day-to-day basis. As a result, Edwards counsels that we should look for evidence of a lasting and deep love and joy:

there will be rises and dips, but what is the general tendency over months and years?

Edwards closes the first part of the book with some first points of application: preaching and public worship should be designed to stir up godly emotions; we should be ashamed at our cold-heartedness and more deeply moved by the gospel.

The second part of the book introduces one of Edwards' most important contributions, the concept of a 'negative sign'. A negative sign, in Edwards' terms, is not a disproof, but something that, although perhaps superficially impressive, proves nothing in any direction. The debates over the revivals had featured claims and counter-claims concerning the fairly spectacular reactions of certain converts. Edwards himself had seen this, when he famously preached on 'Sinners in the hands of an angry God' at Enfield, Connecticut, on July 8, 1741. The sermon was repeatedly interrupted by people moaning and weeping, crying 'what must I do to be saved?' and then rejoicing as they found peace in Christ.

For some proponents of the revival, such remarkable manifestations were visible proof that the Spirit of God was at work in someone's life. For others, opponents of what was going on, they were clear signs of disorder – possibly of insanity – and so compelling evidence that what was going on was inappropriate and wrong. Edwards wants to insist, in contrast to both views, that events like this proved nothing in either direction. He has twelve such negative signs that he identifies and discusses.

In each case, the argument takes the same form: Edwards offers biblical examples of true faith marked by this sign and then offers a counter-example, also biblical, of false belief similarly marked. So, for example, his first negative sign is the presence of very strong emotion. There can be no doubt, biblically, that very strong emotion can – indeed should – be a part of true piety. The Psalms are full of extravagant claims of everlasting, overwhelming love for God and for God's law, and equally of protestations of 'perfect hatred' against God's enemies (Ps. 139:22, KJV); John the Baptist expressed 'great joy' at the coming of Christ (Jn 3:29); the women who were the first witnesses to the resurrection similarly experienced 'great joy' (Mt. 28:8). Edwards lists many more examples from the Bible, but the point is clear: strong, elevated emotion is not incompatible with true faith and should not be dismissed as disorder or madness.

On the other hand, there are several biblical examples of strong religious emotions that rapidly come to nothing. Edwards offers Israel's rejoicing at the Red Sea and at the foot of Mt Sinai, which so rapidly turned to worship of the golden calf, as one example; for another, he proposes the crowds who welcomed Jesus into Jerusalem on Palm Sunday with joy and worship – the same crowds who demanded his death at the end of that week. Religious emotions may be very strong and expressed very publicly but still be transient – and so no sign of the true state of a person's heart.

The other eleven negative signs cover the source, strength, content, and effect of the affections. That strong emotion comes upon people suddenly, from without, that it brings with it recollections of biblical texts, that it causes them to speak eloquently and forcefully about the wonders of the gospel – all of this proves nothing. The devil quoted Scripture for his own ends against Jesus; Paul, Peter, and Jude all warn against eloquent, false teachers; and so on.

What, then, are convincing signs of truly holy affections? Edwards lists twelve in Part III of the book. Three relate to the source of the affections, five to their nature, and four to their results. On the source, truly gracious affections come from the internal work of the Holy Spirit, from an appreciation of the beauty of the gospel, and from a conviction of the truth of the gospel. Again, the proof of each point is essentially through an appeal to biblical material.

Turning to the nature of the affections produced by true piety, Edwards suggests first that they are disinterested and not a result of self-interest; they bring with them an inward conviction of the truth of the gospel and also a humbling awareness of our own sinfulness. They are a part of a genuine change in our nature that results from conversion, and they are marked by a 'beautiful symmetry and proportion'. This last point is a suggestion that there is a proper balance in truly Christian emotions between love for God, hatred for sin, joy in the gospel, sorrow at our own failures, and so on. A person who is implacable in his/her hatred of sin but shows little joy, for instance, lacks this proper balance, and this suggests there is something deficient in his/her Christian experience.

On the result of true Christian piety, Edwards suggests truly religious affections produce meekness; a softening of the heart; a desire for their own increase (love for God brings with it a longing to love God more, for example); and a lifetime of devoted Christian practice. This last point is dealt with at disproportionate length and would seem to be for Edwards the crucial demonstration. Holiness, lasting and growing until death, is the true measure of someone's heart.

CRITICISMS

Edwards' text is a classic of pastoral psychology. He traces with care and insight the internal impulses that make someone Christian. For all our advances in psychological science in recent decades, this text still sounds real and convincing: if Edwards' language and concepts are quaint, his insight into how people work demonstrates much pastoral experience and much profound reflection upon it.

The concept of a 'negative sign' is an extremely valuable one. Edwards is able, with careful judgement based on biblical texts, to cut through much that appears remarkable and to dismiss it as something that may be hugely exciting, but is nonetheless not decisive in determining a person's spiritual state. His norm for judgement is – unsurprisingly, given his context – appeal to the Bible; whether we find this norm convincing or not, his arguments indicate powerfully that we need to be able to insist that what matters is not something spectacular, but instead something well-grounded in sound argument.

The preoccupation of Edwards and his various opponents with sifting true from false religious experience might seem strange to us, but we should remember that they lived in a different context. Today, someone seeking spiritual solace for selfish reasons has any number of alternative spiritualities to choose from, most of them much less ethically demanding than any form of Christianity; in Edwards' day, in New England, the church was the only option. So a pastor in New England was perhaps more likely to encounter someone merely pretending to be converted.

At the same time, we should not forget Edwards' own history. In Northampton, the revival fires had cooled, and Edwards' relationship with his church was becoming strained – they would dismiss him a few years later. He had trumpeted the effects of revival with confidence, but by the time he came to write *The Religious*

Affections he may well have felt he had cause to doubt the real spiritual experience of some whose conversions he had celebrated. The text is a very chastened defence of revival, extremely aware that the zeal of the most enthusiastic converts can fade to (apparently) nothing after a few years.

This recognition perhaps also explains another feature of the text: the positive signs Edwards lists are extremely difficult to apply. True religion may well stem from the internal work of the Spirit and be the result of a change of nature caused by conversion, but these are not easy things to measure with any confidence. The crowning proof, that truly religious affections produce a lifetime of faithful Christian practice, is only testable after death: up to the point of death, it is potentially, at least, falsifiable. True religion might well consist largely in holy affections, but recognizing holy affections, on Edwards' account, seems a very difficult business. (Of course, this difficulty is particularly acute within a broadly Reformed account of the relationship between justification and sanctification; the approach offered by the Council of Trent**, for example, would struggle much less with the issue.)

Of course, Edwards' positive signs are not totally opaque: if it might prove difficult to decide with any real conviction that a person's affections are 'beautifully balanced', it is not at all hard to spot some examples of people who clearly fail this particular test. It is certainly not merely useless. Again, whilst the requirement for a lifetime of Christian living can never be proved before death, it can certainly be disproved. Edwards allows us to judge between 'no' and 'perhaps' – there is little room for an uncomplicated 'yes'.

This is perhaps unsurprising when we consider the heart of Edwards' analysis: true Christianity is, he believes fervently, about an internal change. The biblical texts speak of new birth or new creation – a profound and decisive transformation of our basic identity. This, when it happens, has many – endless, perhaps – effects, but none of the effects can be confused with the cause, and Edwards wants to caution us that every particular effect might happen as a result of some other cause, and so to regard evidence for any one of the effects as evidence for the internal cause is always, potentially, a mistake.

But if the change is internal, then there will be no direct evidence of it. There is no unmediated access to the core of another person's being – to his/her 'soul', to use the language of Edwards' day. We can observe his/her behaviour and we might draw inferences about his/her soul from that, but Edwards wants to warn us to be cautious in drawing such inferences, in any direction. It remains a warning worth heeding, and the book remains a classic.

16

JOHN WESLEY

A PLAIN ACCOUNT OF CHRISTIAN PERFECTION

INTRODUCTION

John Wesley (1703–1791) was a minister in the Church of England and the founder of Methodism (which was originally a movement within the Church of England, although it became a separate denomination). As a young clergyman at Oxford University, Wesley, his brother Charles, and others became famous for the seriousness of their religious practice; the two Wesley brothers later went to the American colonies as missionaries to Native Americans. It was only on his return, however, that Wesley experienced what he regarded as his conversion to true Christianity, when he heard Luther's *Commentary on Galatians* being read at a Moravian meeting in London.

Wesley began preaching a message focusing on salvation by faith alone, with great success, and he became one of the leaders of the Evangelical revival. His willingness to preach outdoors brought some conflict, but also many converts, and he began to organize those converted into 'societies'. His genius for organization was unquestionable, and when, soon after his death, Methodism separated from the Church of England, it had its structures completely in place already.

Unlike most of the other early Evangelical leaders, Wesley was a convinced Arminian*. He regarded the doctrine of Christian perfection as the particular inheritance of the Methodists: this was the truth they were to restore to the world church. He taught the doctrine energetically all his life, but a 1777 publication, *A Plain Account of Christian Perfection*, is his definitive statement of what he believed was the particular gift of the Methodists.

SYNOPSIS

Wesley's aims in *A Plain Account of Christian Perfection* are to define his doctrine, to defend it against misunderstandings or misrepresentations, and to demonstrate that he had been teaching the same doctrine all his life – indeed, from 1725 (when he read Jeremy Taylor's *Rules and Exercises of Holy Living and Dying*), long before his conversion in London. The text is arranged chronologically, with twenty-eight numbered sections largely (1 is a brief introduction, and 27–28 form the conclusion) highlighting things Wesley read or wrote in a particular year that contribute to defining perfection and demonstrating that it never changed.

There is a gradual change in character of the sections through the book. The early sections are brief and mainly record Wesley's reading, which shaped and confirmed his belief in perfection; the middle sections are quotations from tracts, sermons, and hymns that he and his brother Charles wrote, which asserted Christian perfection; and the later sections come from a time when his teaching had become known and controversial, and offer more lengthy statements, often in question-and-answer format, trying to define the doctrine more carefully and to defend against criticisms.

Throughout the 1720s, Wesley found accounts of Christianity as entire devotion to God in Taylor, Thomas à Kempis, and William Law. In 1729, he turned his reading and study more exclusively towards the Bible; he defines the religion he discovered there to be 'a uniform following of Christ, an entire inward and outward conformity to our Master' (5).

Wesley includes extensive quotations from a university sermon he preached in Oxford in 1733 on 'the circumcision of the heart', his first published writing, where he developed the same theme: the conformity of all actions, and all desires, to God is the heart of Christianity. He quotes hymns he wrote before and after his 1735–1738 American journey: 'Is there a thing beneath the sun/That strives with thee my heart to share?/Ah! tear it thence, and reign alone,/The Lord of every motion there!' (7) He queries, rhetorically, 'who could ever object to such sentiments, or deny that they are truly Christian?'

Section 8 is significant: Wesley records a conversation he had in August 1738 with a Swedish Moravian called Arvin Gradin, who was then in Germany. Gradin was the first person Wesley ever encountered who claimed not just to long for a perfect Christian life, but to be living it. Gradin defined his own experience in writing at Wesley's request: 'Repose in the blood of Christ; a firm confidence in God, and persuasion of his favour; the highest tranquillity, serenity, and peace of mind, with a deliverance from every fleshly desire, and a cessation of all, even inward sins'.

Wesley's earlier rhetorical flourishes somewhat missed the point: he knew well that nobody denied that there was at the heart of any Christian ethic a serious call to perfection; what sets Wesley's beliefs apart from those of others – including those he had quoted earlier – is the assumption that perfection is in fact attainable on this side of the general resurrection*. Traditional doctrine had held that the Christian, like perhaps the athlete, must constantly strive for perfection, but also must realize that he/she will always fall short and never actually achieve it. Gradin's testimony – and presumably evidence of his life and testimonies of others to his behaviour – convinced Wesley that something more than holy dissatisfaction with one's imperfect life was possible. Christian perfection is attainable in this life: this is Wesley's core, and controversial, teaching.

Wesley quoted extensively from his famous tract, *The Character of a Methodist* (1739), which, he claimed here (10) was his description of 'a perfect Christian'. He noted that this received little criticism at first, and then expressed surprise at the controversy that followed, and particularly that it came from 'religious men' (11) and that the point of attack was not his definition of perfection, but his assertion that it is possible on earth.

It is hard to know whether Wesley's 'surprise' here is genuine or affected; there were few enough who were 'religiously serious' in his terms that he may have assumed they all thought the same as he did; on the other hand, he was a voracious reader of historical Christian texts, and it would be remarkable if he had not spotted the general assumption that perfection would not come before death.

The year 1740 marked the publication of Wesley's famous sermon on 'Christian perfection'; he asserts (12) that he tested the ideas on the then Bishop of London first, who assented to it all; the sermon is important in marking Wesley's first attempt to state explicitly what Christian perfection is not. The fully-sanctified Christian is perfect in the sense of being motivated by nothing but love for God and love for neighbour, is free both from 'evil thoughts' and 'evil tempers' but is not perfect in knowledge – areas of ignorance still exist – and is certainly not free from illness or temptation.

The sermon also marks Wesley's first published attempt to defend his novel idea of the availability of perfection from criticisms based on Scripture. His strategy is two-fold: to make a distinction between old and new covenants, and to make a set of distinctions between 'sinning inevitably', 'sinning', and 'having sinned'. On the first, he acknowledges that there are many texts in the Old Testament asserting the inevitability of sin, and Wesley accepts its inevitability under the old covenant; he claims, though, that with the coming of Christ and the gift of the Spirit, there is no necessity under the new covenant.

On the second, he acknowledges cheerfully that Christian believers – even the apostles – do/did fall into sin; there is/was, he wants to claim, no inevitability that this should happen, however, 'no necessity of sin was laid upon them'. What of the claims of 1 Jn 1 that 'if we say we have no sin, we deceive ourselves' (v. 8) and 'if we say we have not sinned, we make him [God] a liar ...' (v. 10)? Wesley claims that these two assertions are parallel and that the second explains the meaning of the first: every Christian has sinned – before his conversion, certainly – and has virtually certainly fallen and failed often since. This does not establish, however, the inevitability that Christians continue to sin every moment of their lives.

Section 13 contains extensive quotation from the preface to the Wesleys' 1741 hymnbook. Here, Wesley does seem rather unhappy with his description of the nature of Christian perfection, and he tempers it through many editorial comments inserted into the quotations. He had claimed that the perfect Christian desires no ease in pain; never knows wandering thoughts in prayer; needed no preparation to speak well; and was not troubled by the temptations that came: now, he modifies or denies each of these points.

The new aspect of the teaching here is a consideration of how a Christian becomes perfect. This does not happen at conversion, but it is an instantaneous gift of God at some point post-conversion. The Christian longs and prays to be freed from sin (many of the hymns that follow this preface were just such prayers, including some that remain well-known today: 'Finish, then, thy new creation,/ Pure and sinless let us be,/Let us see thy great salvation/Perfectly restored in thee./Changed from glory into glory ...'); God one day answers this prayer, in an instant, and sets him/her free.

Wesley then (17) includes extensive extracts from the first few annual Methodist conferences, which began in June 1744. The conferences brought together clergy and preachers associated with the Methodist movement to discuss common concerns and issues. It is not a surprise that their distinctive doctrine of sanctification was aired; the questions asked and answers given focus on three areas: better understanding the teaching; relating to others who do not hold to the doctrine of Christian perfection; and practical advice on teaching the doctrine.

There is one idea that is explicit in these conference questions and answers, and which had not been explicit before: the relation of gradual and immediate sanctification. Wesley – or the conference – admits readily that there is a gradual process of increase in holiness that begins at conversion and carries on throughout life; God's gift of perfect holiness is here presented as the culmination of this process, which will never happen until just before death for those who are not looking for it, but might well for those who are earnestly seeking and praying for the gift.

The advice of the fourth conference concerning 'our brethren who differ from us regarding entire sanctification' is noticeably irenic: justification by faith alone is presented as the crucial doctrine that all must adhere to and that must be constantly stressed and preached; entire sanctification should be urged strongly on occasion, but (the implication might be) not when it would be divisive or unhelpful.

The question of the holding up of examples of people who have been granted entire sanctification was raised; Wesley suggests that there are good reasons never to raise someone up as an example: they would become a target for every kind of criticism and examination, and if the judgement had been made in error (which is hardly impossible), the visible failure would bring the doctrine into disrepute. Besides, someone who claims to be entirely holy is liable to arouse a degree of envy or even distaste. The experience may – should – be enjoyed and rejoiced in without being broadcast.

In these extracts, the fewness of those who are given the gift of perfection is stressed: they were few (but not none) in New Testament times, and so must be expected to be few now; nonetheless, there are explicit promises in Scripture that this gift will be given, explicit commands to pray for it, and clear expectations that some, at least, have received it. All Christians should be encouraged seriously to strive for the gift because that is the encouragement of the New Testament itself.

Section 19 contains lengthy extracts from Wesley's 1759 publication, 'Thoughts on Christian Perfection'. This particularly addressed the question of the continuing sinfulness, and so the continuing need for a mediator, of those who have been made perfect. Wesley distinguishes carefully between perfect love, which concerns motive, and perfect knowledge, which concerns comprehension. Christian perfection, as he defines it, embraces the first but not the second – and imperfect knowledge will inevitably lead to imperfect practice. The one made perfect in love will never consciously do anything against God's will, but he/she may not know what is against God's will.

Wesley's own concrete example here is of someone who is committed to the gospel command to mortify the flesh, but who misunderstands what is required by that, so adopts extremes of physical discipline that are inappropriate. An excess of self-mortification, however, might not seem to be a true moral failure. In part, this is because Wesley was considerably more scrupulous about morals than most Christians are today: to be slightly too serious in devotion was, for him, as much a moral failure as to be not serious enough. Nevertheless, we might imagine more convincing examples for our own day: churches at present differ on the moral status of gay/lesbian relationships; imagine two people, granted the gift of entire sanctification by God, but taught differently through their lives on this question: one welcomes a gay couple as brothers in the church; the other lovingly and gently suggests their lifestyle needs to change. One of these people is wrong, but it is an error of understanding, not of love, and so in Wesley's terms, both may be perfect.

So even the one perfected in love constantly makes mistakes and so falls short of the standards demanded by God. He/she therefore constantly stands in need of a mediator, who will provide forgiveness for his/her sins. Wesley is most insistent on this point: perfect or not, all our hope is in Jesus and in his atoning death.

Again, the pastoral questions come to the fore: if someone obtains perfection, should he/she speak of it? Wesley's answer is that, initially, he/she could not be silenced, but that afterwards, a certain discretion is appropriate. Then there is a far more careful exploration of the experienced character of this perfection than has been offered before. Those who are perfect are not imperturbable: a sudden noise may surprise them without shaking their internal fixed gaze on God. What about the pleasures of good food? Those perfected in love will enjoy good food, but will not be disappointed or discommoded if the food is poor, and will render all thanks to God for the goodness of that which is enjoyed. There is extensive advice on how, pastorally, to deal with those who claim the experience: perhaps they are deceived; perhaps they are not; either way, they must be properly cared for.

Wesley also includes the full text of his 'Further Thoughts on Christian Perfection' (1762; 25); this is a lengthy recapitulation of his teaching, with one very clear – and acknowledged – new point. Asked whether those who have attained perfection can later fall from it, Wesley answers, 'Formerly we thought, one saved from sin could not fall; now we know the contrary'. The proof is in pastoral experience: Wesley asserts that he knows many who previously experienced Christian perfection beyond doubt, but who then fell from this experience. He asserts that it is possible to return to it and again claims proof of this in the experience of his acquaintance. This is the final point of development of Wesley's doctrine as it is explained in the *Plain Account of Christian Perfection*; what follows is summary statement.

CRITICISMS

Wesley's claim at the beginning of the book is that his doctrine has been consistent from 1725 until the date of publication, 1777. The evidence of the book does not seem to support this contention. He explicitly repudiates several aspects of his description of the nature of perfection in the 1741 hymnbook preface; more pointedly, as we have shown, his doctrine is developed, or at least refined and more carefully stated, right down to 1762.

That said, there is an unchanging core belief: Christian perfection, defined carefully, is possible in this life. Wesley is less interested in terms than in definitions: more than once he considers the language of 'sinless perfection'; each time he accepts it, but shows little interest in arguing for it. Someone who accepts the substance of his view, but who balks at the term would be accepted warmly by Wesley.

The use of the language of 'sinless perfection' turns on making a distinction between 'sin' – the deliberate transgression of divine law – and 'mistake' – the accidental transgression of divine law through ignorance. The broader Christian tradition would want to use the word 'sin' in both cases, but the distinction is nonetheless an important one which should not be elided. Wesley's terminology here might be provocatively novel, but he is right to believe that little, doctrinally, is at stake in the choice of terminology.

Is he right to believe in the possibility of perfection in this life? The broader Christian tradition has said no and has made a developed case from Scripture in support of that negative conclusion; perfection is held out to us as an ideal to be strained towards, but never, on this side of the coming resurrection, to be achieved. Wesley's doctrine is distinctive and challenging.

First, the challenge: rejecting Wesley, and accepting that we are necessarily imperfect, can lead to a comfortable ethical mediocrity: the Christian finds a place where, knowing that certain things are still wrong with his/her life, he/she is nonetheless able to express sufficient devotion as to be confident of his/her place in heaven. Wesley's doctrine will not allow such evasions or accommodations: perfection is possible and to be striven for.

Second, the distinctiveness: historically, Wesley's account of Christian perfection was the driver for a series of accounts of a distinct 'second blessing' that would/might be given to the Christian. The 'holiness' tradition of nineteenth-century Anglo-American Evangelicalism was deeply influenced by such ideas, but it also modified them somewhat: by the early twentieth century, the 'second blessing' was an endowment of power to minister by the Holy Spirit; for some, this became detached from accounts of holiness; for others, the two necessarily belonged together.

Historically, the most widespread consequence of Wesley's ideas was Pentecostalism. Here the second blessing was (at least initially) an endowment of power for mission; there has been a palpable shift, rightly or wrongly, from Wesley's initial idea of a basically ethical second blessing to one which is about power to transform the world. Pentecostalism is the dominant tradition of Protestant Christianity in the world today and owes one of its core doctrines to a development of Wesley's idea of Christian perfection.

One final criticism should be noted: is Wesley's doctrine logically coherent? The crucial point here is perhaps the last one in the exposition above: can those who have been granted perfection fall away? Wesley asserts that they can, on the basis of experience: many who seemed to have claimed perfection validly had in fact later fallen back to a more normal Christian life. We need not doubt his experience; the logic, however, is interesting: if perfection is, in essence, a heart entirely full of love for God and (therefore) a will entirely directed towards God's desires, how does this 'backsliding' happen? Wesley asserts the reality of temptation, but suggests that, for the perfected saint, temptation is so much water running off a duck's back: it has no purchase.

If temptation has no purchase on the sanctified soul, however, and if the person consumed with love for God cannot long for anything that is out with God's will, the idea that we might lose our perfection seems difficult. Wesley asserts that it happens, but, under the conditions he describes, how can it? There would seem to be a logical problem at the heart of Wesley's position.

17

FRIEDRICH SCHLEIERMACHER
THE CHRISTIAN FAITH

INTRODUCTION

Friedrich Schleiermacher, 1768–1834, was a German theologian of the highest stature. He is rightly considered the father of Liberal Protestantism and was also very influential in philosophy, biblical text criticism, and the developing field of hermeneutics. Schleiermacher was raised in the Protestant Christian tradition; his father was a second-generation clergyman. He went to a Christian school, but also studied Latin, Greek, and Hebrew, in addition to the classical Greek authors and many other great thinkers. He then went to a seminary that stressed personal Christian piety*. Against the rules of the seminary, he secretly read Kant and other Enlightenment philosophers, which led to him having a crisis of faith. He transferred out of the seminary to a more rationalistic university to finish his education. He went on to serve as a professor and pastor in his life. His work can be seen, in part, as an attempt to fit together the Christian faith and the philosophy of his day, trying to defend Christianity against the arrogance of Enlightenment thinking.

The Christian Faith is the mature and developed thought of Schleiermacher, written towards the end of his life, and is his *magnum opus*. It is a book written to Christians – specifically, to future leaders in the church to help them preach better. Yet, in this book, Schleiermacher has other objectives. He is trying to correct problems he saw in Enlightenment thinking and to defend theology as a legitimate discipline, one that is not vulnerable to criticisms from what was happening in the discipline of science at that time. He is also offering a defence of Christianity to the Romantics, particularly, to the German Romantic movement. The world of thought he inhabited – early Romanticism – was overwhelmingly based on the idea that certain religious experiences were normal for everyone. Following German Romanticism, the common theological tendency was towards pantheism*, something Schleiermacher successfully resisted. Nonetheless, a very crucial idea in this book is that we all have some shared experience that is basically the same in all of us.

It seems that Schleiermacher is trying to build a theology that only says things that are immediately justifiable on the basis of Christianity's 'essence'. This 'essence' is a common human experience. We can all have this basic experience, famously known as 'the feeling of absolute dependence'. This feeling, when everything goes right, will be identified by us as 'the feeling of being redeemed by Jesus Christ', and Schleiermacher wants to use this phenomenon as the basis for building an entire theology and argument for the Christian faith. (If this was not actually what he was saying about experience as the foundation of theology, which is debateable, it was how he was understood by those who created a vibrant liberal tradition that proceeded on that basis.) Theology is the science of faith, and therefore what is said in theology must come from reflection on Christian religious feelings and experiences. Only through doing this do we have access to ideas about God or about the world, and even then it is indirect access.

Although Schleiermacher has the deserved reputation for being the father of Liberal Protestantism and although he started the 'turn to the subjective' that is very focused on inward experience, he sees his work as very pietistic and conservative. He strives to focus on the Christian experience of being spiritual and religiously devoted as a central point in his theology. He also claims to be doing a remarkably traditionalist and conservative theology in the Reformed tradition. He sees himself as representing classical Reformed theology with a new approach, trying to translate the expressions of doctrines into a new language for his day. The first section of *The Christian Faith* focuses on his method and explains this new approach – this will be the focus of our treatment of this work, which will only look at two selected areas of doctrine in the rest of the book. After considering his method, we will discuss his Christology and his doctrine of the Trinity.

SYNOPSIS

Schleiermacher says that we need to start with the idea of the Christian Church and not with some other foundation, and this is just what he does. We cannot start with human reasoning, not on some pre-established doctrine of God, or with anything else. There is this thing we call 'the church', a group of people connected by some shared similarity, and we begin our thinking there. However, we cannot assume to start with the Christian Church. We must start with the idea of 'church' in general, which means the idea of a religious group of people. We cannot understand the idea of church in general through forming a concept of church and then turning to a specific religious community because we would never really know whether our theory of the idea of church actually matches what we see. Yet we cannot understand the idea of church through mere observation because we would not be able to tell what parts that we see are the heart of the church and what parts are accidental and unimportant. In short, if we come with a theory of church already built, we cannot tell whether a group really matches that theory, but if we come with no theory at all and try to build it by looking at religious groups, we cannot deduce therefrom what is truly essential.

How, then, should we understand the idea of church, and then the idea of a Christian Church? Schleiermacher turns to three areas to explain the idea of church, labelling them 'ethics', 'philosophy of religion', and 'apologetics'. By ethics, he means arguments not based on natural science, but 'the science of the principles of history', and the most basic and important principle is the absolute dependence of the world on a fundamental, unique force we call 'God'. To get at this, we turn to our own experiences, looking at feelings and self-consciousness. By philosophy of religion, he means a critical study of the various things that all make up the phenomenon of piety in human nature and how that works out in all the religions. By apologetics, he means an examination of what makes Christianity unique, what its essence is.

First, *ethics*. Schleiermacher started the modern 'subjective approach' to religion. However, his approach is not a total subjectivism – one's feelings are actually an experience of 'the infinite' (it is important to note that 'feeling' for Schleiermacher is a technical word, and he means something different than 'emotion'). The essence of religion – true religion, which for Schleiermacher is personal piety – is a 'feeling of absolute dependence on this "Infinite" [in other words, *God*]'. By 'the Infinite' or 'God' Schleiermacher does not really mean the God of the Bible. The word 'God' is used for whatever is outside us that we (and the world) are absolutely dependent upon. This 'whatever' is not the world because we cannot be absolutely dependent on something of which we are a part. However, we have no prior knowledge about God that we can use to make sense of this feeling of dependence – any prior knowledge we think we have actually just comes from this feeling.

As Schleiermacher sees it, there are three grades of self-consciousness, laid out in a spectrum. On one end is the feeling of absolute dependence. On the other end is a consciousness like that of the lower animals, which seem to have thoughts but do not have any sense of self-consciousness. In the middle of these two is anything that falls short of a feeling of absolute dependence, but does not entirely fall down to lacking self-consciousness. This middle area is some combination of a partial feeling of dependence and a partial feeling of freedom. People can be in different places on this continuum, from being like a lower animal that lacks self-consciousness to coming very close to – but just falling short of – a feeling of absolute dependence. If someone did achieve the feeling of absolute dependence, the tension between feeling dependent and feeling free would disappear. We can never perfectly achieve this highest grade of self-consciousness because we are in time and are always changing. But we can have this highest grade *and* be somewhere in the middle at the same time. This is because the absolute feeling of dependence is something usually present in what we might call the subconscious, but it rises up to the front of consciousness when we feel religious and pious. This feeling of absolute dependence, when it rises to a point where it is expressed in our actions, is the consciousness of God or what Schleiermacher calls the 'God-consciousness'. God-consciousness' is a type of self-consciousness. It is a subconscious thing that is always present, but in a small degree.

This religious self-consciousness leads to people joining together to form groups based on this shared feeling. This explains various religions and the existence of what we call a 'church'.

Second, *philosophy of religion*. How does Schleiermacher make sense of all the various religions in his scheme? For him, it is important to say that all religions are about piety, that is, the response to the feeling of absolute dependence. Some religions more accurately reflect the feeling of absolute dependence than others. He says that the various other religions are in different stages of development on the way towards *the* right response. No religion gets things entirely wrong, but no religion gets things entirely right either. Paganism and polytheism wrongly say that the object we feel dependent upon is a thing we can touch and see, or upon multiple things (which all are themselves finite and dependent). Those religions that express the thing we feel dependent upon as one supreme and infinite being – monotheism – are at the highest level. All others are lower forms that should lead to the higher form. The big three monotheistic religions are Judaism, Islam, and Christianity. Schleiermacher says that Judaism is too exclusively focused on a narrow ethnic group, while Islam is too tied up in linking religious feelings to the senses and to doing things. Christianity is the purest form of monotheism that has appeared in history because its interpretation of the feeling of absolute dependence does not let finite things become part of that interpretation and because its interpretation best brings about the Kingdom of God in the world.

Third, *apologetics*. What does Schleiermacher think is unique about Christianity? Christianity is unique in this way: everything in it is in some way related to the redemption accomplished by Jesus. While certain aspects of the Christian faith can be found in other religions (a creator God, for example), no other religion has this feature or anything like it. This is to be taken very minimally – the idea of redemption is just moving from an evil condition, where we have the God-consciousness to a lesser degree, into a better one, where we have it to a higher degree. The unique part of Christianity is that through its founder, redemption becomes the central point of religion. Only in Christianity is the bringing of redemption the true centre point and basis for everything else because Christ is himself the Redeemer.

Before moving on to specific doctrines, a few more words on the introduction to *The Christian Faith* are in order. In the Christian tradition, God is the object of theology and religious thought. Schleiermacher is often accused of replacing God with human consciousness as the object of theology. While this accusation is understandable, it is not quite right. He turns his attention to human consciousness as a way to understand God, even as *the* way to understand God. By 'understand', he is not talking about 'having concepts', but as a certain type of self-consciousness, a *feeling* that is not structured by conceptual thought. But that does not mean there are not concepts involved: the feeling of absolute dependence is a feeling *we* have of being dependent *on something other than ourselves*. This something other than ourselves is what he means by the word 'God'. The big point is that we cannot understand 'God' as just some idea, but only as an implication of the feeling of absolute dependence, and never apart from this feeling. In a sense, for Schleiermacher, this feeling is our only way to 'God'.

'Feeling', for him, is not structured by concepts. The feeling of absolute dependence is what it is, regardless of what we say or think about it. It cannot be reduced to a thought; thus it is truly a *feeling*. But it is not entirely divorced from thought, as if it were some inexpressible *blah*. The idea is that having the feeling of absolute dependence does not at all mean that we will interpret this feeling correctly or that what we say about it will be guaranteed to be true. For him, non-Christian religions are misinterpretations of this feeling that should evolve into the right interpretation: nineteenth-century German Protestantism.

Faith is something that accompanies the feeling of absolute dependence. It is conceptual, as the rest of *The Christian Faith* shows by explaining in detail the various Reformed doctrines. Faith in God is faith that the feeling of being redeemed by Jesus Christ is true. In saying this, Schleiermacher seems to imply that feelings can be true. Yet he also says that this feeling can only be true if there is, in fact, a God who creates, redeems, etc. Faith is believing that there is something there to feel dependent upon when we have this feeling of absolute dependence. Yet again, theology is grounded only in the religious feeling, and any concepts that come up in doctrines are only indirectly related to God through this feeling.

Merely having the feeling of absolute dependence is not the end of the story Schleiermacher wants to tell us. We could have this feeling to some slight degree, but it would be hindered by sin. We can know that we have faith in Christ, and that we have been redeemed, because faith in Christ will remove the sin that muffles the feeling of absolute dependence and leads to a much fuller development of that feeling. When we become Christians, we know that Christian faith is true because of the effect it has on us: it makes the feeling of absolute dependence to be the dominant force in our experience. Because it has this effect on us, it can only be explained as coming from the influence of the one who had the perfect God-consciousness: Jesus Christ.

While it seems that the introduction of *The Christian Faith* is the most important, it is only a small section of the whole work. Most of this book is the presentation of doctrine. Yet the tradition of Liberal theology has read the book's introduction as the lens through which everything after is to be interpreted. How does Christian doctrine relate to Christian piety, this feeling of absolute dependence? For Schleiermacher, doctrine is just an account of religious feelings as put forth in speech, both in theology and in preaching. This speech is a reference to the religious feelings themselves, and in that way it can be helpful to a religious community. We try to organize these doctrines to make a system, to see how they all work together, but these doctrines are not truly the Christian faith — only the inward feelings are. Doctrines that would undercut the connection between religious feelings and the redemption that Jesus brought are out of bounds. Anything that makes redemption unnecessary or makes the Redeemer unable to accomplish redemption is unacceptable; yet within these boundaries, Schleiermacher thinks we should not be too picky. Heresy for him is what contradicts the essence of Christianity (as he sees it) — the range of what is acceptable, then, is quite broad, much broader than the tradition has allowed.

Much of the presentation of doctrine is the reinterpreting of Reformed theology along these lines. We will discuss two examples that are most affected by his methodological commitments: Christology and the Trinity.

Schleiermacher says that Christ has the perfect form of the God-consciousness. He has this as a human, and so it was learned and developed as he grew up, but was always there even as a child. He has a human nature, but he also had God in him, which, for him, meant that he had a pure God-consciousness (as an adult).

Schleiermacher is worried that the church creeds, such as Chalcedon, were in need of correction. The terms used in those creeds had become too technical and caused too much confusion, and so needed to be recast for a new era. He wants to go through the creeds and purge them of unessential additions, keeping what is truly important and putting it in the language of his day. He objects to the 'two natures, one person' formulation, saying that it ignores the infinite difference between the divine and the human by using 'nature' to describe each. How can one person share two very different natures without making a third nature, or separate them so much as to undo the unity of the person, or to put one more important than the other? What does it even mean to say the second person of the Trinity took on a human nature? What is the difference between a person and a nature? Schleiermacher thinks things get even worse – we talk about Jesus' divine nature, but then what relationship does that have to what we say about the Trinity? Do the members of the Trinity have a nature?

He wants to get rid of terms like 'nature', 'essence', and 'person' altogether. Instead, we should just say that the God-consciousness in him was so pure, it meant that God really did exist in him (thus the centre of Christ's work is the incarnation itself, not his atoning death on the cross). This, says Schleiermacher, is what the creeds are really trying to get at, and this is the general faith of all Christians.

Schleiermacher does not start with the Trinity in this book – he ends with it under a section called 'conclusion'. This has brought some criticism on him for not starting with a Trinitarian theology. Yet this is not the problem it might seem to be because he explains earlier that we cannot understand any doctrine in theology apart from its connections to other doctrines and to the whole. What he says about the Trinity, however, shows that he wants to get rid of words like 'essence' and 'person'. For him, the Trinity is a combination of several ideas related to the Christian self-consciousness, not just one simple idea that comes from it. Also, for him, the Trinity is the capstone of Christian theology. The divine essence is united with human nature in Christ and in the Spirit that is in the church. Salvation and redemption fall apart if we lose these two. Yet it is the same simple divine essence that is present in each, not two different beings.

This is about all Schleiermacher wants to say about the Trinity in this work. When we try to think backwards to get to the being that is united with Jesus, and united with the church, we then conjure up a third person, Father, to make sense of it all. Schleiermacher is not happy with any sort of eternal distinctions like this in God because that idea does not come from any sort of Christian consciousness. He cannot see a way to distinguish the persons of the Trinity without making them unequal. Yet he does not want to deny the divinity of the Holy Spirit or of Christ, so he suggests that we affirm both unity and trinity because our experience requires it, but we remain cautious with any attempts to explain it, even those found in the creeds.

CRITICISMS

The first and most important criticism of Schleiermacher comes from Feuerbach** (for details on his criticism that putting religious experience as primary makes the actuality of God unnecessary, see Chapter 19). Feuerbach's critiques target the first section of *The Christian Faith*, where Schleiermacher lays out his method and approach. Many, these authors included, consider Feuerbach's arguments against Schleiermacher to be devastating.

The second criticism is one that is shared with almost all of liberal theology, which assumes, in one way or another, that all of human experience is universal. For Schleiermacher, it is assumed that everyone, without exception, has the same basic experience of a feeling of absolute dependence. Yet this is nowhere argued and is famously difficult, if not impossible, to prove. How do you really know your experience is the same as someone else's?

The final criticism is that other religious views seem to be able to use his same basic method, appealing to the same feeling of absolute dependence, to support *that* view instead of Schleiermacher's

German Protestantism. Indeed, why can't the Muslim say that Christianity is a developing interpretation of this feeling that is leading towards the strict monotheism of Islam? It seems difficult to see how Schleiermacher does not bring all religious discourse to an impasse, where each view takes up this method and starts at the same place, but sees its conclusion as the right one.

18

JOHN HENRY NEWMAN

ESSAY ON THE DEVELOPMENT OF DOCTRINE

INTRODUCTION

John Henry Newman (1801–1890) was a controversial clergyman and theologian in Victorian England. Although a convinced Evangelical in his youth, he became a leader of the Oxford Movement, an influential group within the Church of England that wished to move that church in a decisively Catholic direction. In 1845, he converted to Roman Catholicism, where he rose eventually to become a cardinal.

Newman was born in London and experienced Evangelical conversion in 1816 at the age of 15, under the influence of one of his teachers. He went to study in Oxford, and in 1822 he was elected to a fellowship in Oriel College, then acknowledged as the leading centre of intellectual life in the university. He was ordained deacon in 1824 and priest in 1825 in the Church of England. At this point, he was still associated with the Evangelical party in the church, although there were signs that his theology was developing in some non-Evangelical directions. Around 1830, he took positions and decisions that made it clear that he had moved away from Evangelical convictions. In particular, he made it clear that he regarded Nonconformist Christianity as seriously deficient.

He was not the only one who was coming to such conclusions. In 1833, the Oxford Movement began, initially to campaign for the apostolic succession of bishops* and for the importance of *The Book of Common Prayer*. Newman quickly began a publication series, *Tracts for the Times (Tracts)*, which became the public voice of the movement over the next few years. The closeness of Anglican Evangelicals with Nonconformists – who had neither bishops nor *The Book of Common Prayer* – and the problems surrounding the Church of Ireland, which seemed to raise questions about the establishment in law of the Church of England, combined to create a perceived (at least) threat that the *Tracts* were written to oppose. Newman's purpose, however, was positive as much as it was negative: he had come to a vision of the Church of England as a *via media*, a 'middle way', truly Catholic, but also properly Reformed, and this was what would be promoted in the *Tracts*.

The heart of this *via media* was an acceptance of the first four centuries of Christian development as correct and authoritative: the true church stood in visible continuity, doctrinal and liturgical, with the church of the great ecumenical* councils of Constantinople, Ephesus, and Chalcedon. Thus bishops, a high view of sacrament and priesthood, and a developed liturgy were proper developments, but later Roman novelties – such as Marian devotion or the primacy of the papacy – must be resisted.

Tractarianism, as the Oxford Movement was first known, became popular through the 1830s, and Newman was its acknowledged intellectual leader (Edward Pusey's influence was more significant in the area of liturgical reform). At the end of the decade, however, Newman began to doubt that the position he had created and promoted was in fact tenable; he records reading a sentence from Augustine**, written in the context of the Donatist controversy, where Augustine states, 'the verdict of the whole world is unassailable'. Could the Church of England really stand against the international Catholic Church? Newman commented that this one sentence 'absolutely pulverized' the *via media* doctrine he had worked so hard to develop.

At the same time, he was a victim of political manoeuvring in Oxford (which was not unconnected to his developing Catholic sympathies); he resigned his university posts and moved south of Oxford to create a private religious community at Littlemore. There he wrote his *Essay on the Development of Christian Doctrine (Essay)*, published in 1845. Although technically still an Anglican whilst he wrote much or all of it, the *Essay* gives all the theological backing for his conversion to Catholicism. He converted whilst the book was in press, and when it appeared, it was inevitably read as a justification of his decision.

Newman's conversion was at significant personal cost: his family and professional relationships were deeply damaged. He travelled to Rome and returned as a Roman Catholic priest, living in community in Birmingham for most of the rest of his life (he had a brief spell as head of the Roman Catholic University in Dublin). He lectured in defence of English Catholics, and wrote extensively. His most famous works, alongside the *Tracts* and the *Essay* included his autobiography, justifying his conversion, entitled *Apologia Pro Vita Sua*; his discussion of the founding of a Catholic university, *The Idea of a University*; and the poem *The Dream of Gerontius*, later set to music by Elgar.

A second edition of the *Essay* was published in 1878; he claims in the preface that the changes are not extensive – some, largely cosmetic, amendments to the text and some alterations in arrangement which improve the clarity of the argument. In fact, Newman was in the process of editing all of his Anglican works, and the *Essay* was altered more than any other. That said, the central argument certainly does not change, and some of the more extensive changes are a defence against a charge of 'scepticism' which was probably unfair – not that the book could not be read like that, but that this was never Newman's intended meaning. Instead, the rise of higher criticism and the growing British awareness of German liberal theology made some of his critiques seem more devastating than they had been intended to be, and he removed the possibility of these false readings in his revisions. References below are to the second edition.

SYNOPSIS

Newman's *Essay* is divided into two unequal parts: Part 1, 'Doctrinal Developments Viewed in Themselves' and Part 2, 'Doctrinal Developments Viewed Relatively to Doctrinal Corruptions'. Newman's argument can be summarized quite quickly: there is a normal, observable pattern in the development of ideas; the development of Catholic Christianity fits this pattern; therefore, Catholic Christianity is the legitimate heir of primitive Christianity.

The context for this argument is important: in England, a very standard Protestant polemic against Catholicism was in place, which suggested that certain Catholic doctrines, developed and/or defined late in history, were visible departures from historic Christianity, and so Catholicism was to be repudiated. Before Newman's day, with a strong anti-Catholic sentiment being a part of English identity, this was perhaps merely a support to a widely held prejudice; for Newman, as he notes in the 'Advertisement' to the first edition of his book, the status of the argument had changed: he – and others – had grown to have great respect, even love, for the Church of Rome; only this claim concerning 'visible departures' had kept them outside. Now he sees the claim to be false.

We need to understand what Newman means by an 'idea', particularly since his examples are either rather obscure, or very much of his time, or both. For Newman, an idea is fundamentally inexpressible (a view he may have derived from Coleridge): there can be various representations of the same idea, some better (more precise, or expressing more of the reality) than others, but no representation can completely encompass the idea. For an example of our own, think of *democracy*: we all recognize the idea of democracy, and we all recognize the varieties of democracy around the world; but there is no political system, existing or imagined, which we can point to and say 'that is democracy, complete and untouched by anything else!' This is what Newman means when he writes, 'There is no one aspect deep enough to exhaust the contents of a real idea, no one term or proposition which will serve to define it …' (I.1.§3).

Of course, Newman's point here goes deeper than our example in that he points out that an idea is not reducible to a word or phrase. Can we speak about 'democracy' without speaking about 'freedom'? Is the 'rule of law' a component of the same idea that we reach for when we say 'democracy'? What about 'human rights' or 'freedom of speech'? There is an idea of how a society might be ordered that all these terms seem to be reaching towards, but which none quite exhausts. (Newman in fact offers a similar example, of how the English Long Parliament's desire to check the power of the monarch in 1628–1629 led, over the years, to a vision of a limited monarchy; the example is unhelpful, at least for the modern reader, in that he assumes his readers are familiar with (one interpretation of) constitutional history and merely alludes to events by date.)

His next point is already implicit in this discussion: ideas develop over time, in unpredictable ways, as they move through different contexts. 'Democracy' as Newman knew it involved a small percentage of male landowners voting; universal suffrage for all men and women was something he could not have imagined. If we are right to suggest that the development of human rights legislation is a further development of the same idea that lies behind 'democracy', that is a further new world as the idea develops.

For Newman, characteristically for a nineteenth-century thinker, the idea develops – it does not merely change. He sees this process of development as the filling out of each aspect of the idea in its fullest form and the coming together of these various aspects in their proper arrangement. Ideas grow and blossom into their full form; this is the normal path of history. Ideas also develop because of their context: an idea expressed in a new cultural context will be expressed differently. Some of this will be possibility (consider the democratic possibilities opened up for mass referendums by improved travel and technology); some will be the influence of new cultural ideas or contexts on the idea (consider how democracy has to work differently in a compact city-state compared to a federal state stretching across a continent). Newman identifies various sorts of development, of which he suggests five will apply to the development of Christianity: political; logical; historical; moral; and metaphysical.

The degree of development that may be expected of any one idea will depend on the richness of the idea; the richest ideas will have more and profounder possible developments – they will be able to grow into larger and more varied and complex expressions. Newman proposes that, naturally, Christianity is the most exalted idea known to humanity, and so must expect to show the greatest development. The only reason we could have for not suggesting such a development would be some 'special exemption' from normal historical patterns (I.2.§2).

Newman considers two possible 'special exemptions': the claim that the Bible describes the limits of Christianity, and therefore its full development; and the claim that Christianity, because of divine origin, should not be analysed or expected to behave the way other ideas do. Newman's response to the first is to claim that ideas exist in human minds, not in texts; the idea formed in the mind of the reader of the Bible is not, he claims, complete, exhaustive, and accurate; nor could any number of texts – certainly not the relatively brief New Testament – exhaustively describe every possible development of an idea. Further, the Bible itself shows examples of development: prophecies are brief statements, pregnant with larger truths that will be understood later when their fulfillment is seen, for instance. On the second, Newman appeals to the incarnation: Christianity is a genuinely divine inspiration, but comes clothed in ordinary earthly form – an idea like any other idea. Further, if Christianity is to grow and spread and take form in many different ways in many different cultures and contexts, it must develop from its beginnings.

Newman next argues that, if Christianity is of divine origin and if Christianity will grow and develop, we must expect a divinely-instituted authority to regulate its growth and to recognize legitimate developments. His argument first turns on the necessity of interpretation of Scripture: the question is not, what does the Bible say? but, whose interpretation is correct? It would therefore be bizarre to believe that God has given a revelation, but no means of knowing – infallibly – what it means.

We are then given a variety of examples of the development of doctrine in the history of the church. He begins with the incarnation*; this leads inevitably to an idea of the need for mediation between God and humanity; once we have an idea of mediation, Newman suggests, it develops into a doctrine of atonement*, to the sacrifice of the Mass, and to the merits and invocation of saints. None of these developments are predictable in advance; instead, they happen and are recognized – and authorized – as appropriate developments of the idea in retrospect.

In the second part, Newman offers seven 'notes' that demonstrate that a development in doctrine is genuine, and not a corruption, together with a series of illustrations from the church history of each note. The first is 'continuity of type', by which he means something like essential nature. Doctrine will grow and develop into different expressions of the central Christian ideas, but the basic nature of Christianity will never change. The second 'note' is 'continuity of principles': a 'principle', for Newman, is an ethical orientation. Christian doctrines may develop, but Christianity will always tend to promote humility or self-control.

The third note is 'power of assimilation': genuine development of a doctrine is an expansion that embraces other things and brings them, perhaps transformed, into the original doctrine. The idea grows without distortion. The fourth note is 'logical sequence': simply put, true developments make sense and happen in an order that makes sense. The fifth note is 'anticipation of its future': when we look back at an earlier form of doctrine, we will see that the development, though unforeseen, looks natural and inevitable with hindsight.

Newman calls his sixth note 'conservative action upon its past', by which he means that authentic developments in a doctrine will not contradict the primitive forms of that teaching, but will instead maintain and deepen them. His final note, 'chronic vigour', means simply that developments in doctrine last through time; they do not appear and then fade. Newman's lengthy examples of these notes, which make up about half the book and conclude it, are (perhaps unsurprisingly) mostly devoted to demonstrating the correctness of Roman Catholic developments through history.

CRITICISMS

Newman is celebrated as a great English stylist, and justly so, but this text is nonetheless not easy to read. In part, this is because the preferred style of his day was rather flowery and verbose by our contemporary standards; in part, it is because Newman has a habit of gesturing at events or narratives he intends as evidence or illustration for his argument, assuming his readers will be familiar with them and will be able to trace their relevance. In some cases, the difficulty for a modern reader is again down to historical distance, as when Newman alludes to a political debate of his own time, which he could reasonably assume would be familiar to his readers. In other cases, however – the English Long Parliament example cited above is an example – Newman is simply expecting rather too much of his readers.

The overall argument of the book is certainly open to challenge. Newman's assertion that any idea will inevitably grow and change is no doubt broadly plausible, although his vision of an inexorable development to better and fuller expression would seem to be more an unconscious echo of the nineteenth-century fascination with 'progress' and 'evolution' than a necessary assumption. Better, surely, to accept that the lived expression of ideas change over time and in different cultural contexts – but also to accept that each change demands exploration and evaluation, rather than assumption of a general bias towards changes being positive?

Newman's criteria for a development being regarded as 'authentic' – his seven 'notes' – are neither as obvious nor as straightforward in application as he makes them seem. The study of the history of ideas shows that there is always a degree of continuity, or a logical progression (to take two of Newman's notes), in any story of change, even if the story involves the abandonment of the first idea and its replacement with its opposite.

Finally, Newman simply asserts that we should expect that God will provide an infallible interpreter of the correctness, or otherwise, of developments of doctrine because otherwise we could not know which were authentic and which were not. Since the Reformation*, there had been an ongoing debate on whether a magisterium was necessary for certainty over the interpretation of the Bible, with a strong and careful Protestant argument that it was not; Newman's argument is sufficiently close to this debate that he really should have addressed the potential analogical arguments (particularly concerning the witness of the Holy Spirit) before asserting the negative.

All that said, the book remains a standard account of one particular view of the development of doctrine and a classic defence of the Roman Catholic position. Newman might be criticized, but he cannot be ignored.

19

LUDWIG FEUERBACH
THE ESSENCE OF CHRISTIANITY

INTRODUCTION

In modern Western culture, God is often depicted as a white, white-bearded old man sitting on the clouds. He is radiant, with a deep and booming voice, and he is powerful, but he is pictured as ultimately just a heavenly human. What if God were nothing more than a 'heavenly human' we invented? Atheist and seminal psychologist Sigmund Freud called religion 'the longing for a father'. Long before him, Ludwig Feuerbach raised this challenge to Christian faith and religion in general.

Ludwig Feuerbach, 1804–1872, was born in Bavaria, Germany to a distinguished family. He was religious in his childhood and early life, raised as a German Protestant. Leaving his family to study theology in Heidelberg in 1823, he soon became interested in the thought of Hegel, which led him to move on to study under him in Berlin. In order to placate his father, he went there under the pretence of studying theology under Schleiermacher, but he soon transferred to the philosophy department. After finishing his PhD, his drift away from Hegel's thought was accelerated by the negative reactions to an infamous book he wrote in 1830, in which he denied that humans have a soul that continues to exist after death.

With this and other works, he developed a reputation as an atheist and a dangerous thinker, which made most universities reluctant to hire him, hampering his academic career. In 1837, he married a woman who had enough income from her share in a porcelain factory to support his writing and research – he was never able to fully break into a university, spending most of his life as an independent scholar and writer.

Feuerbach's biographical journey is telling: he started off studying theology, but eventually denied it by trying to explain religion and theology as being completely reducible to anthropology. His thought and writings were radical at the time and caused many to regard him as an enemy of Christianity. Readers may naturally ask why we would include a work from such an anti-theologian amongst the classics in Christian theology. We have done so largely because of the impact his work made on theology and the way he critiqued influential theologians before him such as Schleiermacher.

Feuerbach is attacking the whole of Christian theology, but he has in mind several specific figures, including Hegel and Schleiermacher – both his former teachers in Berlin. He takes their thoughts to their logical conclusions: in these systems, if they were honest and consistent, theology is completely reduced to anthropology. We will first look at Hegel before turning to Schleiermacher.

Hegel's influence in philosophy was tremendous, to say the least. Yet Feuerbach accused Hegel's philosophy of ultimately being just another theology. Hegel's thought is entirely committed to idealism*, insisting that consciousness was more primary than the material world. For Hegel, objects do not exist by themselves, but are generated from thoughts. Feuerbach reversed this, saying that objects exist regardless of anyone thinking about them, and thus was a strong realist*. He saw his work as a correction to that of Hegel. Hegel saw divine being and human being as identical, part of the 'absolute spirit', a sort of universal consciousness that includes all aspects of reality. Feuerbach says that they are not two different parts of the same thing: 'God' could be entirely explained by human beings. Humans project a purified, infinite, perfect version of themselves and call it 'God'. They then think that this projection has some real objective existence, but in thinking this they are confused. In his thinking, to deny 'God' entirely would be to deny man, which is not what Feuerbach wants to do. Instead, he attempts to show that what is expressed as 'God' is really nothing more than a human projection.

Feuerbach's ideas – especially his emphasis on the material world – prepared the way for Marxism*; he is rightly considered to be a bridge between Hegel and Marx. The idea in Marxism that religion is just an illusion is indebted to Feuerbach: indeed, he is the father of all projectionist theories of religion.

Schleiermacher made religious experience primary, working from that basis to then talk about God and about the world, both of which are secondary in his method. Yet when this is done, Feuerbach points out, the secondary matters could just as well be omitted. All that is left is religious experience, and that, in itself, can readily be explained purely by anthropology. God as an actual being becomes unnecessary.

Feuerbach claims that subjective experiences do not tell us anything about a transcendent God – they only really say something about the essence of the one having those experiences. If feeling is the essence of religion, as Schleiermacher says, then feeling just *is* the divine. There is no objective God 'out there' to be felt; there is only feeling itself. If feeling is the true heart of religion, then Christian doctrine is unimportant: doctrine only matters if it can cause the right religious feelings. If something else – say, a specially concocted drug – could do the same thing, it could entirely replace Christian doctrine and thought. If feeling is the essence of religion, it cannot be the subjective essence whilst still retaining some objective aspects (i.e. a transcendent God). Once feeling is the essence of religion, feeling becomes God.

Schleiermacher's project is centred on religious feeling, but Feuerbach says the basic principle of his critique is not limited to feeling. The same is true of anything we might suggest to be the essence of religion. If the essence of religion is thinking the right thoughts, then that thinking becomes God. If the essence of religion is doing the right rituals and activities, then those activities become God. And so on. Any consciousness of God, however we might get at it, is really just self-consciousness, nothing more.

In the wake of the Enlightenment, many in the Protestant tradition, including Schleiermacher, tried to find a way to make the Christian faith what our conclusion would be if only we would properly study mankind. The starting point and ultimate authority was man, and theology felt the need to justify itself to the Enlightenment's ultimate trust in autonomous humanity. Feuerbach shows what happens to theology when it walks down this road: there seems very little, if anything, to prevent theology from being entirely reduced to anthropology. In fact, in his view, theology has been anthropology since Protestantism stopped thinking about what God is in himself and turned towards thinking about what God is for man. This course in theology was set for some time; Feuerbach just calls it for what it is. Religion worships man, he says, although theology tries to pretend this is not the case. Feuerbach says he is just the messenger of this fact, of Christianity's true essence, discovering it and bringing it to light. In response to the accusation that he is an atheist hostile to Christian theology, he would cry, 'Don't shoot the messenger!'

SYNOPSIS

The Essence of Christianity was published in 1841 and caused quite a stir in Germany. In this book, Feuerbach gives what he thinks to be the best explanation for Christian doctrines and practices, including an explanation of their alleged contradictions. The basic thesis is that religion and theology are really just anthropology, all the way down. He argues for this in two parts. The first part explains that the essence of religion is the projecting of human relations as divine relations: man casts his own shadow onto the heavens and calls it 'God'. In this part, he tries to show how Christian doctrines are merely projections of some aspect of humanness or human desires and feelings. The second part explains that the content of theology – especially the theological idea of the Son of God – is contradictory to nature and reason. Here he tries to show contradictions within Christian theology. We will first discuss his picture of projection and then turn to his allegations of contradiction.

First, we will provide some explanation on how Feuerbach sees God as merely a projection. It starts with understanding the human nature. Humans have consciousness. Consciousness is only something available to a being that can recognize that it is a member of a species, having an essential nature. Man has consciousness because man can think about mankind. Dogs can think about themselves to a degree and even think about their pack, but a dog cannot think of what it means to be canine. Religion is nothing more than this ability of man to think of the essential nature of mankind, which for Feuerbach is an infinite nature.

What happens when we try to project this nature into a 'God'? We cannot think of God without using human analogies – there is no way to get directly to what 'God is in himself'. Feuerbach says the distinction between what 'God is in himself' and how God appears to me (or you) is untenable. There is no other way to get at 'God in himself' apart from how he appears to me because God will always appear to us as a big human in the sky. There is no way to remove anthropology from the idea of God: 'God' will always be determined by human nature. In this way, there is no 'God in himself'. That is just an illusion, a mistaking of a shadow for a real thing.

The doctrines of the Christian faith are projections, says Feuerbach. For example, the Trinity is a projection of God in the image of man. Man sees that he has different aspects to his being: intellect, will, and emotion. These three are not the same, yet they are united in one human person. Taking this self-awareness, we project it up to God, who then must be Father, Son, and Holy Spirit united in one divine being.

The projections we put up onto 'God' are shaped by what we are as humans. 'God' is something that satisfies our emotional needs; the basic doctrines of the Christian faith are realizations of the desires of the human heart. It is easier and more pleasant to have a saviour than to save one's self, to just be loved rather than to put forth the effort to be a good person, to go with one's own feelings than to be guided by one's own reason. Feuerbach gives the example of the resurrection to eternal life. Man wishes not to die, that is, man has the instinct of self-preservation. Since it is clear that we all die, man concocts the notion of resurrection. So man made up Jesus' resurrection, which then secures our own resurrection. The resurrection is a fiction, a lie that man produced to fulfil his own felt need for immortality.

Feuerbach is very critical of this projecting done by theology. He is particularly hostile to theology, which, for him, is the attempt to take religion and give it rational expression. Theology is actually dehumanizing, he accuses; it takes away our humanity and puts it all on God, leaving nothing for ourselves. The projection of a divine being actually alienates us for at least two reasons. First, when we project what is best about us onto God, we deny that we actually have these things – for example, only God is good; we are wretched and sinful. Second, when we focus on individual feelings and our own self-consciousness, as Schleiermacher does, we lose the connection we have with other people and with nature. An inward turn only leaves us all alone.

This projecting of the best of human nature onto God means that man is diminished: for God to be all, man must become nothing. Man denies his own knowledge and places it all in the concept of God; man must give up his personality to make God a person. Human dignity is lost so that God can become the selfish and egotistical being who seeks his own ends and his own glory. Mankind is projected up onto God, who then becomes the end and goal of all human activity. In religion, man is supposed to be humble before God, but, in truth, man is actually just projecting himself up to the highest degree!

While he is hostile to theology, he is less antagonistic towards religion. He does not wish to make religion an absurdity or just an illusion. He says that religion *is* anthropology, nothing more, and that anthropology is not absurd or just an illusion. He reduces it all into anthropology and thus turns anthropology into 'theology'. He thinks this is just like what happens in Christianity, where God is lowered into man, which makes man into God. Jesus Christ, as Feuerbach understands him, is the model for his entire project.

So how does he understand Jesus Christ? He says that in Christianity's doctrine of the incarnation we have a veiled recognition of the truth of the matter – God is a human being. Not because there is an actual being, 'God', who actually took on human nature, but because this doctrine is an expression of the basic projectionist principle that explains what is really going on in religion. Religion, for Feuerbach, is really just an expression of human worth.

Feuerbach does not deny the idea of 'God', but says that theologians have not properly defined the term. 'God' is not some independent divine being. He says that what we call 'God' is really mankind's true nature that we mistake for a God that exists apart from us. He wants us to realize that 'God' is really just mankind, and thus we should become atheistic humanists. We need to turn our gaze from heaven to earth, from supernaturalism to real life.

This is the basic picture of his theory of projection. We must now turn to his accusation of contradictions. Because of the projection of feelings that Feuerbach has described, he says that Christians ignore the contradictions in their theology. Reason is put under feeling. He alleges several contradictions. For example, he says that the Bible contradicts morality and reason, and even contradicts itself over and over: how could the 'Word of God' do this?

An interesting critique is that the Christian concept of 'God' is a contradiction in itself. Christian theology says that God has various attributes: he is good, just, loving, etc. Feuerbach says that the idea of God is dependent on the ideas of goodness, justice, love, etc. Without just one of these, God would be a defective being. Yet these qualities are the best things in mankind, and so we project them onto God. The problem, he says, is that these attributes can be realized by a species of individuals (humanity), but cannot be all realized by one God because they are contradictory if held by just one individual (love and wrath, for example). God cannot be all-knowing, all-powerful, and unaffected by creation while at the same time being loving, compassionate, and merciful. The attributes that really matter in Christian theology are *personal*. However, he says that these are purely human attributes said to express the very nature of God and that they really only express human nature.

Rather than embrace the contradiction or try to give some response which is doomed to fail, Feuerbach says that Christians should see that all of God's attributes are really attributes of the human species. In any individual, these attributes are limited: for example, one person does not know everything, one person is not able to do everything. However, the essence of humanity is to know things, to do things, etc., and if all of humanity is taken together and given enough time, the possibilities are infinite. That extension to the limitless of human possibility is mistakenly projected into an idea called 'God'.

In the end, religion has a progression to it, gradually expanding the concept of 'God' to include the very best of the human species as a whole, free of the limits of just one person. This progression eventually leads to realization that 'God' is not real and is a manifestation of the human nature. The thinker, the philosopher (like

Feuerbach), is the one who will step outside of the self-delusion of religion and call it for what it is.

CRITICISMS

As we would expect, criticisms have been raised against Feuerbach's work, as many have come to the defence of Christian theology. The first we will discuss deals with the role played by human nature or the 'consciousness of the species'. Feuerbach made the 'consciousness of the species' the ultimate rule by which everything else was judged, but he does not defend this important move. Humanity's essential being was really what is meant by 'God'. Yet why does this 'corporate man' idea, which is clearly a conceptual construction, get such a privileged place? This idea of generalized man seems to be just a projection. Feuerbach gives no reason to think that 'God' is a projection, whereas his 'general man' is not. Certainly, and more problematically, he gives no reason why this 'general man' should be the ultimate standard.

The second criticism is that if God really were just a projection, we should expect him to look very different than he does in Christian theology. God is said to be wholly other, a being unlike all others. He is beyond human grasping, beyond human control or manipulation. He is the source of all that exists. God is not there to serve us, but rather we are created to serve him. Feuerbach calls this giving of all worth and honour to God a contradiction in Christian theology, but he gives no convincing explanation as to why a God who is merely the product of projection would be cast this way. If God is merely a projection, we should expect him to be safer, under human control, and less demanding of us.

The final criticism we will mention comes from Karl Barth**. Since Barth's *Church Dogmatics* have a chapter (22) in this volume, we can be brief here. Essentially, Barth says that only in Jesus Christ do we see true humanity. That is the starting place for anthropology. One cannot approach theology assuming there is no God and that humanity is the final measure of all things, as Feuerbach does. Rather, we need to think of God as the primary subject of theology, not humanity, the self or self-consciousness, any religious experience, or anything like that. Only then can we do theology on its own terms.

20

SØREN KIERKEGAARD
THE PHILOSOPHICAL FRAGMENTS

INTRODUCTION

Søren Kierkegaard, 1813–1855, was a Danish philosopher and theologian born in Copenhagen. He was very critical of the dominant philosophy of his time and of the Christianity found in the Church of Denmark. He is also considered to be the first existentialist* philosopher and the father of theistic existentialism*. He was very introverted, deeply religious, and highly emotionally sensitive, and this is evident in much of his writing. He had little influence in his own day: *The Philosophical Fragments* was published in 1845 and only sold a few hundred copies in the three following years. The sales of his works were unimpressive, and he was often misunderstood by his contemporaries, but he had a significant impact on twentieth-century figures such as Barth. His writings are often cryptic, using pseudonyms, and sometimes it is difficult to decipher what he is really trying to say. He takes up this unique and often difficult writing style for a purpose: he did not want to be understood as presenting a philosophical system (hence the word 'fragments' in his title). He is not trying merely to convince his readers of some intellectual truth; he is trying to change the reader's attitude and perspective on the subject matter. He is ultimately trying to get his reader to take up a different type of existence, to jostle him/her out of a coma caused by the philosophy of the day, and to live life on the highest level: in the religious sphere.

In much of Kierkegaard's works, it is difficult to interpret what he is ultimately saying due to the layers of pseudonyms, irony, cryptic allusions, and intentional self-contradiction. *The Philosophical Fragments* was published under the pseudonym 'Johannes Climacus', a persona he adopted for this work and a related book that followed, *Concluding Unscientific Postscript*. The question of precisely how the positions advanced by each pseudonym relate to Kierkegaard's own views remains open. We will present our best attempt to interpret what Kierkegaard himself is ultimately saying in this book, but readers should be aware that some in Kierkegaard scholarship may have alternate interpretations.

The Philosophical Fragments was written to address the problem of how to be a Christian in Denmark at that time. The country was widely thought to be in 'Christendom', where someone was a Christian by nothing more than birth in that country and infant baptism in the state church. Kierkegaard saw this as unacceptable and as incompatible with the gospel. He tried to get through to his countrymen that the Christian faith demands personal commitment and faith.

There are three big issues that Kierkegaard addresses in this book which can be organized as three different relationships. The first and main issue is the relationship between idealism* and Christianity. In this book, Socrates is used as the voice of idealism, but Kierkegaard is also indirectly criticizing the idealism of Plato, Hegel, and others, so it will prove helpful to discuss idealism. Idealism, crudely put, is the view that reality is fundamentally in the mind or constructed by the mind. In idealism, truth is something already contained in each person. In Socratic and Platonic thinking, each person (in soul form) pre-existed before his/her birth, and in this pre-existent form, we each knew all things. Embodiment causes the soul to forget, and learning is the process of recollecting what the person already knows but has forgotten. In Hegelian idealism, truth is already contained in the Idea. Hegel believed that the Idea unfolds itself from itself in a necessary process. Individual minds may learn the truth by following the process of unfolding, where each step is necessary. In this way, truth is contained in each person; one need only reflect on it. For Hegel, Christianity and philosophy actually contain identical content, but only differ in form. For Kierkegaard, idealism is completely incompatible with Christianity. The truth is not within us, but rather the truth comes to us from outside, as we shall soon see.

This leads to the second issue in the book: the relationship between faith and reason. Kierkegaard's concern is specifically about the relationship between Hegelian reason and genuine New Testament faith, and he says that the two are incompatible. Arguably, he is not entirely anti-reason, nor does he say that Christian faith rules out reason. Yet he gives reason a more circumscribed role than Christians typically did in his day (and also in ours). We must read his unusually negative comments about reason in light of their context of combating Hegelian idealism.

The third issue in the book comes from Kierkegaard's rejection of idealism and its implication that history is necessary: the relationship of faith and history. He says that history is genuinely contingent, that whatever happens really could have been otherwise, and philosophy cannot lead us to see necessary connections and explain everything. The basic question regards how reason, faith, and matters of fact fit together, and how we can grasp historical matters of fact. Since Kierkegaard saw that history was not necessary and our access to historical events, such as the life of Jesus, was limited, he said that we need more than reason to get at it – we need to take a leap of faith.

The Philosophical Fragments must be understood in relation to the thought and influence of Hegel. Kierkegaard was trying to overthrow Hegel's philosophical system, which he saw as a threat to genuine Christian faith. The Christian faith, as it seems in Hegel, is the result of a necessary and inevitable process working itself out through history. There is a sort of reason working in everything that happens and it determines the outcomes according to the Idea, and we can follow the necessity with the relationships of one thing to another in order to build a comprehensive system that encompasses all of reality. The line between creator and creature was being blurred by Hegel, protested Kierkegaard. Hegelian thought suggested that the idea of the incarnation, where God and man are one in the God-man, is natural and reasonable, the outworking of some necessary process. Kierkegaard thought that this line of thinking threatened to domesticate God. Instead, Jesus Christ as both God and man is the 'absolute paradox'; he is an offence to human reason. Only in faith can we attain this truth, or rather, can we attain the one who is truth. This faith comes in the moment of encounter the individual has with Jesus, in the present, where we must take a leap of faith beyond what reason can prove.

For Kierkegaard, truth is subjectivity. This point is presented in detail in *Concluding Unscientific Postscript*, but it is also present in this book. By this, he does not mean that truth is subjective, in a post-modern way, but rather that in order to really have truth, it must be personally appropriated, grasped, and acted upon.

SYNOPSIS

Kierkegaard begins by comparing two stories about how we learn truth. The first story is what Socrates would tell us from his view-point in idealism. The second story is the Christian one, and by contrasting these two stories he wants to show the incompatibility between the two. The first story goes something like this: truth is already in each one of us. We just need to recall it. Something outside the person – say, a teacher – can assist in the remembering process, but nothing external can truly teach a person. A teacher serves as the occasion to help the person remember by asking probing questions – a bit like a midwife. So when we ask about our eternal happiness, and how we might achieve it, the answers are already in us. The teacher is ultimately unimportant for our eternal happiness: at best, Socrates is just the occasion and nothing more. Further, the moment in which we remember is insignificant because we discover that we already knew the truth from eternity. Indeed, how can one even seek the truth, for if one has it already, then seeking and finding are little more than illusions, but if one does not already have it, then how can one know what to look for, or that one even needs to look at all?

The second story – the Christian one – goes much differently. Truth is not something within a person, but is something that comes from outside. Unlike in idealism, the moment we learn the truth makes all the difference in the world. Before the truth comes, a person is outside of it: he/she is untruth. The teacher must bring the truth to the learner, but since the learner is untruth, the teacher must also provide the condition for understanding it. It is a person's own fault that he/she lacks the condition and that there is nothing he/she can do on his/her own to get it. This lack of the condition can be called *sin*. No human can give the condition to another person – only God can do that. The condition can be called *faith*. The teacher is God himself, who gives the condition and gives the truth – he is a *saviour*, for he saves the learner from sin; he is a *deliverer*, for he delivers the person from imprisonment; he is a *reconciler*, for he takes away the wrath and guilt. Encountering a teacher like this will be unforgettable. *The moment* in which a person receives the condition and the truth is completely unique and decisive – it is a moment that is filled with the eternal. What is taught by the teacher? God's presence is essential to the teaching – in fact, it *is* the teaching. Unlike Socrates, the person of Jesus, as the teacher, is of the utmost importance. *The moment* is God revealing himself, which he does entirely out of love for the learner. God as the loving teacher must stoop down to the learner's level and become like the learner (the incarnation). In *the moment*, the learner becomes a *new* person – this can be called *conversion*. Yet turning away from an old state to a new one requires sorrow – this can be called *repentance*. Since a new person has come from the old, we can speak of *rebirth*.

The concept of *the moment* is crucial. There are two different aspects to *the moment*. First is the moment where God became man in the incarnation. This was not just a special case of a general union between God and man, nor was it just an instance of something that could potentially happen between God and all humans. Denying a theme common in German Liberalism and affirming a more traditional position, Kierkegaard said that Christ was uniquely divine and the incarnation is a decisive moment in time, where the eternal enters into time. This was God revealing himself. Yet this moment happens *for the individual* not in the first century, but when God in Christ reveals himself to that person. This is a decisive moment in time in the life of a person, where the individual is radically changed. The key point in either aspect is that *the moment* is a revelation from God.

The Christian story says that our existence is one where we are essentially ignorant of the truth. There is something very wrong with our existence – an idea that people are naturally resistant to accept. What is wrong is that we are sinful, but because we are sinful, we are not willing to admit that we are in this state of sinfulness. The result is that we naturally do not like the Christian story, and our acceptance of it must come from God, not from ourselves.

Kierkegaard's pseudonym says that he is only trying to show that these two stories are incompatible, not that one should be preferred over the other. However, it appears that Kierkegaard himself was subtly trying to get the reader to realize that the Christian story is the right one. Since we all have a life, and since what happens in our existence is important to us, there is no purely objective way to decide between the two stories. The question at issue with both stories is, What is the relation of the individual to the truth? We all have a personal stake in the answer, and the choice cannot even be considered apart from what it would mean for each of us. Socrates' story and those like it require us to surrender the idea that our temporal existence matters, that we make choices that are real, and that things could genuinely have been otherwise. The Christian story, however, makes our existence – especially *the moment* – truly important.

After contrasting these two stories, Kierkegaard then moves on to talk about faith and reason. While he does not directly say this, it seems probable that by 'reason', he means the sort of reason used by Hegel, the type of reason that unfolds all truth. Reasoning like this about God, he says, brings us to a paradox, which he calls the 'absolute paradox'. What is the absolute paradox? In a way, it is that the eternal God comes into existence in time. In another way, it is that the unknown reveals itself and makes itself known. At its heart, it is this idea: that which is absolutely different from humans, a difference caused by sin, becomes like them out of love. Despite our sin, God loves humans so much that he becomes human. He frees from sin and makes eternal happiness possible. In short, the absolute paradox is the incarnation.

In trying to understand the absolute paradox, the reason is met with major difficulties. God is absolutely different from human beings – and yet, in the absolute paradox, God somehow becomes man. If a human being is to come to truly know anything about God, he/she must first know that God is absolutely different from him/her. Yet the human being cannot understand something that is absolutely different. Therefore, this knowledge must come from

God. However, if he/she does come to know this, he/she cannot understand it because it is absolutely different, and thus he/she cannot know it. The absolute paradox presents the reason with a paradox, and there are two responses to it. The first is for the reason to be offended at the paradox, which amounts to rejecting it and turning the absolute paradox into something the reason can understand, but by doing so it removes God from the picture and destroys the personal significance for the individual. The second is for the reason and the paradox to be joined together, when the understanding surrenders itself. It seems Kierkegaard is saying that the reason can understand that the paradox cannot be understood by reason, that it must see its own limits and step aside. Faith must go above reason to try to grasp something that will make sense of everything else (but not 'make sense' in a rational way). Faith is required in order to understand God, to understand the absolute paradox. In showing that genuine faith is different from reason in this way, Kierkegaard is showing the incompatibility between Hegelianism and Christianity.

Kierkegaard next talks about the problem of faith and history. The problem is this: merely being around Christ during his life does not make one a disciple. Many people saw him, heard him speak, and witnessed his miracles. Yet very few were actual disciples. If simply being an eyewitness to these historical events does not turn one into a disciple, what does? Kierkegaard says that only a revelation from God – an encounter with Christ – in which he reveals himself can make someone a disciple. This encounter is available to those in Christ's time as well as to us today. Kierkegaard says that there is a problem with historical events: the farther one is, historically, from actual events, the more likely it is that the story of the event has become distorted. Yet when it comes to being a disciple of Christ, this is not a major issue because everyone – whether a contemporary or someone living hundreds of years later – becomes a disciple in *the moment* that individual encounters Christ firsthand. This moment is when God in Christ reveals himself to an individual. There is no follower at second-hand. In this moment, the understanding is discharged and faith is received. Details about the historical events may be the occasion for the moment just like being an eyewitness to Jesus may be the occasion. But historical knowledge, however it is gained, is not the key to faith in Christ, and it does not make one a disciple. For that, we need faith.

CRITICISMS

The first criticism of *The Philosophical Fragments* is that Kierkegaard is telling us we should be irrational. It is not difficult to read him to be saying this. Yet perhaps this is misguided: he had a central role for logic in his thinking. Perhaps it might be better to say that Kierkegaard thought there were elements of the Christian faith that were *supra-rational*, neither irrational nor rational. Sometimes it is not clear what to do with his statements along these lines, but at the very least he seems right to insist that the Christian must always have God, not some sense of rationality or 'reason', as his/her ultimate master. However, it is not clear that Kierkegaard can completely escape the accusation of fideism – that, in his theology, faith is ultimately in opposition to reason.

Kierkegaard would say that faith is a paradox; it initially stands in incongruity with reason. But when faith is taken up, despite the paradox, there is a 'continuity in reverse' with reason. Faith is absurd until it is embraced, when it then somehow makes congruity between reason and Christianity. In short, the incarnation seems absurd until one embraces it by faith, where one sees that all things – including the absolute paradox – are possible for God.

The second criticism has to do with how he handles the relationship of history and faith. Kierkegaard certainly seems right to say that historical evidence alone is not sufficient for faith in God. Faith involves having certain moral and spiritual qualities, qualities that he insists are required if we are to grasp Christian truth. Yet he seems to go further and say that historical knowledge is *not even necessary* for faith. All that is necessary is to have a firsthand encounter with the incarnate God, in *the moment*. One problem with this line of thought is that the New Testament seems to indicate otherwise – for example, in the preaching of the events of Christ's death and resurrection 'according to Scripture'. Certainly, a saving faith in God is *more* than cognitively grasping and affirming certain truths, but can it be *less* than that?

The third criticism is that the work of the Holy Spirit is conspicuously absent in his discussions of *the moment*. Certainly, the literary nature of his work can help explain this – using pseudonyms, irony, satire, and cryptic allusions – but any discussion of an encounter with God in conversion seems impoverished if the Spirit is absent.

Finally, Kierkegaard's pride of place for existentialist concerns is susceptible to leading to something like the theology of Rudolf Bultmann** (see Chapter 24 for critiques). It is not clear what might prevent Kierkegaard's theology from reducing concerns about truth into mere concerns for existential satisfaction.

21

ADOLF VON HARNACK
WHAT IS CHRISTIANITY?

INTRODUCTION

Adolf von Harnack, 1851–1930, was a German theologian and
church historian who had a major impact on the study of church
history and doctrine. He was a prolific and influential modern critical scholar and a powerful figure in Liberal Protestantism, teaching
for years as a professor in Berlin and influencing many students,
including Karl Barth and Dietrich Bonhöffer. He had a brilliant
career as a scholar and was an excellent church historian, the premier expert on early Christianity. Responding to the thought of
Immanuel Kant, he tried to develop a theology that was firmly
based on historical research. He distrusted anything he considered
to be speculative theology, be it Chalcedonian or Hegelian, and
was sceptical towards philosophy.

The book *What is Christianity?* consists of the lectures von
Harnack delivered in 1899 and 1900 at the University of Berlin.
They were delivered to an audience that comprised people that had
no formal theological education, but who were curious about
Christianity and historical criticism. This book contains von
Harnack's deep personal convictions, and whatever we might say
about his conclusions or his method, we cannot deny that he
revered Jesus.

How does von Harnack answer the question posed in his title? In his answer, he attempts to get to the very essence of Christianity, to the heart of the gospel message. For von Harnack, the essence of Christianity is the religion of Jesus – the religion that Jesus himself held and taught. It is available to the scholar and the simple man alike. It does not require theology or philosophy. It is, in his words, 'trust in the message, which Jesus delivered, of eternal life in the midst of time, by the strength and under the power of God'. Von Harnack has often been summarized as teaching the Fatherhood of God and Brotherhood of Man, and as a summary statement this fits well. Yet von Harnack did not mean this idea to be simplistic or trite – he considered it profound yet accessible to everyone. He thought that Jesus' message was about God as our Father and his care for every person, not about Jesus himself.

Understanding von Harnack's method is crucial in order to appreciate his impact and influence. He believed we had good access to the historical Jesus through the standard practices of the discipline of historical research. He is confident that the gospels provide an accurate account of Jesus and his teachings. Although he rejected the early chapters of Matthew and Luke, and much of John, thinking they are unable to provide historical evidence, he thought there was enough reliable history in the New Testament to give a true and sufficient picture of Jesus and his teachings. Von Harnack thought theological/philosophical systems had corrupted Christianity, and he sought to overcome theology by history. He gave priority to certain parts of the New Testament and only had a limited role for the Old Testament in his system of thought.

Theology was not the essence of Christianity for von Harnack – in fact, it was often the enemy of true Christianity. Yet in reading his works, one can see that it becomes difficult to get rid of theology altogether. He recognizes that Jesus is *the* Son of God in a way unlike anyone else, but it is not clear that he thinks Jesus was divine in the sense of being worthy of worship. He certainly opposed the Christology of the early church creeds. For von Harnack, the true message of Jesus needed to be purified from the additions of doctrine and church structure that developed over time. Nicaea and Chalcedon were unhelpful and dangerous, betraying the gospel to Greek thought.

Adolf von Harnack was on the wrong side of history on many issues: theology after him was not mortally wounded and cast aside, but has decidedly turned away from the Liberal Protestantism of which he was a leading figure. Yet his work is still useful and important, even if most judge the answer he provides to the question in his title to be failed. The work of Karl Barth** must be understood as, in part, a reaction against his former teacher. Also, his impact can still be felt today on historical and early church studies. Over against the speculative philosophy of his era, von Harnack showed that we can arrive at some knowledge of the historical person called Jesus and that this historical person was more than a mere accidental part of some bigger philosophy.

SYNOPSIS

Adolf von Harnack is trying to answer the question What is Christianity? through historical investigation of Jesus. This work is not a work of apologetics – he is not attempting to show that Christianity is valid, and it is not a work of philosophy – he is not using some speculative reasoning process to get at Christian faith. His work attempts to get at the true gospel message we find in the New Testament using historical criticism. When he applies this method the first three gospels are given priority, and it is important to see why he does this. John's gospel has too much theological commentary and imaginary situations to be an authority for the history of Jesus. The accounts of Jesus' childhood in the other gospels are suspect because they are too 'mythical'. He is also cautious about the miracles in the gospels. He says that if miracles are a violation of the laws of nature, there are no miracles. That a donkey spoke or that a storm was stopped by a mere word cannot be believed, yet von Harnack allows for the possibility that the lame walked or the blind saw (when forgiveness comes inwardly, it can have these external manifestations, which are not really miracles). He also rejects the notion of demonic possession: this was really just mental illness, but in that day everyone – including Jesus – called it demonic possession. Yet even with these supposed problems in the gospels, von Harnack thinks we can get at Jesus and his teachings. The gospel Jesus taught is simple and powerful, and cannot easily be mistaken – anyone honestly reading the life and teachings of Jesus is able to see it. This is the essence of Christianity, according to von Harnack.

What is Christianity? moves through three major steps. The first step is an attempt to get at the heart of Jesus' message. Von Harnack offers three points that summarize the teaching of Jesus: 1.) The Kingdom of God and its coming, 2.) God the Father and the infinite value of the human soul, and 3.) the higher righteousness and the commandment of love. He says that if we understand any one of these three points, and all its implications, we also grasp the other points and thus the whole message of Jesus, a message that is both simple and profound. Each of these points will be briefly explained.

THE KINGDOM OF GOD AND ITS COMING

Von Harnack says that the idea of two kingdoms – a kingdom of God and a kingdom of this world – was an idea Jesus shared with his contemporaries, not something unique to him and his teaching. However, the idea that the kingdom was coming and was even present is something new in the message of Jesus. The kingdom of this world is plagued by evil and suffering. Regarding the kingdom of God, von Harnack contends that Jesus adopted existing ideas present in first-century Judaism, but also added some new elements – all with a view for personal ethics and morality. The Kingdom of God is the rule of God in the hearts of individuals, in the present. It has no substantial external, historical, or future meaning: Judaism understood it this way, but Jesus' teaching about the Kingdom moves beyond anything like this. As von Harnack understands Jesus' message, those more concrete senses of the kingdom of God have been eclipsed by the 'inner coming' of the Kingdom in the hearts of individuals.

GOD THE FATHER AND THE INFINITE VALUE OF THE HUMAN SOUL

Von Harnack believed that every human soul is valuable because all have God as Father. Being a child of God means being at inner peace, having the soul united with God as Father. It means the child of God has no fear or anxiety because he/she knows that God rules over all and knows that the soul is ennobled beyond heaven and earth by having God as Father.

THE HIGHER RIGHTEOUSNESS AND THE COMMANDMENT OF LOVE

For von Harnack, the gospel message is an ethical message. Yet it is important to see that he did not think ethics are about external religious observances and acts. Like Jesus teaches in the Sermon on the Mount, the higher righteousness is about intentions and purposes, not just acts; in short, it is a heart issue. Importantly, for von Harnack, it can all be reduced down to one root and motive: love, and the command to love is for a love that is not linked to any public religion, including Christianity. The only place this morality of love has to do with religion is where one is to have an attitude of humility and love one's neighbour. This is true Christianity: nothing more than to have a love for one's neighbour.

In the second step in this book, von Harnack applies what he has identified as the heart of Jesus' message to six specific problems he considers universally relevant to every individual. Each of these problems will be explained.

ASCETICISM

Asceticism, although present in the Christian tradition and seemingly supported by some New Testament texts, is misguided in von Harnack's view. We should not shun the world for several reasons. First, because, unlike John the Baptist, Jesus ate meals with the rich and poor, enjoyed wine, and did not tell people with a firm faith to sell everything. He did not make his disciples into monks. Second, the disciples did not understand Jesus as an ascetic and did not engage in ascetic behaviour themselves; they kept their wives, for example, and understood their calling as Christians to involve staying in their current situation in life. Third, the Fatherhood of God and Brotherhood of Man principle of Jesus' teachings, which for von Harnack is the essence of his teachings, leaves no room for asceticism. Jesus calls us to self-denial and service in love, not asceticism.

SOCIAL ISSUES (THE POOR)

Von Harnack gives two extremes to avoid: first, that the gospel is fundamentally a social message, and second, that it says little to nothing about social issues. Both of these are wrong. Jesus warns that wealth is a liability for the soul, but it is not necessarily fatal to it. Yet Jesus did not give us a social program and was no social reformer. He taught that everyone should love their neighbours as themselves, and from this principle we can derive what an appropriate social program might be in our political, historical, and cultural context. Von Harnack says that this principle should be first individually applied, in the heart of each person, and then extended to meeting the needs of others – not through legal forces, but through a motivation that comes from appreciating the Brotherhood of Man.

PUBLIC ORDER (LAW)

Jesus was not a political revolutionary, and he respected the established ruling authority, seeing rulers as having a different province than God. When it comes to civil laws and the gospel, von Harnack thinks that Jesus taught that everyone should have their rights. The individual should give up his/her own rights for the sake of others, but this does not undercut individual rights and punishment regarding the government. For von Harnack, the gospel is an appeal to the inner man, the individual, to exercise love in whatever life situation one might be in. The gospel does not have to do with the affairs of this world.

CIVILIZATION (WORK)

Again, the gospel is not about the affairs of this world, so it cannot directly speak to work, art, science, or the progress of civilization. These are worthwhile matters, but they cannot really satisfy the soul. Knowledge of God is the highest and only necessary good.

CHRISTOLOGY

Von Harnack wants us to ask, How did Jesus want to be understood? Who did he intend us to think him to be? Von Harnack provides his answer: Jesus did not want anything more of us than to keep his commandments. Any doctrine about the person of Christ beyond the Fatherhood of God and the Brotherhood of Man is unnecessary. Jesus had a knowledge of God unlike anything before, and Jesus' mission was to communicate this knowledge to others – in this sense, he is *the* Son of God. Yet the gospel only has to do with God as our heavenly Father; it is not about the Son. Jesus was a messenger in a unique situation, nothing more. His message is the way to the Father. The idea of a God-man, which is really a creation of the later church, led to Christology, the doctrine of the Trinity, and other major problems. Von Harnack says that none of these doctrines can be supported from just reading the first three gospels and that they all hinder Jesus' true message.

CREED (DOCTRINE)

The gospel is only doctrine insofar as it proclaims that God is the Father. It is not a theoretical or speculative system of doctrine. We can only think rightly about Christ once we begin to live according to his gospel, and when we do, we will see that the controversies in church history about Christology were misguided.

In the third step in this book, von Harnack turns to the history of the Christian religion, both East and West. He tells the story of Christian history as he sees it. In the early Christian community, Jesus Christ was recognized as the Lord because of his teachings and because he died for sinners and rose again. Von Harnack is not convinced that Christ was actually resurrected, but he does think that belief in Christ's resurrection is important in the history of Christianity. Regardless of this issue, von Harnack believes that every individual in the early church had a living experience of God and that people in the early church led a holy life, expecting Christ to return very soon.

Paul delivered Christianity from Judaism by emphasizing a current salvation in Christ by abolishing the Law, by making religion for individuals and thus the whole world, and by putting the gospel in the terms of spirit versus flesh. Yet new limitations on the gospel came from the establishing of new forms of worship, by stressing Christology, and by retaining the Old Testament in the church.

Soon the gospel came in contact with the Hellenized world, and it was taken over by Greek philosophy. In struggling to maintain its identity in the face of many different threats, the church became institutionalized and Christianity a codified system of thought.

Once that happened, nobody was free to be a Christian without having his/her experience and knowledge tested by church creed. Traditionalism, intellectualism, and ritualism took over. The church became a political and cultural power, a visible institution that claimed to have divine authority and to be itself the Kingdom of God. The true spirit of the gospel survived, but it was distorted, diminished, and sometimes perverted. Yet not all hope was lost: the first three gospels were still in the Bible, and the emphasis on God *becoming* man in Christ, while misguided, still supported the idea that God was in Christ in a special way. The gospel as von Harnack defines it was still realized in individuals despite these barriers.

As a German Protestant, it is not surprising that von Harnack thought that the Reformation was a step towards restoring the true gospel. It brought back an emphasis on the individual's religious experience, reducing the excess that had grown around the core of the true gospel. For him, the gospel is simple and all Protestant churches have it. For both von Harnack's true gospel and for Protestantism, justification by faith is key and the individual is the final authority. Yet Protestantism got several things wrong. It established state churches and it retained problematic doctrines such as the Trinity and two-nature Christology.

CRITICISMS

The first criticism of *What is Christianity?* targets the stance von Harnack takes on miracles, particularly the resurrection. The bodily resurrection of Jesus Christ seems to be a miracle upon which the whole Christian faith stands or falls. At the very least, Jesus himself predicts his resurrection and considers it an important part of his work. Von Harnack, in making the resurrection merely something the early Christians believed as opposed to an historical event of significance, runs the risk of presenting a Christianity that is fundamentally different from the Christian tradition and that is incompatible with it. In short, if von Harnack is right about Christianity, most every other Christian is wrong about it.

The second criticism we will mention is that von Harnack distorts the teachings of Jesus, moulding them into his own likeness. He presents a Jesus who teaches a morality strikingly similar to that held in nineteenth-century Western Europe. When someone like von Harnack looks into the 'pool' of Jesus, as it were, they see themselves reflected back. It is very suspicious, to say the least, that von Harnack's core teachings of Jesus, a first-century Palestinian Jew, look remarkably like the ideology of his day.

The third criticism is one of distorting the presentation of Jesus in the gospels. He focuses on the ethical teachings of Jesus and ignores or downplays Jesus' actions – but the gospel narratives resist this division. Jesus' death on the cross is the climax and centre of the gospel story and of his own message: it seems we cannot choose to accept his ethical teachings without also accepting his claims about his divine identity.

The final criticism is also one of distortion. Von Harnack is against the church and the idea of the church. He thought we really only needed the fellowship of believers that comes from proclaiming the gospel of the Fatherhood of God and the Brotherhood of Man. Yet this does not at all do justice to the idea of church in the gospels themselves, much less in the rest of the New Testament.

22

KARL BARTH

CHURCH DOGMATICS

INTRODUCTION

Karl Barth (1886–1968) was a Swiss Reformed pastor and theologian. He is routinely described as the greatest Protestant theologian of the twentieth century. In preparing for ministry, he was trained in a classical German liberal tradition, and accepted it. On taking a pastorate in his native Switzerland, however, in an industrial area, he became increasingly convinced of the irrelevance of the theology he had learned. This came to a head with the outbreak of war in 1914: Barth saw a declaration in favour of the Kaiser's war policy signed by many of his former teachers, and concluded that a system of doctrine that obscured the evils of this militarism must be worthless.

As Barth tells the story, he shared his dissatisfaction with a friend and neighbouring pastor, Eduard Thurneysen, and together they began to search for a better expression of Christianity. Barth records his astonishment that they eventually found it in returning to, of all places, the Bible. Out of their conversations, Barth wrote a commentary on Romans, which was a devastating rebuttal of the liberal theology he had been schooled in. He had been taught, he suggested, to identify God with the highest aspirations of human culture; Romans portrayed a God who was infinitely qualitatively different from any human reality, and so stood in judgement over every human reality.

Barth's *Romans* was a remarkable success, and he was soon offered an academic post in Germany. There, he records with some humour, he found himself in a quandary: his work had been to destroy all he had been taught; to teach himself he would need to find something positive to say. He found it in a return – far from uncritical, but serious – to the older Reformed tradition of theology, which he felt enabled him to find his place in a conversation that took Scripture seriously. At the heart of his programme was the idea that, although God was infinitely beyond humanity, God graciously became available to humanity in the incarnation in the person of Jesus Christ.

He set himself to offer a positive account of Christian doctrine, based on this realization, and the *Church Dogmatics* is the result. It is a massive book, intended to be even larger. It consists of four volumes split into thirteen part-volumes, several of which approach a thousand pages in English translation. The whole runs to nearly ten million words, and yet still the fourth volume is incomplete, and Barth intended a fifth volume. The survey that follows, then, is necessarily rapid.

Barth divides the book up into very lengthy chapters. The chapters are divided up into sections, and the *Church Dogmatics* is sometimes referenced by section number (as in '§40'). Each section begins with a summary statement of its context in bold type, which is then expanded in the main body of the chapter. The discussion is interrupted by material in small print, in which Barth interacts with other writers from across the history of the church and in which he offers extended expositions of the Bible to defend and develop his ideas. These biblical sections can be very lengthy – nearly fifty pages of small print discussing the biblical witness concerning Judas Iscariot, for instance – and show Barth's respect for, and creative use of, Scripture.

SYNOPSIS

Barth's first volume, *The Doctrine of the Word of God*, deals with revelation. For Barth, the basis and possibility of theology as a rational discipline does not come from a philosophical proof that

God exists (the common Roman Catholic tradition in his day) or from an analysis of human religious experience (the common Protestant position after Schleiermacher), but from the fact that God has revealed himself and still reveals himself today.

God's revelation is primarily God's act − God makes himself known in his covenantal dealings with his people and most fundamentally in the becoming-human of the divine Word in Jesus Christ. Because revelation is a divine act, the Bible cannot itself be revelation; however, the Bible is the Word of God in the sense that it is the record of God's acts and, because of this, it can and does become the occasion for God's revelatory acts today. This is particularly so when the Bible is preached. Revelation, for Barth, is an act of God the Trinity, so much so that he offers his first account of the doctrine of the Trinity by analyzing the fact of revelation. God is the one who reveals; God is what is revealed; and God is the reality of the effect of revelation − the Father reveals the Son, and the Spirit makes possible our response.

The second volume, *The Doctrine of God*, defines God as 'the One who loves in freedom'. This is spelt out at length, first through a rich discussion of the divine perfections, tabulated as three perfections of the divine loving, grace, mercy, and patience, each paired with a balancing perfection of the divine freedom − grace with holiness; mercy with righteousness; and patience with wisdom. Similarly, the perfections of the divine freedom are unity and omnipresence; constancy and omnipotence; and eternity and glory. The discussion of eternity, in particular, is strikingly original in its attempt to understand God as at once intimately involved in time and free from any bondage to time.

God's being as 'the One who loves in freedom' is next expounded through the doctrine of election. Barth's account of election is, as he acknowledges, a major departure from the tradition in a number of ways, and has been widely discussed. The first move is placement: for Barth, election is who God is, not what God does − it is a part of the doctrine of God, not the first word in the doctrine of reconciliation. God *simply is* the one who, in Jesus Christ, chooses and saves his covenant people. This was not inevitable − God loves in freedom, and so was not constrained to be who he is. However, God *loves* in freedom, and so God's life as the electing God is not arbitrary.

Second, for Barth, the content of the doctrine of election is just the person of Jesus Christ. He is both electing God and elected human being; he is also the reality of reprobation: in Jesus Christ, God chooses that he will bear the sin and rejection of humanity. Barth thus reframes the traditional 'double decree' (the idea that some people are predestined to be saved and others predestined to be lost) by locating the reality of both election and reprobation in Jesus Christ.

In Jesus Christ, God chooses a community, which exists in a twofold form: Israel and the church. Jesus is both the crucified Messiah of Israel and the risen Lord of the church. The one community both resists its election and crucifies its Messiah, and is established by its election, and so serves its risen Lord. The community witnesses to the deserved judgement and undeserved mercy of God in its refusal to hear and its life of hearing. In all of this, it is one community, Israel and the church together. Barth offers a running commentary on Rom. 9–11 as the basis for all this in the small print sections throughout this chapter; it is striking to reflect that he was writing this account of the unity of Israel and the church a few miles from the German border as Hitler was implementing the chilling 'final solution'.

What of individuals? The witness of the elect community is that each human person is already elected in Jesus Christ: God has already born his/her deserved rejection in the person of Jesus. We may live in joyful acceptance of this gospel truth, or we may attempt to live as if it were not true. The second choice is, or should be, impossible, but in the mercy of God it is maintained as a possibility. The classic example of rejection is Judas Iscariot, who, Barth claims, fulfilled his apostolic ministry of 'handing over' Jesus and making salvation possible despite his attempts not to do so. Judas tried to live as one rejected by Jesus, but Jesus constantly chose to accept Judas – from choosing him as an apostle to offering him bread and wine at the last supper. The Bible, Barth claims, is silent on the outcome of this clash of wills, stating only that he has gone 'to his own place' (Acts 1:25).

Barth ends his doctrine of God with a section on ethics. This is a deliberate decision, followed through in the rest of the *Church Dogmatics*: ethics should not be separated from doctrine, but should flow naturally out of it. This must be so because in Jesus Christ, every claim about God is at the same time a claim about human life properly lived.

The third volume turns to creation. Barth wants to offer a properly Christian account of creation: creation is not something generally known by all human beings; instead, it is a revealed truth that is taught in Bible and creed. Creation is intimately tied to redemption: it is an act of grace, which finds its own basis in being the necessary backdrop for God's acts of salvation. Barth describes this by pointing to an intimate link between creation and covenant, God's saving promises made to human beings. The centre of creation, then, is humanity, God's covenant partner. We know true humanity in Jesus Christ and not otherwise. To be human is to be loved and addressed by God.

God is constantly intimately involved with humanity, and so Barth turns to the question of providence*. God remains Lord of every creature: our existence is dependent on God, and he rules over all with a Fatherly love. This raises the question of the existence of evil, which Barth answers with another much-discussed innovation: the concept of 'nothingness'. Nothingness is that which God actively does not will, that which is met and decisively defeated in the victory won by Jesus Christ on the cross. Nothingness takes concrete form in human sin, but it is a bigger, more amorphous power than that. It derives what reality it has from God's active rejection of its existence. Through considering evil like this, Barth offers a new take on theodicy*: we should not ask in abstract how evil comes to be, but instead proclaim that in Jesus God has decisively defeated it.

Barth again ends the volume with a substantial treatment of ethics. As creatures, human beings are set free by God, but we are set free as creatures, and so our true freedom is not an abstract ability to do anything, but a decision to live joyfully before God our creator. So Barth discusses worship and prayer under the heading of 'freedom before God', marriage and wider questions of human society under 'freedom in fellowship', and (amongst other issues) questions of abortion and euthanasia under 'freedom for life'.

The fourth volume of the *Church Dogmatics* deals with the doctrine of reconciliation. This massive treatment is carefully built: three sections discuss Jesus Christ as God, Man, and the God-Man, and under each we have an account of the work of Christ; an account of the essence of human sin, an aspect of reconciliation; and communal and individual aspects of the Holy Spirit's work.

Jesus Christ is God, but God comes to us 'not to be served, but to serve'. Barth's first section, then, is under the title 'The Lord as Servant' and discusses the priestly character of Christ's office. The opposing aspect of sin here is pride, and reconciliation is worked out as justification. The Holy Spirit gathers the community and grants faith to the individual.

Jesus Christ is true Man, and in him humanity is exalted to be God's covenant partner. The second section, then, is entitled 'The Servant as Lord'. The kingly character of Christ's office is here discussed in opposition to the human sin of sloth. Reconciliation is here explored in the aspect of sanctification; the Holy Spirit upbuilds the community and grows love in the individual.

Jesus Christ is the God-Man, and, as such, the one true witness. His office finally involves a prophetic character, which addresses directly the human sin of falsehood. Reconciliation culminates in giving vocation to human beings, and the Holy Spirit sends the community in mission and gives hope to the individual.

This schematic does not convey anything of the scale, or the power, of the exposition. This section contains some of Barth's finest writing, notably a subsection entitled 'The Journey of the Son of God into the Far Country', which weaves together allusions to the parable of the prodigal son and an account of the incarnation as God's answer to humanity's need. Barth's originality in the fourth volume is to weave his Christology* and his soteriology* completely together. He rejects the standard scheme, describing first the fall of humanity and sin, then the person of the redeemer, then the work of the redeemer, as inadequate — it gives too much prominence to human failure, when the task of theology is to talk about God. So Barth places the doctrine of incarnation* as the controlling scheme for the entirety of his consideration of reconciliation.

The fourth volume was left incomplete, with the ethics missing. Two fragments ('fragments' here means substantial books!) of the ethics are published: a treatment of baptism, included in sets of the *Church Dogmatics*, and a text entitled '*The Christian Life*', which is published separately. Barth rejects the practice of infant baptism as improper (although not invalid), arguing that baptism is properly a human ethical act of response to God's gift of reconciliation. Barth never began the fifth volume, which would have discussed eschatology* and the work of the Holy Spirit.

CRITICISMS

The *Church Dogmatics* is enormous in bulk, and looms even larger in contemporary theology. On almost every doctrine, Barth's treatment is profoundly influential, and his legacy is hotly debated. The book has been aptly described as 'a mountain we cannot go around, but must go over'. His rejection of the optimism of the liberal tradition he was schooled in, and his repeated insistence that Jesus Christ is the key to every theological question, have alike been very influential.

We have noted above some areas where Barth is strikingly original, and inevitably debate has focused around these areas. Barth's expansive writing style often leads him to develop an idea at length, only then to qualify it with a series of warnings. Several standard lines of criticism inevitably, then, focus on the coherence of Barth's ideas: he affirms many things that all would want to affirm, but seems, to some, to smuggle in logical problems as he does this. So, for example, his account of 'nothingness' having existence only as that which God does not will and which God actively fights to defeat in Jesus Christ is profoundly powerful, but can we really speak meaningfully of something coming to existence because God does not will it? Barth wants to insist that the existence of nothingness is in some sense limited and improper, but again, what does 'improper existence' actually mean? Similarly on eternity, Barth's account of God enjoying the benefits of time whilst experiencing none of its limitations is very attractive, but again raises questions, for some, of logical coherence.

Barth's account of election is perhaps the most strikingly original and controversial of all his ideas. It might seem to tie God to the world, to teach universal salvation, and to offer an unhappy account of God's purposes for Israel; it might equally be held to offer a Christological focus and a properly hopeful and joyful tone to a doctrine too often reduced to the inscrutable and arbitrary choices of an unknown omnipotence. Barth has often been accused of universalism*, a doctrine he repeatedly denies; the question, then, is not 'is he universalist?', but 'can he avoid universalism without lapsing into logical incoherence?'

The relation of God's election to God's eternal life has been a very controversial topic in recent studies of Barth. By locating election in the doctrine of God, rather than as the first of the works of God, Barth is claiming that God's decision to be for humanity is an account of *who God is*, not just of what God decides to do. Further, by linking election so closely with the person of Jesus Christ, Barth seems to be tying the life of God to creation, or at least to one particular creature – the human nature of the incarnate Son. Barth makes both these moves because of his overriding concern that election should be simple, unequivocal, good news – gospel. There is no hidden God who could have chosen otherwise; God really is just as we see in Christ.

The first question above has recently been phrased in terms of the logical priority of election and Trinity: does God's decision of election determine that God is triune? And if so, is this a problem? The second seems to us to be more significant, if less discussed: the willingness to entangle God's life with the life of the world has been endemic in theology since Barth, and, although as with other areas noted above, he was careful to deny the most worrying implications of certain aspects of his thought, those who have followed have been less careful.

Barth's greatest achievement, however, might not be any doctrinal innovation, but a renewal of the way academic theology is done. Barth's work takes the Bible with utter seriousness, is deeply informed by readings of the Christian theological tradition, and is explicitly done with the intention of serving the church. All these things had become unfashionable, to say the least, when he began to work; they have become mainstream since; he changed the way theologians worked – in the opinion of the present authors, decisively for the better.

23

DIETRICH BONHÖFFER

THE COST OF DISCIPLESHIP

INTRODUCTION

Dietrich Bonhöffer (1906–1945) was a German Lutheran pastor and theologian. His strong resistance to the Nazis in Germany before and during World War II was based on deep Christian convictions and eventually cost him his life. Bonhöffer was born into an affluent upper-middle-class family. His father was a successful neurologist who eventually became professor of psychology at the University of Berlin. While his immediate family was nominally Christian in their faith and not particularly devout, Bonhöffer does have several notable theologians and pastors in the extended family. Despite this heritage, Bonhöffer's decision to pursue theology and the pastorate was met with some dismay and reluctance from his parents and siblings.

Bonhöffer began his study of theology at Tübingen, but soon moved to Berlin to study under the leaders of German liberal theology, including Adolf von Harnack**. He completed his doctoral work in 1927 at the young age of 21. He then took a pastorate in a German-speaking congregation in Barcelona for two short years before returning to academia. He soon joined the faculty at Berlin, but only after some postdoctoral study at Union Theological

Seminary in New York, where he was influenced by his friendship with Reinhold Niebuhr, brother of H. Richard Niebuhr (See Chapter 25). Bonhöffer was challenged through this relationship to confront the demands of the gospel regarding social action for the poor. Upon returning to Berlin to teach, his theology grew and developed under the influence of the theology of Karl Barth**, though he was not afraid to criticize Barth on certain points.

As the Nazis rose to power, Bonhöffer began to publicly criticize the party, Hitler, and their ideology. Growing disenchanted with the German church's poor response to this threat, he gave up academic teaching and left Germany to become a pastor at two German-speaking churches in London. During his time abroad, the Confessing Church was founded by those German Christians who opposed Nazism, and while Bonhöffer was not present at the time, his own ideas were represented in the movement. In 1935, he was asked by the Confessing Church to return and lead an underground and illegal seminary, which he did, but it was eventually ferreted out and squashed by the Gestapo. Bonhöffer continued to speak out against the Nazis, attempting to draw the attention of the worldwide church to the threat. It is in this period that he wrote *The Cost of Discipleship* (1937). In 1939, he left Germany for America, disillusioned by the lack of response from church leaders to the terrible events beginning to unfold, only to immediately return home out of a sense of duty to suffer for the gospel in his country.

When he returned, he became involved in the German Resistance movement, becoming a double agent by taking a role the Gestapo believed would enable him to gather vital intelligence for the Nazis through travel and through his ecumenical contacts. Instead, this role enabled Bonhöffer to bring the message of the German Resistance movement to the rest of the world. At this time, he became convinced of the need to assassinate Hitler, conspiring with a few others in the movement. Unfortunately, the Gestapo became aware of this plan, and he was arrested in 1943 and sent to prison near Berlin, never to leave. He was convicted of high treason and hanged on April 9, 1945, just before the end of the war – a tragedy that cut short the life of a promising theologian, whose work was just begun and whose potential was great.

Bonhöffer's theology has had an influence, although it is sometimes overshadowed by the drama of his participation in the

Resistance movement and his untimely death. Interpretation of Bonhöffer's works has proven controversial, largely because of his unsystematic style and unfinished thoughts. *The Cost of Discipleship* was written in his earlier period and evidences his conservative approach; his later period has works that can be read to support the 'Death of God' movement and its attack on traditional Christian beliefs (this, however, is a misreading of Bonhöffer, who is to be situated in a neo-orthodox context).

The Cost of Discipleship has a distinction between cheap grace and costly grace. This was an attempt to resolve Luther's dilemma over the relationship between grace and Law. Bonhöffer says that obedience is integrally linked with belief. Costly grace, true grace, leads one down the road Christ walked – the way of suffering and demanding obedience. Cheap grace, grace that does not demand repentance and discipleship, is not grace at all. Costly grace demands we follow Jesus – and no other but him – with absolute obedience. When others – such as the state, a poignant example that lay in the background of this book – demand our obedience, we cannot capitulate. Discipleship will be costly, as Bonhöffer knew quite well.

SYNOPSIS

The Cost of Discipleship begins with extended reflection on grace and discipleship. There are two kinds of grace: cheap and costly. Cheap grace is grace as a doctrine or as a principle. If grace is a general truth to be grasped by intellectual assent, then it is cheap. Grace must result in justification of the repentant sinner who turns away from sin, or else it becomes sin that is justified. Cheap grace is the preaching of forgiveness that does not also demand repentance. Costly grace is costly because it demands much of us; it is grace because it calls us to follow Jesus Christ. It is costly because it cost God the life of his Son; it is grace because it is God who dies for us.

Grace and discipleship are inseparable. When Christianity becomes secularized, when it becomes little more than a cultural identity, costly grace is lost. Discipleship is not something for specialists such as monks, but is the call upon every Christian. Luther understood this – following Jesus is costly, but it is the only response to encountering true grace. Only grace can save, but saving grace invariably has the obligation of discipleship. Costly grace, without discipleship, is converted into cheap grace.

Bonhöffer thinks the Lutherans of his day had succumbed to the pitfalls and temptations of cheap grace. Germany had become Christian and Lutheran in a loose identity, holding the correct doctrine of justification. However, it had lost sight of true discipleship. Germans were spiritual pushovers when it came time to stand up, anaemic from a diet of cheap grace. They could check the boxes for orthodoxy, but were unable to follow the Lord Jesus Christ. Bonhöffer intends to offer a challenge to those concerned about this problem, one that brings meaning back to the word 'grace'. He offers an attempt to recover the right understanding of the relationship between grace and discipleship.

The call to discipleship is a demanding one. The call to follow Christ is a call to follow a person, not a programme, set of rules, or ideology. It is a personal obedience. Following Jesus involves certain definite steps. First, we must leave our previous existence. We must drop our nets, abandon our tax collecting, leave all and go with the incarnate Son of God. Only he/she who is obedient to this call believes, and only he/she who believes is obedient. While it is faith that first justifies and obedience that follows, this is not a chronological distinction – there is an essential unity to them. Only by heeding the words of Jesus is faith possible.

Christians are called to a single-minded obedience. We cannot accept excuses, we cannot dilute the command to leave everything and follow with qualifications about keeping our riches, staying in our current places, and changing our inner attitudes. While following Jesus might, in fact, mean staying in our current place in life, this possibility cannot in the slightest concern us – if it does, then we fall short of the single-minded obedience required of us.

Discipleship must be about the cross. The call to follow Christ is the call to follow him to the cross, an invitation to suffering and rejection. Since Jesus had to suffer, so must his disciples, who share in his suffering and crucifixion. Following Jesus is to deny oneself, to be aware of only Christ and no more of self, and to take up one's cross, to suffer for his sake. This is not just any suffering, but suffering and rejection for the sake of Christ. Christ calls us to come and die to ourselves. Suffering is a mark of true discipleship; those who take up the cross take up Jesus' yoke and burden, which are easy and light.

Discipleship is an individual calling. Christ calls us to become an individual, to leave our nationality, our family, and our friends. We are called separately and we must follow alone. Only then, through the mediation of Christ, can we be joined in the right way with our nation, our family, and our friends. Our relationships with others and with the world have been built on an illusion, one that needs to be completely abandoned in following Christ. Only in Christ do we find true connections with reality and with others.

After discussing grace and discipleship, Bonhöffer turns to reflect on Jesus' Sermon on the Mount and another section from Matthew, where he considers what this means for the disciple.

In the beatitudes – Jesus' 'blessed are the ...' sayings – Jesus was speaking to those who had answered his call to follow him. They had nothing, leaving it all. They are poor – not just generally poor, but poor for the sake of Jesus. They mourn the evil world they have left to follow Jesus. They are meek, giving up their own rights to live for the sake of Jesus Christ. They renounce their own righteousness and seek that from God. All this and more is said of them, yet he calls them blessed – blessed because they followed the call and receive his promises.

Those who are called to follow Jesus are, in fact, the highest good and the redeeming factor in the world, the remnant that prevents it from decaying into nothing. Christians are the salt of the earth and the light of the world. This is not something Christians are called to do, something at which they can succeed or fail, and it is not something they possess. Christians *are* the salt and the light – it is part and parcel of following Jesus, and there is no Christian faith without the good works of taking up one's cross.

After the beatitudes in the Sermon on the Mount, Jesus talks about the Old Testament Law. Christ does not destroy the Law, he fulfils it. Bonhöffer understands these difficult words of Jesus to mean that disciples cannot disregard the Old Testament Law in following him. The Law is not a means of righteousness – believers find that in Christ alone, who completes the Law in his life and death. In obedience and discipleship we are to follow the one who perfectly fulfilled the Law – not just in its letter, but in its penetrating intent, down to our motives. Murder is forbidden, but so is hating one's brother in one's heart. Adultery is wrong, but so is sexual lust in one's heart. We are not to take revenge, but are to renounce our personal rights for the sake of Jesus. We are to love our enemies, pray for our persecutors, and do good to those who hate us. This is how Christians are to follow the Law – by the costly discipleship of following Jesus.

This good we do is always to be kept in view of its purpose and nature – it is for following Jesus, and for his sake. It must not be done for its own sake, done to earn our own righteousness, or done as a demonstrating performance for others. This is accomplished by fixing our eyes, so to speak, on Jesus in our discipleship, looking neither to ourselves nor to others. Our righteous acts, our life of prayer, and our pious life are not to be done for display, but should be done even in secret, when nobody else is looking. Also, we cannot be a follower of Jesus and be a follower of worldly wealth. Rather, in following Jesus we must trust God to provide for our daily needs, not having any anxiety about the future and not seeking to build up our own security.

If this is the path of discipleship, what then becomes of the disciples in the world? Specifically, what is the relationship between Christians and their non-Christian neighbours? Bonhöffer says that the disciples are not to judge others because Christians only have their righteousness through fellowship with Jesus Christ. They have no special privilege or power of their own. This band of followers will be a minority in the world. The path of discipleship is narrow and easy to miss, and it is also a difficult path to walk. The group of disciples will have imposters too, but a true disciple will be evident by the fruit of his/her life.

Reflecting on Matthew 9–10, Bonhöffer says that disciples have a certain purpose to their calling: followers of Jesus are to be messengers. The people are lost, like sheep without a shepherd, and the harvest is ripe. In the New Testament, the disciples are called for this task by Jesus. He sends out his disciples into the world to preach the coming Kingdom of God. They are to follow Jesus' initiative and instructions, doing so on his authority, not their own. Their jobs as messengers will be dangerous and will require them to suffer, but God will empower them. Discipleship means losing one's life and finding it in Christ.

Bonhöffer then turns to discuss how discipleship relates to the church. First he asks, How are Christians today to be disciples? Jesus came to his first disciples in bodily form – he walked directly up to

Peter, Matthew, et al., and said 'follow me' right before their eyes. Bonhöffer says that Christ is alive and present to us today in his church through the preaching of the Word and the sacraments. Here we encounter the very same Christ, in his whole person. Discipleship is the decision for obedience to Christ, and in that way we are just like the first disciples.

Baptism is an offer Christ makes to man. It is being baptized *into* Jesus Christ, where we are basically passive and where we pass from the dominion of this world into ownership of Christ. Our old selves are put to death and a new self arises, one that has died to sin and the world. Baptism is connected with the Spirit, who dwells in believers. Baptism is about a visible act of obedience, a public act, and once-and-for-all marks us as Christ's own.

What does it mean to be baptized into the body of Christ? Through the incarnation, the Son has taken humanity and has taken up the whole of the human race by taking on bodily form. For the first disciples, it was not enough just to follow his teachings and instructions. They had to follow *him*, and because of the incarnation, that meant following him bodily. In his earthly body, he was crucified and he died, after which he was given a new glorified body. Today, we participate in the body of Christ through baptism and through the Lord's supper. The whole of humanity is with Christ in his death, which means death for them, but Christians not only die, but also live with Christ. Christ is present to Christians in a special way – they are in Christ and Christ is in them. The body of Christ today is the church, where he is really present in the world. Individual disciples become members that make up that body, and that body has a visible presence in the world through the preaching of the Word as handed down from the apostles and through baptism and the Lord's supper. It is also legitimate to give liturgy and order to the body, to have ministers and practices that give form to the church.

Disciples are to be holy, as God is holy. Bonhöffer points out that all Christians are called 'saints' in the New Testament, but are not called 'the righteous' – because the gift of righteousness is clearly not their own. The saints are sealed with the Holy Spirit, and this seal cannot be broken. This seal keeps the saints separate from the world, waiting for the return of Christ. For the community of the saints, this means they should be clearly separated from the world as part of the visible church, they should walk in a way worthy of God's holiness, and their sanctification is not for the world to see, but to prepare us for the return of Jesus Christ.

CRITICISMS

The first criticism raises a theological problem. Does Bonhöffer sufficiently answer the accusation often levelled against Lutheran theology, namely, that its accounts of justifications have nothing to do with sanctification? There have been two main ways to answer this, each represented by the Roman Catholic and Reformed traditions (see Chapters 12 and 14 on the Council of Trent and The Westminster Standards, respectively). Bonhöffer makes a distinction between costly grace, which leads to a changed life, and cheap grace, which does not. This seems to put him in the Reformed camp and not the Lutheran camp – yet he makes no direct indication of this move, which he would have done well to state explicitly.

The second criticism is about pastoral theology. Christian discipleship is always messy, and pastoral theology and ethics are always very messy. It is one thing to say the demands are high; it is another to explain how to wade through conflicting and messy demands. History seems to have offered Bonhöffer a 'break in the clouds' in that, for him, radical discipleship means opposing a fundamentally evil culture that must be rejected. However, not every context is this extreme. In many contexts, radical discipleship is a much more complex thing. Bonhöffer challenges us to ask the tough questions and consider the radical options, but he leaves us little guidance for day-to-day decisions in the Christian life.

24

RUDOLF BULTMANN
NEW TESTAMENT AND MYTHOLOGY

INTRODUCTION

Rudolf Bultmann (1884–1976) was born in Germany in 1884. He studied theology at Tübingen and Berlin before finishing in Marburg. Later becoming a professor at Marburg, he spent most of his adult life there. He actively participated in the strong opposition from the German churches to the Nazis. Bultmann is one of the great scholars of his day in New Testament studies. He systematized and popularized modern sceptical biblical interpretation for the twentieth century.

He was heavily influenced by the philosopher Martin Heidegger and developed an existential interpretation of Christianity. Such an interpretation of Christianity was concerned with decisions confronting a person living today that are part of human existence. Thus, while he tried to avoid the criticism of turning the New Testament into existentialist philosophy, it is fair to say that his entire theology depends on existentialist assumptions.

With his project, Bultmann is not trying to dissolve the gospel from the Bible or to reduce it to a 'God and Soul' message like older Liberalism did. He is interested in the universal implications of Jesus and the meaning of the revelation of God in Christ. However, many critics conclude that he does not succeed in retaining the gospel.

Bultmann's project involves demythologizing the New Testament. In short, demythologizing is the task of translating meaning from a mythical expression to a modern way of thinking. For example, the three-level universe of heaven above, a flat earth, and hell below; spiritual beings such as angels and Satan; the incarnation; the return of Christ; all miracles; forgiveness as the remission of punishment, to name a few, are all myths that need demythologizing. Perhaps the most conspicuous example is the resurrection. Bultmann, if you asked him directly, would say that he believed in the resurrection of Jesus Christ. In fact, he says as much. Yet he did not believe that Jesus bodily rose from the dead and is alive today; rather, he believed the resurrection was the rise of the disciples' faith as a result of Christ dying on the cross. The literal resurrection is a false offence in the mind of modern man; it must be demythologized in order for a person to be confronted with the *true* gospel, to which he/she must personally respond. So it is not that Bultmann thinks that myths are not true, but that myths are a form of expression different than literal or scientific expressions of truth. Myths are only false if understood literally, something in Bultmann's estimation the Christian tradition failed to avoid.

What motivated Bultmann to demythologize? The modern world cannot believe the pre-Enlightenment, pre-scientific view of reality in the Bible. If the gospel is tied to that view, he thought, then it has nothing to offer us today. Since the modern reader cannot accept the ancient mythical framework of the Bible, to have any hope for the gospel to be accepted it must be demythologized. Bultmann, then, was motivated by apologetic concerns.

We must recognize that Bultmann's desire for the gospel message to be 'translated' from the ancient context of the Bible to today's contemporary context is a good instinct shared by every preacher and a skill possessed by the good ones. However, as objections and critiques of his method have abounded, it seems that his approach might not be the best way forward.

SYNOPSIS

In *New Testament and Mythology*, Bultmann raises a problem and then offers his solution. The problem, in short, is that the Bible presents a mythical view of the world as it proclaims the gospel, a view that is obsolete and odious to the modern man. Living in the modern age, we cannot accept the miracles, the ubiquity of demonic and angelic forces in the world, the appearance as a man of a pre-existent divine being, or the future return of Christ to the earth that characterizes the New Testament. Scripture teaches that death is the punishment for sin, that the Holy Spirit supernaturally works in us, that Christ was the sinless sacrifice for sinners, and that Jesus was resurrected from the dead. No, says Bultmann, these myths – which can be traced to Jewish or Greek sources – are incredible to us. Further, for Bultmann, the mythology of the New Testament is sometimes contradictory: Christ's death is sometimes a sacrifice and sometimes a cosmic event, Christ's virgin birth is inconsistent with his pre-existence, God is in complete control of all things yet we are commanded to choose for ourselves, etc. When we preach the gospel message, should converts be expected to accept this whole mythic package? Or is there a more palatable truth in the New Testament that can exist independently of this mythical setting? Bultmann considers it senseless and impossible to expect modern man to accept the cosmology of a pre-scientific age. The solution, then, is in demythologizing.

Demythologizing is to decode a myth into contemporary ways of thinking. Bultmann believed the Bible needed to be demythologized: to take the ancient mythical patterns of thought found in the Bible, 'translate' the message into our modern scientific view of the world, strip away any remnants of mythology, and present the core truth of the myth. The New Testament, when given this treatment, provides us with the knowledge of how a person might understand himself/herself in this world – the core truth is really about existential matters, about life here and now, not about questions of the Trinity or the two natures of Christ.

How does Bultmann suggest we go about the task of demythologizing? He begins by explaining a wrong approach. He says we cannot save the gospel message by selecting some features and removing others in a pick-and-choose manner. This is what many of the older liberals had tried, and they failed. One of the biggest problems is the criteria for these judgements: where does one draw the line? The mythology of the New Testament is not an exterior husk we can discard; it runs deep and cannot be pruned away: it must be demythologized.

The nature of myth is to express man's self-understanding in the world, not to present an objective picture of the world as it really is. Thus, myths need to be interpreted existentially, as a quest to find meaning beyond the tangible world in which we live. The question then becomes: when we interpret the New Testament mythology, do we arrive at an understanding of existence that is true? As Bultmann sees things, faith says that we do.

Others have tried to handle New Testament mythology with poor results. The nineteenth-century Liberal Protestant tradition destroyed the gospel preaching as they eliminated mythology; they failed to truly interpret it. The gospel is reduced to a few principles of religion and ethics. Lost was the heart of the gospel – 'the proclamation of the decisive act of God in Christ', as Bultmann puts it. The New Testament does not merely proclaim Jesus as a good teacher, but proclaims, rather, that his appearance is the event where God brings redemption. Liberal Protestantism comes up short, but so does the History of Religions movement. They emphasized participating in religion and piety rather than teaching religion and ethics. Theology was unimportant – the essence of the New Testament is in living a religious life. Yet they too failed to do justice to the decisive act of God in Christ we find in the New Testament preaching – just who is this Jesus we ought to worship, and what difference does he make?

Bultmann then arrives at what demythologizing should be: an existentialist interpretation of the New Testament. He first explains what Christian existence should look like, and then discusses the relationship of this to Christ. We will turn to each of these points, the first receiving much briefer treatment than the rest.

First, a few words on Bultmann's existentialist unmythological interpretation of Christian existence. When the New Testament speaks of 'this world', the idea is a world of corruption and death. It was not like this when originally created, but became this way because of sin. By saying this, Bultmann means that our lives are weighed down by anxiety, by concern for security, and by fear of death. We seek security and relief from this world. However, this is an inauthentic way to live. An authentic life is lived on the basis of unseen realities, and this is what the New Testament calls 'life after the Spirit' or 'life in faith'. Such a life requires faith in the grace of God. Such grace means the forgiveness of sin, which, for Bultmann, means release from the past pursuits for false security. Such faith requires obedience, abandoning worldly security and surrendering to God. Such a life leads to detachment from the world and to true freedom. A life lived like this is 'eschatological existence', meaning that one is a 'new creature' (from 2 Cor. 5:17). This is the Christian interpretation of existence.

Second, how does this relate to Christ? In the New Testament, faith is always faith in Christ. Faith is the consequence of the event of Christ, an event that occurred at a definite point in history. At this point, the crucial questions for Bultmann become: Is this event a remnant of mythology that requires demythologizing and interpretation? Can there be this Christian understanding of existence without Christ?

Bultmann insists there cannot. The Christ event cannot be discarded as a relic of mythology. However, the Christ event is described mythically, and this requires some careful attention. Modern existentialist philosophy, such as that of Heidegger, seems to arrive at a similar view of man's natural understanding of his existence. However, theology is not merely a precursor to existentialism, Bultmann says. While both existentialist philosophy and the demythologized teaching of the New Testament see anxiety as a chief characteristic of man's existence and require the abandoning of all worldly security and committing to the future, Bultmann says that the New Testament view requires revelation. Man's nature − to live an authentic existence − is discovered by both. However, it cannot be realized unless God decisively acts. It is not enough to know what man ought to be. The New Testament, even after being fully demythologized, teaches that man is incapable of releasing himself from his fallen state. God must act.

Existentialism says that we can achieve authentic existence on our own, without a saving act of God; the New Testament says that such an act is necessary. Both agree that man can only become what he already truly is, that the authentic life is possible because in a way we already have it. The key difference is that the New Testament says this only of Christians. Natural man, in a natural state of sin, only has despair. The New Testament insists upon a fall that leaves man totally unable to save himself, whereas existentialism sees no need of God for man to realize his authentic nature. Which is right? Bultmann says that the New Testament's case cannot be proven any more than the existentialist's. It comes down to a matter of decision, of making the choice in faith.

The problem, according to the New Testament, is that man is a sinner. Is this notion of sin mythological? Bultmann says that it is not for the Christian, when the love of God meets a person in his/her fallen state, treating him/her as if he/she were something other than what he/she is, and setting him/her free. An authentic life is only possible when this happens, when God decisively acted on our behalf when we were completely unable to do so.

God reveals his love in the event of Jesus Christ. Faith in this love of God is only valid if it is connected to this revelation, that is, if it is faith *in Christ*. The act of God in Christ makes man capable of faith and love – capable of an authentic life.

If this is the role of the Christ event in a Christian's self-understanding, then does the New Testament regard this event as essentially mythical? Bultmann thinks it undeniable that the New Testament presents the Christ event in mythical terms. The issue is whether this can be demythologized, and if so, what remains. Insofar as Jesus is the Son of God, he is a mythical figure – but not like, say, Zeus, for he is also a figure of concrete history: Jesus of Nazareth. This combination of history and myth is unique. What, then, shall we make of the supposedly mythical elements such as his pre-existence, his virgin birth, his miracles, etc.? Bultmann says that many of these can be explained as an attempt to put forth the meaning of the historical Jesus and his life for faith. There is only meaning in the events of his life when we ask what God is trying to say to us through them. Bultmann focuses on two key events: the cross and the resurrection.

There are elements to the cross that are mythical. The Son of God was crucified and he then died; he was our representative sacrifice; he delivers us from death in his dying – these cosmic dimensions are mythical interpretations of the historical event. The true, demythologized meaning of the cross is the call to 'make the cross of Christ our own', to 'share in his crucifixion' by making it a present reality by faith. The cross' only 'cosmic' effect is the difference it makes in the everyday lives of Christians, helping us to accept suffering and to rise above our attachment to this world and live an authentic life.

At this point, Bultmann knows he will be asked about whether this existential significance can be discerned in the actual events of

Jesus' life. What of the Jesus of history? He says that the Jesus of history has significance for the first preachers in the New Testament because their histories intersected with Jesus'. They witnessed the cross in their own lives, historically. Today, we cannot have this connection; we only have historical report. The true meaning of the cross does not come from historical contact or from historical research, but in how Jesus is proclaimed not only to have been crucified, but also to have risen from the dead. Since the cross and the resurrection are united in the New Testament, Bultmann turns to explain the resurrection.

Bultmann asks if the resurrection is a straightforward mythical event. The answer is in the negative, not because the resurrection of Jesus from the dead was an actual historical event (he thinks it was not), but because it is united with the cross. In this way, it is not purely mythical but, in itself, is mythical in character. The event of Easter Day is not a historical event – it is the result of the events of the cross that caused the faith of the early church and led to the apostolic preaching. The resurrection cannot be a miraculous proof of the claims of Jesus. For Bultmann, the resurrection narratives in the New Testament are later embellishments and are unreliable. The only way to see the importance of the cross and the resurrection is by faith. Thus, the meaning of the resurrection, like the meaning of the cross, is in the everyday life of Christians, who walk in freedom from the anxiety of death. Faith in the resurrection, when demythologized, is the same as faith in the power of the cross to enable us to live authentic lives.

We are confronted with the preaching of the cross and the resurrection. Bultmann says we are not to question its credentials – rather, we are the ones questioned, we are asked to believe this Word of God or reject it.

CRITICISMS

Bultmann's theology has been criticized from a number of angles; we will briefly mention a few. First is the criticism that his definition of myth is too vague; it seems to cover all symbolic and metaphorical language in the Bible. His blunt instrument of demythologizing crushes nearly all metaphor, simile, poetry, and other literary devices. For example, certainly the description of the

New Jerusalem in the Book of Revelation is not suggesting literal dimensions and building materials for the city. However, it seems clear that the literal resurrection of Christ is intended by the New Testament writers to be understood as an actual event. Between these two there is a need for much interpretive nuance, something Bultmann's method seems to disallow.

The second criticism is that his method of demythologizing often reads modern values and concepts into an ancient text. In other words, his process of interpretation actually sometimes runs in the opposite direction of what he purports to be doing. The New Testament, when so readily thrown into the machinery of demythologization, is gagged from speaking on its own terms.

The third criticism is that Bultmann more or less assumes the naturalist worldview and then proceeds on that assumption to translate the Bible into existentialist terms. It is not clear if he actually holds a naturalist worldview or if he believes that the preacher must do so in order to be heard and to be effective today. Either way, this is to beg the question. That naturalism cannot accept the literal resurrection of Jesus is no argument against the resurrection; to call it 'myth' and do away with it is to prejudge the matter before one even begins.

The fourth criticism is that Bultmann's existentialism is too self-focused and too man-focused. The gospel is about what God is doing in the world, his plan of salvation; a person's individual decision is certainly important, but cannot take the central position Bultmann gives it. Bultmann seems to be ultimately indifferent about what Jesus actually did or said – rather, as long as a person takes the words and actions as decisive for his/her own existence, the question of the connection with the actual life of Jesus is unimportant. Yet how can this be so? For if what we have of Jesus is merely the tradition that developed from the early Christian community, in the 'now', what is the individual actually doing, if not an act of wilful ignorance? If God has not *actually* decisively acted in history, what is decisive for the existence of a Christian?

The final criticism is that modernity is laden with 'myths' just like the New Testament, 'myths' that fit Bultmann's definition just as much as the New Testament's do. If a 'myth' is essentially a transcendental-value-laden story, modernity is in the same boat as the New Testament. The myth of progress, the myth of enlightenment, the myth of a certain knowledge based solely on empirical deliverances from the scientific method – these and many more are all myths the modern man holds. In explaining our world, the human condition, and the truth, why should these modern myths receive priority over those held by New Testament writers?

H. RICHARD NIEBUHR
CHRIST AND CULTURE

INTRODUCTION

Helmut Richard Niebuhr (1894–1962) was an American Protestant theologian and Christian ethicist who taught for several years at Yale Divinity School. He was born in Missouri, and his father was a German immigrant and Lutheran pastor. Niebuhr graduated from Elmhurst College in Illinois and Eden Theological Seminary in Missouri, later earning his Ph.D. from Yale University. He was the younger brother of Reinhold Niebuhr, one of the great Christian social thinkers in America in the twentieth century. Yet Richard also had substantial influence, his theology becoming foundational for what is sometimes called the 'Yale School' of postliberal theology.

Christ and Culture, published in 1951, came from the lectures H. Richard Niebuhr delivered at Austin Seminary in 1949. This book has had enormous influence on the discussion of Christianity and society, the church's relationship to the world, and how believers ought to engage in culture.

SYNOPSIS

To begin, Niebuhr puts forth what he calls the 'enduring problem': the relationship between Christianity and civilization. Christ is perfect and sinless; culture is made by humans who are imperfect and sinful, and is thus tainted by sin and imperfection. How, then, can a perfect Christ mingle with sinful culture? When we turn to Scripture, we see calls for the Christian to walk away from this sinful world as well as calls to be in the world. To compound things further, what we have in Scripture is given to us in cultural embodiment.

Jesus challenged and confronted certain elements of his own Jewish culture, which started the question of Christ and culture for Christians, who have been wrestling with the problem ever since. A harmonious relationship between the two has not been achieved, says Niebuhr: detractors of Christianity have accused Christians of neglecting the temporal by an overemphasis on immortality, neglecting their own duty to be agents of change in the world on the grounds that God alone must do this, and being intolerant of other religions in the cultures of the world. Throughout the chapters of church history, this fundamental problem appears in many forms: the problem of reason and revelation, of religion and science, of state and church, etc. The problem is not really the relationship between Christianity and civilization because Christianity itself moves between the poles of Christ and culture. The problem, in essence, is the relationship between the authorities of Christ and culture.

Niebuhr defines these two terms. He explains at length what each term means, but in short, by 'Christ' he means the person of Jesus Christ who exercises authority over a Christian and by 'culture' he means the total process and result of human activity commonly called 'civilization'. It is made up of values, language, habits, ideas, beliefs, customs, social institutions, etc. Culture is always social, always a human achievement, and always a world of values concerned for man's good and man's material realization of those values. Culture is the 'secondary environment' that humanity superimposes on the natural world (a river is of nature, but a canal is of culture).

Niebuhr offers five possible answers to this problem, but he clarifies that he is really providing five families of answers. There are similarities and differences that bridge some of the families, and no person or concrete view holds one answer to the complete exclusion of anything in some of the others. However, one can and must identify one's position as residing predominantly in one category. We will examine each in turn.

The first view is *Christ against Culture*. This is the most uncompromising and is the starting place because the other views are seen in distinction to this one. In it, Christ is the sole authority over culture, and our loyalty is to go to him alone. We are to be loyal to Christ and to our brothers and sisters in Christ, but we are to forsake the world and any claim it might have on us. Tertullian and Tolstoy are examples of this view. Niebuhr says that while we must take this view seriously simply because of the stature of those in the Christian tradition who have adopted it, the view is inadequate, and nobody can live it out consistently. It is impossible to rely solely on Jesus Christ to the exclusion of culture – we are inextricably culturally situated creatures, and there is little to nothing we can do as humans that does not involve culture. Even talking, the use of language, involves culture. Further, how are Christians to preach the gospel to the world without engaging with culture? More damaging to the view are some theological problems. First, the view tends to denigrate reason and elevate revelation to an extreme, but we cannot understand revelation or think well about the Christian faith without some use of reason. Second, the view says that sin lies in culture and thus we must escape culture, but in so doing, the Christian does not escape sin. Sin is present in even the most sequestered monastery. Third, the view fails to do justice to Jesus' role in creation, his role as ruler of history, and to the Spirit's role in creation and in the church. God is concerned with the material just as he is with the spiritual.

The second view is *The Christ of Culture*. This view is on the opposite extreme to *Christ against Culture* and is where Christ and culture are minimally – if at all – in opposition and competition. In this view, Jesus is hailed as the Messiah of one's society. Christians should maintain fellowship with fellow believers as well as those unbelievers in their society, in the same way and to the same degree. In this view, there is no great tension between the church and the world. In the *Christ of Culture* approach to the enduring problem, culture is interpreted through Christ, where the most important elements of culture are those that best fit with his work and person; Christ is understood through culture, where the elements of Jesus' life and teachings and of Christian theology that agree with what is best in civilization are highlighted. This view seeks the maximal harmony possible between Christ and culture, not entirely ignoring the discordant differences, but definitely downplaying and/or synthesizing them. Leibnitz, Kant, and Schleiermacher are examples of this view. There is something to the idea that the Christian message will often comport with the best that moral and religious philosophy in culture has to offer. Also, proponents of this view tend to be leading examples of making an impact in culture for the Christian message, showing that Jesus speaks to all areas of human existence. However, Niebuhr raises some problems for this view, the biggest being this: in their efforts of accommodation, proponents of this view distort Jesus and his message to the point where he begins to be – and often is completely – lost. A non-authentic Jesus is presented in the name of cultural acceptance.

The great majority of Christians have not opted for either of these first two extremes, but have tried to forge a middle way. This middle way is represented by Niebuhr's third, fourth, and fifth views. In this middle way, the fundamental issue is not between Christ and culture, but between God who is holy and man who is sinful. God orders culture, and thus culture is neutral. Obedience to Christ, who is God, can only be done in the space of culture. Sin is a radical and universal reality in humanity, so sin cannot help but be manifested in culture. Yet it is humans who do the sin in the space of culture; culture itself is not inherently bad. Within this centrist and majority impulse, there are three distinguishable families that make up Niebuhr's remaining categories: synthesists, dualists, and conversionists.

The third view is *Christ above Culture*, and it is the synthesist view. This 'both-and' view sees the relationship between Christ and culture differently than the *Christ of Culture* view. It is represented by Thomas Aquinas. It is unwilling to compromise the nature of Jesus we find in the New Testament, the Jesus who is Lord. He is Lord of both heaven and this world, both fully God and fully man. The *Christ above Culture* view affirms both Christ and culture, where Christ is the incarnate God-Man, and culture is both divine and human in origin, both holy and sinful. Human culture cannot be separated from the grace of God. Christ and culture are distinct, but they are unified in a synthesis in the Christian life. We are to give to Caesar what is Caesar's and to God what is God's, and both of these are part of obedience to Christ. Christ becoming incarnate means that he is part of human culture, Christ being the eternal God means that he is nevertheless above culture as the God who sustains it. Christians are to be involved in society because God created mankind to have a culture that is supposed to function through direction from God. The church has both a spiritual purpose and an earthly purpose. Niebuhr sees great strength in this position, but is hesitant about the apparent implication of institutionalizing Christ and the gospel. The position is liable to draw attention away from the eternal hope of the Christian and focus too much attention on the cultural embodiment that man creates. He also complains that this view does not adequately come to grips with the radical evil present in all human work.

The fourth view is *Christ and Culture in Paradox*, and it is the dualist view. Luther and Kierkegaard are representatives of this view. This view accuses the *Christ above Culture* perspective of making the co-operation between Christ and culture a happy union, when there is actually conflict in this relationship. This view agrees that we have loyalty to Christ and an obligation for culture, but there is a severe paradox whenever a conflict between Christ and culture exists on account of sin in culture (and this is not uncommon). The conflict is between God and us, between God's righteousness and our own self-righteousness. God is a God of grace, but man is in sin, and sin is in man. Humanity is much more sinful and depraved than the *Christ above Culture* view would have us believe. Human culture is fundamentally broken. Christ and culture are not two parts of a closely knit system, yet they are not entirely contradictory. This Christian life straddles both of these and must continue to do so, but we must never forget that we live 'between the times'. This view resonates with the Christian experience of living in a world under both wrath and mercy. The big problem with the view, says Niebuhr, is that it leads to a rejection of law and cultural conservatism. If the world is so extremely sinful, the resistance and obedience to God could be seen as futile. Similarly, the tendency to give up on culture and leave it where it is could be strong, writing it off as a lost cause.

The fifth and final view is *Christ the Transformer of Culture*. This conversionist understanding of the relationship between Christ and culture is like the dualist view, but it is a bit more optimistic and hopeful towards culture. Like the dualists, proponents of this perspective have a strong view of the severity of sin in the world. Yet like synthesists, they believe that even this wicked culture is under God's rule and that Christians must participate in changing culture out of obedience to the Lord. This view is hopeful that culture can be transformed because the existence of culture is part of God's good creation, although it does need redemption. Christ is not just the saviour and redeemer; through him all things were made. Culture is perverted good, not complete evil, and all things are possible with a saving God. Through God's grace, human culture can be transformed and given to the glory of God. In practice, this means Christians work for the betterment of culture because God is working through Christians to do this. Sin must be defeated not by abandonment of culture, but by the transformation and conversion of culture. There is hope for Christ to redeem it.

Niebuhr closes his book with a section called 'A "Concluding Unscientific Postscript"', a title that references Kierkegaard** (see Chapter 20). By this, he means his taxonomy is not exhaustive and the discussion on this issue is hardly resolved. He does not think any one type is the best – even the last one – but that the enduring problem remains. Niebuhr does not see this as a fault in his work – if only he had worked harder and written more he might have arrived at *the* Christian answer. The Lordship of Christ and the liberty that Christians enjoy mean that generation after generation must wrestle with these issues, especially since the types are not mutually exclusive, and overlap is possible and quite actual. This tentativeness inherent in any theory of Christ and culture, however, cannot prevent a Christian from action and decision on the issue. In other words, while we can never reach a definitive theoretical answer, we must all reach an 'actionable' conclusion.

These decisions we arrive at individually are relative to our culture, but Niebuhr is careful to clarify what he means by 'relative'. By 'relative', he means they are relative to the individual's placement in the world and in history. These decisions depend on the partial, incomplete, fragmentary knowledge of each individual and are relative to that knowledge. The individual has a measure of faith and unbelief; he/she has a place in society and a set of values that are relative to other values. All this is not to say that relativism should reign, but that the decider must decide and act as a concrete person with a set of relations. We have relativity, but we are not without an absolute, or as Niebuhr says, the infinite Absolute. We need to be aware of our relativism and the ways we are culturally conditioned, yet our faith in Jesus Christ means that we are anchored to the one who is Absolute and that we have others who stand in the same relation to Christ that can help us.

The decisions we must make about Christ and culture are existential ones in that they cannot be based on speculative theory, but must be made by a subject using his/her freedom to appropriate the truth for himself/herself. Yet while we make individual decisions, we do not do so individualistically – we are united as a group of believers who must exist in society. There is no abstract individualism – we exist in a complex network of relationships, and this matters for our faith and for our handling of culture.

CRITICISMS

While Niebuhr's work, especially the typology it offers, has set the frame of the discussion since its publication, there are many critics who think its days are numbered.

First, critics say that each of Niebuhr's types assumes a 'Christendom' perspective, where 'church' and 'state' are partners – be they sparring partners (*Christ against Culture*), mentor/mentee partners (*Christ the Transformer of Culture*), or something similar with the other types. This assumption, it is argued, is dangerous because it makes the church complicit in violence. No matter the relationship, unless the church completely repudiates the violence of the state and rejects alliance with secular powers, it is falling short. None of Niebuhr's types accomplishes this, so the accusation goes.

Second, and similarly, it is argued that *Christ and Culture* is a product of its time – post-World War II America. Totalitarianism was abroad, and racial segregation was at home. In Niebuhr's time, the looming question was how to set the future for Western civilization after the horrors of World War II in the face of international communism and the threat of nuclear holocaust. History reveals how these concerns played out. Further, we have seen multiculturalism and the postmodern turn since then; Niebuhr neither knew of nor anticipated anything like our context.

Third, Niebuhr's categories of 'Christ' and of 'culture' are both misleading. By 'Christ', he tends to mean 'Christians attempting to follow Christ', but Christians themselves are always shaped by their culture. Niebuhr would say that there is a transcendent Christ who is God incarnate and thus stands above history and culture. However, *Christians* do not. So, to speak of Christians as 'Christ' and everything else as 'culture' seems a bit misleading. Perhaps a better way to state what Niebuhr means by 'Christ and culture' is 'the culture of Christianity and other cultures'. By 'culture', Niebuhr almost indiscriminately means 'anything people do together' – from commercial transactions, to language, to art, to war. Yet with this definition, it is impossible, as Niebuhr says himself, to consistently hold an anti-world position. Rather than conclude that the problem lies with the position, as Niebuhr does, this critique says that the problem lies with the definition itself. There are some elements of culture – family, agriculture, medical care – that are supported by the Christian faith. There are others – pornography, genocide, materialism – that must be categorically rejected by the church. Other dimensions of culture have limitations from the Christian faith. Niebuhr's monolithic definition fails to appreciate these nuances.

Finally, Niebuhr is accused of presenting categories that are historically inaccurate. They are ideal theological types imposed from above onto a history that is much more messy and complicated. Christian groups and figures never fit with comfort into any one of Niebuhr's types, suggesting that they are too synthetic to be useful. However, while the other critiques might have more traction, this one seems to have a response. Niebuhr is clear that his types are not necessarily mutually exclusive and that many groups tend towards one type in one area of culture and another in another. This does not undercut the validity of the types, which provide us a way of entry into a reality that is admittedly muddled and complex.

26

KARL RAHNER
THE TRINITY

INTRODUCTION

Karl Rahner (1904–1984) was a Catholic Jesuit priest and theologian. He was born in the Black Forest city of Freiberg, Germany. One of seven children, he grew up in what he called 'a normal, middle-to lower-class, Christian family'. As a young man, he joined the Jesuit priesthood for the normal reasons one does – later in life, he stated his motivations at the time were unremarkable and ordinary for that sort of thing. He was assigned by the order to become a professor of philosophy and they sent him to schooling for such, where he eventually studied under Martin Heidegger at the University of Freiberg. His doctoral thesis was rejected for being too existentialist*, but was eventually published as the book *Spirit of the World*, earning him high acclaim. He was a charismatic lecturer, well liked by his students and those who knew him personally. Perhaps on account of being a Jesuit, Rahner had a high degree of integration between his personal piety and theological writings. While he considered himself an uninteresting man with no dramatic events in his life, he was an influential theologian, whose work pioneered what is broadly considered to be the modern understanding of Catholicism.

Rahner was connected with the school of thought in Catholic theology called Nouvelle Théologie, which was initially resisted by the Catholic Church (in 1962, he was told that anything he wrote would have to be pre-read by a Catholic censor), but which was eventually embraced at the Second Vatican Council. Nouvelle Théologie was a move away from Scholasticism and towards Scripture and the Fathers, and it sought more dialogue with those outside of Catholicism in the contemporary theological scene. It was, in many ways, a changing of Catholicism in response to modernism. After Vatican II, the Nouvelle Théologie movement split over interpretation of the Council into a more progressive camp and a more conservative one, Rahner aligning himself with the progressives and Joseph Ratzinger (formerly Pope Benedict XVI) with the conservatives.

Rahner's approach to theology was to listen to the living faith of the church, not just theologians, and give attention to the questions being asked by people outside the church. As a Catholic, he holds the tradition as authoritative and papal decrees as infallible, but within this he also criticizes and radically reinterprets the tradition. For example, Rahner emphasizes God's uniqueness. God does not just exist side by side with everything else in this world, and God is not just one member of the larger household of all reality. God is radically unlike us, is complete mystery, and is a transcendent reality that holds together all things and all of our experiences. We cannot fail to be related to God, even in sin. Rahner was significantly influenced by Heidegger's existentialist philosophy, which was crucial to his anthropology; but unlike Bultmann** (see Chapter 24), Rahner's existentialist commitments did not entirely remove the possibility of true statements about God and reality. In another reinterpretation of the tradition, on the incarnation, Rahner says that Christ would have come into the world as a man even if Adam's race had never sinned. The incarnation is not an emergency response plan to the crisis in Eden, but is crucial to who God is. In a reinterpretation of the Trinity, at one point Rahner says that the traditional understanding of the relationship between the Father and the Son can be translated into the idea that the Son is the real symbol of the Father. In the way that a symbol is and is not the same thing as the symbolized, so it is with the Father and the Son.

For our purposes, the most significant contribution of Rahner comes on the Trinity: he began the movement of modern theology on the Trinity that has marked the twentieth and now twenty-first century thus far. He diagnosed a problem with the Trinity in the church. He believed the Catholic Church practices of his day would change very little if we removed the doctrine of the Trinity altogether. In practical life, Christians were nearly 'mere monotheists', as he puts it. The Trinity was just some abstract and meaningless idea, he accused, when it should be the central doctrine of the whole Christian faith with unending practical applications. The problem, then, was that the traditional doctrine of the Trinity needed to be freed from the theologian's ivory towers and released into the actual lives of everyday Christians.

In this diagnosis, Rahner had placed his finger on a major issue in theology. What is the relationship between the doctrine of God and the story of God working and revealing himself in history? At times in the history of Christian thought, the tendency has been to focus on abstract speculation about God and neglect the concrete revelation of Jesus in history, and Rahner is certainly right to critique this. His solution, however, has been met with great praise, inspiring influential figures like Jürgen Moltmann, Wolfhart Pannenberg, and Robert Jenson, but also with great controversy, drawing extensive criticism.

Rahner might well be the most significant Catholic theologian of the twentieth century. Yet he tended to write short essays on various topics, never really producing a systematic work, and the relationship between his various thoughts found in these short essays is far from clear. Why, then, has he been so influential on so many different theologians from different denominations and traditions? First, his topical and decentralized approach gave him a platform to make observations and suggestions on a variety of issues that do not depend upon commitments to his overall system. In other words, even those who disagree with his conclusions and even with his approach can find gems along the path he takes his readers. Second, Rahner's work has remarkable breadth. He wrote short essays on a vast array of topics – from the Trinity, to the theology of childhood, to the relationship between Christianity and Marxism – with the result that almost any theologian could find something within his/her areas of interest from somewhere in his publications.

SYNOPSIS

Rahner says that Christians affirm the orthodox confessions of the Trinity, but that in practice they are almost 'mere monotheists' – not all that much would change if we dropped the Trinity altogether, he says. Even the doctrine of the incarnation does not help this problem: most Christians hold the idea that *God* became man, with only the afterthought that it is the second person of the Trinity – the Logos – who took on flesh. In most Christians' thinking, there is nothing special about the second member of the Trinity being the candidate for incarnation; it could have just as easily been one of the others. In doctrines such as the incarnation, salvation, creation, and others, there is little to no connection with the doctrine of the Trinity. It is an isolated orthodoxy in theology that cannot be jettisoned, but that is for the most part ignored. At least since Thomas Aquinas, we start with the doctrine of one God, and only once that is thoroughly established do we discuss the doctrine of the Trinity. Rahner makes this analysis of the situation and sees in it a major problem.

The cause of this problem, he says, is the division between the economic and immanent Trinities. We start with metaphysical properties of God, thinking about philosophical abstractions and building a robust theoretical concept of God. In this abstract space, we come up with technical ideas about persons, divinity, substances, the divine essence, processions, and the like. Once this is up and running, only then do we turn to salvation history as revealed to us in Scripture and in the church tradition. In other words, we build a concept of the immanent Trinity and then turn to Scripture and salvation history to see the economic Trinity, which is interpreted by our preconceived philosophical notions of what the Trinity must be. This is entirely wrongheaded, and in response to this, we are offered an axiom that has been labelled 'Rahner's Rule'.

Rahner's Rule, in its own words, says this: 'The "economic" Trinity is the "immanent" Trinity and the "immanent" Trinity is the "economic" Trinity'. This is not merely to correct the confusion of, say, a beginner theology student who interprets the language of economic Trinity and immanent Trinity to be referring to two different Gods in six persons. Rahner's Rule is doing something much more. It is saying that no distinction can be made between the doctrine of the Trinity and the doctrine of the economy of salvation. What the triune God does in the world *is* who he is. Rahner says that the idea behind his axiom can do better justice to biblical statements about the Father, Son, and Spirit, and the way they work salvation. In other words, God relates to us and to the world in a threefold manner, as Father, Son, and Spirit. This is not just a copy or an analogy of the inner life of the Trinity – it *is* the Trinity itself, freely communicated to us.

Rahner says that we must start with the economic Trinity. By this, he means that we start with God as the 'Father', as we find in Scripture. This God has communicated himself through the 'Son' and the 'Spirit'. It must be the Son who appears in the flesh in history, and it must be the Spirit who is breathed out into the world – this is inherent in the nature of God himself. For Rahner, it is misguided to emphasize the idea 'God became man' over the idea 'the Logos became man'. The incarnation of the Logos is implied from Rahner's Rule, and he believed that it could not have been otherwise – that the only candidate for incarnation was the Second Person, and God could not have willed another.

God is communicating to *someone*; in other words, there is a personal recipient. That self-communication *is* who God is. Since the economic Trinity in fact *is* God's self-communication, directly and without mediation, the distinction between economic and immanent collapses. The one act of self-communication of the one God has three different ways of being given concretely for us (Rahner is resistant to the way 'person' is understood today, and so avoids using it to speak of the threeness of God).

What difference does he think Rahner's Rule would make to our approach to theology? First, our faith experience of Jesus and the Spirit give us the Trinity; it is a reality we already have in salvation, and we need look no further. In fact, we cannot understand our Christian existence without also understanding the Trinity, for in it we in fact have the triune God. Second, we read salvation history (e.g. the Old Testament) as the secret prehistory of the revelation of the Trinity that became known in the Christ event. Because God's work in the world is his being, even before anyone knew about it, God was working in the world in a threefold way.

Third, it would protect against the tendency of tritheism to take hold at a popular level: starting the conversation on the Trinity with the word 'person' is dangerous and leads to tritheism, but starting our understanding of the Trinity with salvation history protects the unity of God.

Why do so many theologians and thinkers find Rahner's Rule attractive? In answering this question, two motivations become evident. First is a motivation from practical concerns. Rahner's Rule attempts to start with a redemptive-historical approach to the doctrine of the Trinity. The Trinity seen in salvation history *is* the real Trinity, end of story. This move purports to safeguard a practical application of the Trinity: if one does not allow a distinction between the economic Trinity and the immanent Trinity, as Rahner's Rule does not, then the doctrine of the Trinity can only become impractical and meaningless if one entirely ignores concrete history – something the Christian faith, with its emphasis on the revelation of God in the historical person of Jesus Christ, cannot do. With Rahner's Rule, the Trinity cannot help but be practical. This motivation seems a good one, and the appeal to take seriously the doctrine of the Trinity as a core truth in Christian theology is worthwhile. We shall see, however, that Rahner's way of accomplishing this has some substantial criticisms.

The second motivation comes from a desire to say that we truly know God. Rahner's Rule says that we certainly know what God himself is really like from what we see in his actions in the world because there is no distinction between what God does and who he is. There is no God 'behind' the interworking between Father, Son, and Spirit in bringing salvation to the world. However, this is to confuse approach with conclusion. Starting with what God has revealed in the person and work of Jesus Christ does not have to lead to the conclusion of absolute identity between the economic Trinity and the immanent Trinity. Rather, the redemptive-historical approach will acknowledge that we are limited in our knowledge of God by what he has revealed to us. God is not incomprehensible, but is also not without unrevealed mystery, the tradition has said, and he is truly but not fully known to us. Despite his insistence on the mystery of God, Rahner rejects this middle way, saying that we fully know everything about God's inner life.

CRITICISMS

The first criticism of Rahner's Rule goes something like this. In Rahner's Rule, the immanent *is* the economic in the sense of 'immanent = economic' (or 'economic = immanent'; the order does not matter with this sense of identity). The question must then be answered, Since they are in fact identical, what are we to make of any apparent dissimilarity? Does the immanent Trinity determine the economic, or the economic the immanent? If the economic Trinity determines the immanent, then God *must* create just this universe and the second person of the Trinity *must* become incarnate in it. There were/are no other options for God – he is not free – and he is dependent on the world to become who he really is – he does not exist in himself. Rahner and many of those who follow in his footsteps would deny this, but in the estimation of these authors, no convincing case has been offered as to why this devastating implication does not follow from the rule. If the immanent Trinity determines the economic, then there is the possibility that the historical revelation of God in Jesus Christ fails to show us who God truly is. There might be an unknown 'God behind the God' that we see. Rahner is attempting to remove this as even a possibility, but the cost of doing so is quite high, as we shall see in the next criticism.

The second criticism is that on any interpretation of it, Rahner's Rule either says something very traditional in somewhat strange language, or says something that is just false. In other words, it is either nothing new or not true. Here are four possible ways to interpret Rahner's Rule: 1.) The rule could mean that the same persons who make up the immanent Trinity also make up the economic Trinity. Since nobody says there are actually two Trinities, on this interpretation, it says nothing new. 2.) The rule could mean that the properties/attributes of the economic Trinity and the immanent Trinity are identical. This interpretation puts us right back into the previous critique, where God needs the world to be God, which is not true (or is at least clearly outside the boundaries of anything recognizable as the Christian theism of the Bible). 3.) The rule could mean that what we know about God from the economic Trinity is not misleading and gives us a reliable picture of what God is like. God truly is as he has revealed himself to be: the economic self-communication of God is the intra-Trinitarian self-communication present in world in Jesus of Nazareth. Many have read Rahner to be saying this or something like it; however, this interpretation is nothing new – it is the majority view in the tradition, both East and West, and more crucially, this interpretation does not seem compatible with what Rahner actually says. If this is what he meant, it is at best a very awkward way to express it. He is attempting to say that the Trinity has purchase for salvation, that it is revealed to us because it matters for life and faith – but the tradition had by and large insisted on this point, too. 4.) The rule could mean that our statements about God are really something different than what we might normally think. This will require a bit of explaining. It seems that Rahner's position entails claims about the nature of truth that are problematic. Apparently, Rahner is saying that there is no such thing as the world-in-itself or God-in-himself, apart from our knowledge. We cannot at all talk about something-in-itself – even God-in-himself – either because we only have contact with our perceptions of things, not with the things themselves, or because there really just is no such thing as a thing-in-itself. Rahner seems to be engaged in a shift in the meaning of truth. The standard and traditional understanding of truth is sometimes called 'alethic truth' and goes something like this: what we say is true if (and only if) what we say is, in fact, the case in reality. There is a reality apart from human conceptualization and perception, and that reality determines whether or not what we say about it is true. Rahner's Rule appears to require us to give up this notion of truth, at least for talk about God (and probably in total). If we keep this notion of truth, Rahner might say, we cannot know that God really is who he reveals himself to be because we cannot access God-in-himself (the immanent Trinity) at all, we can only access our perceptions and concepts (the economic Trinity). A different notion of truth emerges, whether Rahner intends it or not, one where truth is *entirely* determined by the usefulness of what we say (it delivers results) or by the compatibility of what we say with the rest of what we believe (it is part of a coherent system). If we cannot understand or talk of the immanent Trinity (God-in-himself) because truth is redefined along these lines, then the idea of the immanent Trinity is entirely impossible and nonsensical, and should be abandoned altogether. Any talk of the immanent Trinity entirely collapses into talk of the economic Trinity, which is really talk about our concepts and experiences. Jürgen Moltmann is one of several theologians who seem to draw this conclusion, and it is not at all clear if Rahner can help but do the same. There are two major problems with this fourth interpretation of Rahner's Rule. First, no one can consistently abandon the alethic notion of truth. Even in attacking it, they assume that their new definition is, in fact, the right one, the one that fits with reality. If someone were to consistently abandon alethic truth, truth becomes nothing more than expression of personal taste ('I dislike truth'), or worse, a cruel game of persuasion to get what one wants. Second, this position results in even worse scepticism than that which was trying to be avoided. Certainly, God exists apart from our knowledge of him – we do not create God by speaking about him. However, this position says that we cannot know *anything* about him beyond our ideas and language. The alethic position provides us a fallible but generally reliable connection to God-in-himself. God is more than our ideas and our language, and if we want any sort of connection to God at all, Rahner's Rule does not seem to be satisfactory.

27

THE SECOND VATICAN COUNCIL
LUMEN GENTIUM

INTRODUCTION

Ecumenical councils, in which (a selection of) the bishops of the whole church come together to determine doctrine and practice are rare and significant in history. Virtually all traditions of Christianity recognize the first four ecumenical* councils: Nicaea (325), Constantinople (381), Ephesus (431), and Chalcedon (454) are generally recognized as being determinative for Christian theology; the next three – Constantinople II (553), Constantinople III (680), and Nicaea II (787) are shared by Roman Catholic and Eastern Orthodox churches, although less respected by Protestants.

After Nicaea II, there were no more ecumenical councils before the Great Schism of 1054*. The Eastern Orthodox churches believe that the church is now divided, and so an ecumenical council cannot take place; the Roman Catholic Church has believed that it alone is the true church, and so has counted its own general councils as 'ecumenical'; it still only recognizes twenty-one councils over two millennia of existence, however, indicating that such councils are still rare and unusual.

Since the sixteenth-century Reformation*, indeed, there have been only three councils. The first, the Council of Trent** (1545–1565) defined Roman Catholic doctrine on the points disputed during the Reformation; the second, the First Vatican Council (1869–1870) ended abruptly because of military action, but served to codify in part the church's response to the modernist crisis. Vatican I also sufficiently elevated the office of the papacy (notably in defining the doctrine of papal infallibility, the idea that, in certain specific circumstances, the Pope's definition of true doctrine can never be in error) that it seemed to some commentators that there would never be a need for another council. The Pope could now do what only councils had previously done, or so it appeared.

Pope John XXIII indicated that he intended to call a new council in 1959, just a few months after his election to the papacy. This was a surprise: there was no new pressing error or heresy to be opposed or corrected, and, as noted above, there seemed little that only a council could do. The agenda for the council was left unclear, perhaps deliberately so: the Italian word *aggiornamento* was used by many, including the Pope; this could mean simply an adjournment of the ongoing process of developing the church's code of Canon Law, but its core meaning is something like 'updating' or even 'modernization', and this sense was certainly heard by many.

Vatican I had been intended to discuss and define the Catholic doctrine of the nature of the church; because of its sudden interruption, this never happened, and it is possible to see the agenda of Vatican II as being a continuation of this unfinished work. That said, the Council was called at a time when Catholic theology was changing rapidly: during the 1950s, an old paradigm, called Neoscholasticism*, had collapsed remarkably fast, and a new and more flexible paradigm had grown up, a paradigm based on both an openness to modern criticisms of traditional modes of life, if not of the church, and an extensive retrieval of the texts of the church fathers.

The Council ran from 1962 to 1965. Its initial sessions stuttered on procedural grounds, and John XXIII died in 1963, causing further delay. His successor as Pope, Paul VI, reconvened the Council and set a clearer agenda in four points: defining the nature of the church, particularly the role of the bishop; renewing the church; working towards Christian unity; and addressing the real and felt needs of the contemporary world.

Vatican II produced many documents, of which some were rather specific (addressing the particular place of the Eastern Catholic churches and the modes of initiation into monastic life, for instance).

Five of these stand out. *Sacrosanctum concilium*, the first document produced by the Council, addressed the question of liturgy and authorized Catholic churches to worship in the local language, not just in Latin. This was, of course, a huge change for ordinary Catholics, and so was the most immediately influential effect of the Council. *Dei verbum* offered a profound theological account of revelation*, beginning with Christ and suggesting that Scripture and tradition are two modes of accessing God's one revelation in Christ.

Third, *Unitatis redintegratio* addressed the question of ecumenism, the relationship between different Christian traditions, and was felt by many to mark a significant change in the Catholic Church's relationship with other Christian denominations. At the risk of oversimplifying, the Catholic Church had previously been most interested in its edges: if you were in the Catholic Church, you were truly Christian; if not, you were not. After the Council, and particularly after *Unitatis redintegratio*, the focus shifted to the centre: the Catholic Church was still the true possessor of truth, but others, not formally part of the Catholic Church and who nonetheless held to much or some of the same truth, could be seen to have some real Christian existence. Similarly, *Nostra aetate* addressed the question of the relationship of the Catholic Church to non-Christian religions, and particularly to Judaism.

Fourth, *Gaudium et spes* addressed the issue of 'the Church in the modern world'. Again, the change was in general approach as much as in specific doctrine: Vatican I had pictured the church as an unchanging fortress, around which various cultural trends flowed without ever affecting its life or foundations. Vatican II perhaps saw the church more as a great merchant city, whose greatness relies on its laws and customs, which must therefore not change, but whose life can be affected in a whole variety of ways by those who happen to pass by in this season or that.

Our text, however, is *Lumen gentium*, which discusses the nature of the church, and so addresses what was announced to be the core business of Vatican II.

SYNOPSIS

Lumen gentium begins discussing 'the mystery of the church', which is interpreted as the relationship of Christ to the church (presumably following Eph. 5). Christ is the light of all humanity, and that light shines in the church. The church is the sacrament of Christ – 'a sign and instrument of communion with God and of unity among all [people]' (1). The church has its origins in God's eternal purposes; its beginning in Adam and the people of Israel; its manifestation in the outpouring of the Spirit at Pentecost; and will have its 'glorious completion' when Christ returns in glory to judge the living and the dead (2).

Paragraph 3 suggests that the heart of the mystery of the church is the eucharist: in the words of the document, 'as often as the sacrifice of the cross ... is celebrated on the altar, the work of our redemption is carried out. Likewise, in the sacrifice of the eucharistic bread, the unity of believers ... is both expressed and brought about'. From here, the document moves on into a consideration of the various biblical images for the church, with a particular stress on the relationship of church and kingdom, and on the church as the body of Christ. The church is described as the 'seed and beginning' of the kingdom (5).

After this, the structural reality of the church is discussed. The church is a 'visible society' (8) which 'subsists in' the Catholic Church. There is much that is good and truly ecclesial outside the bounds of the church, but all that is good in this area properly belongs to the Catholic Church, so possession of ecclesial reality is, or should be, a pressure towards reunion with Rome.

Chapter II, 'The People of God' (9–17), locates the church within a narrative of salvation history. God is at work through history to bring together a people who will, in the end, be the final fulfillment of all God's purposes. God's intention was to make people holy, but always corporately, not individually, and so the church is the central vehicle for God's purposes. Christ is the head – king – of the new people, and they share in his priesthood. The whole church is a priestly kingdom: the 'common priesthood of the faithful' and the 'ministerial or hierarchical priesthood' are two complementary ways of participating in the sole priesthood of Christ (10). Paragraph 11 describes the priestly ministry of the church through the seven sacraments.

The church shares also in Christ's prophetic office (12). Inerrancy in matters of doctrine is located here in the *sensus fidei*, the common mind of the whole church, not solely in the Petrine ministry of the

Pope. The Holy Spirit gives gifts to the church so that the church may fulfil this prophetic commission to teach truth to the whole world.

The people of God are to be Catholic, that is, spread across the whole world and present in every nation on earth. Because of this, the church works with the various local customs, purifying and perfecting them. The church is diverse in character, ordained and lay, religious and secular. All people are called to unity in the Catholic church; at present, some are members of the Catholic faithful; some separated believers in Christ; and some neither, having been 'called by God's grace to salvation' (13).

Membership of the church is a great privilege, and the gift of grace, but not enough to ensure salvation of itself. The sacramental life of the church is, rather, a great aid to remaining in charity. Paragraph 15 acknowledges that there are true Christians beyond the boundaries of the Catholic Church. Following Scripture, worshipping God, and believing in Christ, they are united with Christ by baptism; some have bishops and so a proper ecclesial order; many celebrate the eucharist; some are devoted to Mary the Mother of God. Such people are 'in some real way' united with the Catholic Church by the Holy Spirit, but the Spirit's work is always towards unity in the one Catholic Church.

Those who have not yet heard the gospel are of various sorts. The Jewish People are still heirs to God's promises; all who acknowledge the Creator worship the one true God, and Paragraph 16 specifically teaches that Muslims worship the same God as Christians do. Those who have had no chance to hear the gospel of Christ, but who try to follow their own conscience and to live well may receive God's salvation. Nonetheless, life in the light of the gospel is infinitely preferable to all these states, and so the Church obeys the command to preach the gospel to all.

Chapter III, 'The Church is Hierarchical', is the longest in the document and arguably the most important. In discussing the offices of the church, it has been read by some as quietly re-assigning power in the church in far-reaching ways – although this reading is rejected by others. It begins by claiming that bishops are the successors of the apostles, and so the lasting foundation of the church; Peter was called by Christ himself to be head of the apostles, and the successor of Peter, the Pope, remains both the source and the visible guarantee of the unity of the church, and particularly of the college of bishops.

In the person of the bishop, Christ is present amongst the faithful (21). The bishop is assisted in his task of governing, teaching, and shepherding the church by priests and deacons. The bishop has the task of sanctifying the faithful and of teaching and guiding the church; to fulfil this task, he is given a special gift of the Holy Spirit through the laying on of hands at his consecration. Each bishop can only perform his duties in collegial unity with the rest of the bishops; the Pope is head of this college, and the college has no authority unless united with the Pope (22). This is because, as 'Vicar' (that is, representative) of Christ and pastor (shepherd) of the entire church, the Pope retains authority over the whole church.

The most important task of the bishop is the proclamation of the gospel. The bishop is to announce truth, identify and refute error, and guide the faithful in belief and practice. The task of the bishops is to hold and teach the body of sound doctrine entrusted to the church; in seeking to define this doctrine, they will be preserved from error by the grace of the Holy Spirit when united with each other and with the Pope they meet in ecumenical council (25); similarly, the Pope, speaking publicly and exercising his office as supreme pastor, is enabled to speak infallibly by the Holy Spirit.

The bishop has responsibility for the sacramental life of the church, and especially for the celebration of the eucharist, either offering the sacrifice himself or ensuring it is offered. The eucharist feeds, sustains, and unites the church. The whole teaching and sacramental life of the church is regulated by the bishop, but, as the apostles called various helpers to aid them in their ministry, so too the bishop has other ministers to share in the priestly ministry that God instituted in the church. Priests share in the teaching office by virtue of their ordination, but are supremely eucharistic ministers. The priests form a college around their bishop and represent the bishop in the various parts of his diocese; the bishop in turn should see his priests as sons and friends, just as Christ called the disciples his friends (28, referencing Jn 15:15).

The office of deacon is not eucharistic, but the deacon serves in many ways, participating and presiding in worship, administering baptism, blessing marriages, bringing the sacrament to the dying, and officiating at funerals (29). The diaconate had become a stepping stone on the way to priesthood; the Council looked to the restoring of the permanent diaconate so that these functions may be better performed in the church.

The laity are those members of the church who have a secular vocation. Because of this, they are particularly called to work for the coming of the Kingdom of God in the world. By their service, and by their faithful witness in the world, the laity fulfil the peculiar mission given to them by Christ. There is a proper priesthood of the laity, offering spiritual worship in their work and in life, and supremely in bringing all this as an offering when they come to receive the eucharist. There is a prophetic office of the laity also, both as Christ's witnesses dispersed throughout the whole world and as those who receive and make visible the teaching of the church.

Chapter V is entitled 'The Call to Holiness'. The church is holy because Christ has died for her and called her to be his bride (39). Because the church has been made holy, every member of the church is called to live a life of holiness before God. Holiness will look different for those in different stations – bishops; priests; laity; married couples; the sick and infirm; and so on – but all are alike called to the state. Holiness will always primarily involve love for God and for neighbour. The state of celibacy is a particularly intense and valuable form of holiness.

The next, fairly brief, chapter deals with religious life, that is, the life of monks, nuns, and others (priests or laity) vowed to religious orders. The life of poverty, chastity, and obedience to which the religious are vowed is a gift from God for the church, and a particularly ideal way of life. The church has always been prepared to regulate and guide the growth and development of religious life; by renouncing the most powerful ties of earthly life, those who are vowed to religious life demonstrate particularly powerfully how God's Kingdom is greater than, and other than, the world.

Chapter VII, on 'The Pilgrim Church', acknowledges that the church on earth is always on the way to perfection, which will be received only when Christ makes all things new in the eschaton*. That said, the church is in a sense an anticipation of the world to come and possesses the Holy Spirit as the first fruits of this. Those who have died in faith and now enjoy the foretaste of heavenly glory are not separated from the church on earth; they intercede for those still on earth before the throne of grace. The church on earth, in turn, prays for those who are being purified in purgatory* that they may more quickly be freed from their sins and enter into glory.

The subject of the final chapter is the most honoured of the saints: the Blessed Virgin Mary. The Mother of God is redeemed in the most exalted fashion by the merits of her Son and 'far surpasses all creatures, both in heaven and on earth' (53). She is, still, a member of the church, but 'pre-eminent and ... wholly unique'. She is the mother of the church. She was redeemed from the moment of her conception and uniquely holy throughout her life. As death came through Eve, life came through Mary. She was, uniquely, received body and soul into heaven, when her life was over, and was elevated by her Son to be Queen of all things.

The role of the Blessed Virgin does not detract from the unique mediation of Christ, but is a manifestation of it. She is a type of the church in her obedience and holiness. She, perfect in holiness, is mother to the church and the living image of what God is calling all the church to be. For all these reasons, the cult of the Virgin in the church is to be accepted and honoured.

CRITICISMS

Vatican II has been characterized as a change from the church understanding itself as a bulwark against culture to understanding itself as a movement within culture and within many different cultures. This is rather too simplistic, but certainly there is a shift of emphasis going on that such a description captures quite well. One rapid result of the Council was the development of liberation theology*, which worked very much in these terms; it was an attempt to reinterpret Catholic theology in the context of the political struggles that formed the everyday life of people in Latin America. The negative Vatican response to liberation theology suggests the limits of understanding the Council's programme as a thorough inculturation like this, however.

Lumen gentium located teachings concerning the Blessed Virgin Mary within ecclesiology; this was novel, and it seems very helpful. Although Protestants will not be able to accept what is taught about Mary here, seeing her as the pre-eminent member of the church is surely a less objectionable way of dealing with the distinctive Catholic claims. Similarly, there is considerable ecumenical movement here: the Roman Catholic Church, of course, will not give up the claim that it is, alone, the true church, but there is a generosity to other Christians – and indeed to Jews and Muslims – that is at least a change of tone, if not actually a change of doctrine, from what had gone before.

As indicated above, the interpretation of *Lumen gentium* has been somewhat disputed. If Vatican I was, in its teaching on the role of the Pope, felt by some to be centralizing, moving power in the church to Rome, the emphasis on the college of bishops in Chapter III of *Lumen gentium* was understood by some to be a dispersal of power away from Rome to the local dioceses. Recent interpretation has tended to downplay this line, however, and the Council certainly repeatedly re-affirms the supremacy and necessity of the papal ministry. Perhaps what should be said is that *Lumen gentium* did not change the relationship between the local bishops and Rome, but it did strongly re-affirm the dignity and role of the local bishop in the context of a series of official texts over several decades which had stressed only the importance of Rome.

JOHN HOWARD YODER
THE POLITICS OF JESUS

INTRODUCTION

John Howard Yoder (1927–1997) was an American Mennonite
theologian who studied in Basel, Switzerland under Karl Barth**,
amongst others. He began his teaching career in Mennonite
seminaries, but later also joined the faculty of Notre Dame.

The Mennonites embody a distinctive tradition within Christian
theology, one that shaped Yoder's thought and writing. Their origins lie in the radical wing of the sixteenth-century Reformation*.
Mainstream Reformers such as Luther** and Calvin** simply
accepted the long-standing link in Europe between church and
culture, and enshrined it in some sort of unity between political and
ecclesiastical government. So, England developed a polity where
the monarch was also 'Supreme Governor' of the Church of
England; more Reformed* countries tended to have two, somewhat separate, authorities – one civil, one ecclesiastical – but
retained the assumption that the two were mutually supportive and
that to be (say) Scottish and to be a member of the Church of
Scotland were the same thing.

The radical Reformers challenged this: the church was to be
separate from civil society; people were citizens by virtue of being
born in a territory; they were church members by virtue of being

born again of water and the Spirit. In the Anabaptist tradition, out of which the Mennonites developed, this was linked with a rejection of the practice of baptizing infants and with a suggestion that the practice of state coercion, whilst necessary for the state to preserve its peace in this evil world, was less than perfect, and so should be shunned by the church and by each individual church member.

Whilst this decoupling of state and church seems merely normal to us now, at the time it was felt to be dangerously subversive of public order. Anabaptists and other radicals were persecuted across Europe, and many groups died out. The Mennonites, founded by Menno Simons, found a home in the low countries (roughly what is now The Netherlands), where a measure of religious toleration existed; nonetheless, they became adept at living quietly in their own communities, not doing anything that might be perceived to be threatening by the governing authorities.

The Mennonite denomination became established in the United States, where of course separation of church and state became established as the norm. Their pacifist beliefs – and their related refusal to serve in political office – meant they were still somewhat marginalized, however, and their habits of quiet, rather separated existence continued.

John Howard Yoder is widely regarded as the scholar who first brought Mennonite beliefs to the attention of the wider academy, and so the wider church, in a way that presented his denomination and its distinctive positions not as a curious historical exhibit, but as a live option within the theological tradition. *The Politics of Jesus* was not his first book to try to do this, but it has become the most popular of his writings by far, translated into at least ten languages, for instance, and so deserves its place as a 'classic' on our list.

SYNOPSIS

The Politics of Jesus: Behold the Man! Our Victorious Lamb was first published in 1972; a second edition appeared in 1994. The most substantial change in the second edition was the addition of 'Epilogues' at the end of each chapter, which surveyed scholarship in the area covered by the chapter since the first edition had been published. The second edition also updated the text on minor stylistic matters and made it gender-neutral. References here are to the second edition; we make little reference to the Epilogues, since in most of them, Yoder is merely defending his original position against some new possible objections.

Yoder begins his first chapter with a programmatic statement: he wants to offer a survey of contemporary biblical scholarship – particularly historical Jesus scholarship* – that will demonstrate that Jesus taught a radical social ethic (in 1972, he made the link explicitly with the views and longings of disillusioned youth culture in America); Yoder further wants to claim that this radical social ethic lived by Jesus should be taken as normative for Christian ethics, although he recognizes that this claim is contrary to mainstream Christian ethics, which tends to relativize the ethical message of Jesus either by suggesting that it is no longer relevant (the cultural distance is too great; Jesus expected an imminent ending of the world, and so lived an unsustainable interim ethic …) or by suggesting that the proper way to do Christian ethics is not to focus primarily on the ethical teaching of Jesus (Jesus' message was primarily theological, and we need to hear the theology and then work out our own ethical applications of said theology …).

Underlying this is an assumption that Christian ethics must be 'reasonable' or 'rational' or 'liveable'. The teaching of Jesus is extreme and unrealistic, and Christian ethics cannot be like that. Paul shows us a proper respect for the institutions of society, a mediation that accepts such realities as slavery or Roman imperial government and that finds a reasonable negotiation of them.

Yoder will criticize such ideas strongly before the end of the book, but, having identified the question, he first wants to examine in detail the radical ethic of Jesus. In the second chapter, he turns to Luke's gospel and offers a survey reading, picking out several crucial passages. Yoder chooses the language of 'Kingdom' – language central to the gospel of course – to propose that, at least in Luke's portrait, Jesus is revealing and establishing a new political reality prophesied by his mother in the Magnificat, begun at his baptism, announced in his sermon at Nazareth, developed in his teaching, and found to be vindicated when God raises him from the dead – although he is crucified precisely for creating this new community.

The following chapters fill out this story in more detail. The third chapter looks at the biblical concept of 'Jubilee', the fiftieth year commanded in the Old Testament law, when the land would not be worked, all slaves would be freed, all debts cancelled, and all people reunited with their ancestral inheritance of land. Yoder emphasizes, drawing on Luke's version of the Lord's Prayer, that 'forgiveness' and 'cancelling of debts' come, in Greek, from the same linguistic root; the redistribution of wealth in various ways is at the heart of the ethic of Jesus.

The fourth chapter turns to the question of war. Pacifism is a classical Mennonite distinctive, which Yoder wants to defend; he assumes that his summary of Luke will have convinced readers that Jesus' own ethic was one of nonviolent resistance to the political authorities. The problem, he believes, will be convincing anyone that this was a seriously-considered option. Yoder first looks at the Exodus and at various military victories won by Israel or Judah. The history is certainly not nonviolent, but Yoder claims that the key insight that God's people were learning – and remembering in their Scriptures – through telling these stories is the belief that 'God will fight for us' (the title of the chapter).

As this message becomes stronger, Israel starts to act as if it were true, and so as if nonviolence was a possible way of living. Ezra refuses an armed escort when he returns from exile; this conviction that the protection of the nation is in God's hands and not their own – and that this may well involve miraculous deliverance – is something we need to work hard to comprehend if we are going to understand Jesus' ethic of nonviolent resistance properly. The fifth chapter briefly surveys something of the Jewish history of non-violent resistance against Rome, indicating that, for a Jew of Jesus' time, this was clearly an imaginable option.

At this point in the book, Yoder proposes enlarging his focus from Jesus to the broader New Testament. He first offers a very brief sketch of a Pauline ethic of suffering with Jesus before turning again to questions of how this Jesus-ethic is evaded in contemporary scholarship. Then he turns to more detailed filling out of the claim that the same social ethic that is modelled by (Luke's) Jesus is visible in the rest of the New Testament. The seventh chapter looks at the standard New Testament themes of participation in Christ and imitation of Christ. The Christian has died with Christ and now lives Christ's life. Being 'in Christ' is the central Pauline picture of salvation. As a result of this participation, there is a call to imitation: the Christian is to forgive as Christ has for-given him/her, to love as God loves, to serve as Christ served, and so on.

These themes also feed into questions of power: self-sacrifice, surrender, and suffering servanthood are the Christian way, in place of assertion or attempted domination. If death comes, that is vic-tory, and the final defeat of the power of sin in our life. This question of power is the subject of the eighth chapter, although the emphasis here switches from New Testament ethics to theology. The particular focus is on the 'principalities and powers' language found in the New Testament and recent theological interpretation of that language.

'Principalities and powers', for Paul, are created spiritual realities intended by God to bring order and regularity to the created world. Yoder gives examples such as religious structures, intellectual movements, moral codes, political structures, 'the market', and so on. These realities, however, are now fallen, as is the rest of crea-tion; Yoder finds Paul suggesting a deliberate rebellion on the part of the powers, perhaps a part of the 'angelic fall'. They still perform their created function of bringing order to human society, but do so in a warped and twisted way. We are damaged and enslaved by powers that should serve us, but instead promote themselves to be idols and demand our loyalty and worship.

Yoder's key insight here is that we cannot be human without the principalities and powers: these are the necessary structures of our existence. So Christ cannot destroy them, and the church cannot live as if they do not exist. Instead, they need to be dethroned and put back into their proper place. This is what Jesus has done (Col. 2:15). He did this by accepting willingly the attack of the powers, notably Jewish religion and Roman tyranny, refusing to ever accept their lordship. This inevitably led them to kill him.

For Yoder, the resurrection is not the key moment in the defeat of the powers; rather, it is their 'unmasking': the moment when Jesus makes it clear that religious claims to righteousness or political claims to be promoting a just peace are empty lies designed only to protect the tyranny of those structures that make and enforce the claims. Now we can, through Jesus, see every power for what it really is – and the church is called to live in the light of this knowledge, to refuse, as Jesus did, to acknowledge the tyranny of the powers without ever violently resisting their attempts to impose it. Truth will set us free.

The ninth chapter returns to the theme of social ethics in the New Testament, here with the theme of 'revolutionary subordination'. Yoder looks at various texts and suggests that the life of the church is to be marked by free subordination of all members to all other members – and indeed of all members to those outside the church who would claim authority over them. Yoder makes the now common point that, in giving moral instruction to slaves and others on the wrong side of societal injustice, Paul is investing them with a dignity that would be entirely new and foreign. His broader point, however, is that the core ethical stance of Christians – following Jesus Christ – is a cheerful willingness to submit to each other and to all.

The tenth chapter applies this ethic of submission to the Christian's relationship to the state, with particular reference to Romans 13. Yoder wants to offer his submissive ethic as a way of making sense of that text, which does not concede the things often claimed for the text, in particular that every specific national government is of direct divine appointment and that the text legitimizes Christian service in the armed forces, police service, or other coercive government roles.

The last substantive chapter looks at the question of 'justification by faith'. Yoder was clearly aware, already in 1972, of a trend in New Testament studies to find the emphasis on justification by faith as something of a distortion of Paul's gospel. Yoder does not want to dismiss the idea, so much as to insist that it needs to be supplemented with an account of active participation in the new Kingdom that Jesus establishes on the part of the one justified.

The book closes with a conclusion which is largely intended to claim the utility of this new social ethic of submission and non-violence. This, in the good providence of God, is how the world will be changed because this is the way of Jesus, or so Yoder claims.

CRITICISMS

The Politics of Jesus is not a great book, considered in literary terms. The chapters are, in some cases, rather obviously slightly edited papers. (The third chapter is, according to a footnote, a free translation of a French text by André Trocmé.) The order of treatment is sometimes obscure – the ninth chapter follows well from the seventh in that both treat details of the ethical commands of the New Testament letters; however, the interspersion of a very lengthy chapter on a theology of principalities and powers between them seems rather odd.

The influence of the book is not literary, however: Yoder proposed a new view of Jesus' ethics and suggested taking Jesus' ethics seriously as our ethics. He did so with considerable attention to New Testament scholarship and with the conviction and mature reflection of his denominational tradition behind him. The book was a serious challenge to inherited ways of thinking.

It was also a well-timed challenge, culturally speaking, and Yoder emphasizes this point just enough that the popularity of the book is not a surprise. By borrowing the (somewhat obscure, as he admits in the 1992 foreword) term 'biblical realism' to describe the position he is criticizing, he carefully located himself in a broader cultural/ political discourse in which echoes of Martin Luther King's refusal to be 'realistic' in slowing down demands for justice still reverberated, and in which feminist, gay-rights, and anti-war demands offered the same invocation of idealistic urgent action against slow, deadening realism.

The success of Yoder's text can be measured in two ways: on the one hand, if the text is read as an attempt to introduce Mennonite ethical distinctives – pacifism, supremely – into the mainstream academic theological conversation, it certainly succeeded: such views might not be widely embraced beyond the historic 'peace churches', but they are now a fixed feature of the landscape, unignorable to any serious study. On the other, Yoder's text marks a seminal moment – along with early liberation and feminist theology – in the politicizing of Christian doctrine. This has become utterly mainstream; certainly, there has been cultural pressure pushing in this direction – all of Western culture has become more politicized in the last half-century – but Yoder's contribution to pushing at what might have been an unlocked door is nonetheless seminal.

It is possible – easy, perhaps – to argue with Yoder. Luke's gospel is particularly amenable to his themes, and one might find a very different version of 'the politics of Jesus' if one focused solely on Matthew or John; Yoder might successfully convince us that a pressing concern for social justice is at the heart of a properly Christian ethics, but he assumes more and argues the centrality of nonviolent resistance as the mode of achieving that; today's reader will be astonished at Yoder's easy acceptance of structural injustices in the case of gender and his failure to mention human sexuality at all.

That said, the success of the book lies not in the detail of its arguments, but in its changing of an agenda. The observer of popular Christian culture in America today would be astonished that a book arguing that the core question in Christian ethics was, 'What would Jesus do?' was perceived to be controversial just four decades ago; this is the final measure of Yoder's success.

ROSEMARY RADFORD RUETHER
SEXISM AND GOD-TALK

INTRODUCTION

Rosemary Radford Ruether (b. 1936) is an American feminist and theologian. Her father was an Anglican and her mother was a Catholic; she places herself in the Catholic tradition. Her upbringing was free-thinking. Tragically, her father died when she was 12. She attended Scripps College for her undergraduate studies and earned an M.A. and a Ph.D. from Claremont Graduate School, thus doing all of her schooling in Claremont, California. After completing her graduate work, she began a family with her husband Herbert.

Ruether came of age and began her academic career during a time of change in American society. The Vietnam War and its accompanying draft was being widely protested by the youth; the counter-cultural revolution of the 1960s changed the way people thought about sex, authority, drugs, women, and much more; the Civil Rights movement was changing racist structures in society; and Vatican II** was bringing changes to the Catholic Church (see Chapter 27). From this context, Ruether became interested in the connection between theology and social practice. She questioned and severely critiqued the patriarchy present in traditional Christian theology – theology that was written for men by men, leaving women out of consideration and out of the conversation.

In 1965, she started teaching religion at Howard University in Washington DC, and there she began her research on women in the Christian tradition and feminism. In 1976, she moved to Garrett-Evangelical Theological Seminary (a United Methodist school connected to Northwestern University) in the Chicago area, where she spent much of her career. She is known as one of the most influential proponents of feminist theology. While Ruether is a major voice in Christian feminist theology, it should be recognized that there are other sorts of feminist theology – Jewish, for example, or Pagan, which involves worshiping a 'Mother Goddess'.

Christian feminist theology is not a move from within Christian orthodoxy to work towards the goal of women's equality. That line of development has representatives in the Christian tradition that generally do not identify with feminist theology, largely because feminist theology has insisted that radical and sweeping reinterpretations and revisions are necessary in Christian theology. It is very important, then, to distinguish between 'feminist theology' and the broader Christian movement to fight for gender equality in society and in churches. Ruether's is not the only theology on offer that values and fights for women's equality. However, she is a main proponent of a feminist theology movement that has been very visible, highly controversial, praised by some and strongly criticized by others.

SYNOPSIS

Ruether begins the book with an interpretive exposition of the gospel from the viewpoint of feminism, one that reveals the heart of her feminist theology. It goes something like this: God, who is male, overthrew the Queen of Heaven to get his power. He rules the heavens and the earth like a domineering father, and following his example, men teach women their place on earth. Down on the earth, a young woman is pregnant with a fatherless child. That child grew into a man, a teacher with a message of criticizing the authorities. Most puzzlingly, he treated the women as equals, letting them become disciples! Mary Magdalene was particularly close with Jesus, closer than the male disciples. When Jesus willingly submitted to his arrest, the men first took to weapons, but he rebuked them, so they took to cowardice. The women, however, stayed close to Jesus, even witnessing his crucifixion and death. Days later, the men had given up hope, but the women stayed by the tomb, waiting. Mary was there when an apparition of Jesus appeared to her and told her that *she* was the continuing presence of Christ in the world and that she should lead the way in giving up power, subjugation, and revenge. She ran and told the men, who scoffed at the very notion that such an important message would be entrusted to a woman. Some were struck by her message, but Peter hijacked their attention away from her, saying that Jesus had been resurrected and that instead of following Mary's message, they should all wait for Jesus to return back from heaven. This Jesus was a revelation from heaven of which the men must take charge, having power and authority. Yet Mary, though turned away by the men, truly understood. Jesus' heavenly Father was nowhere to be found when Jesus died. In fact, the idea of a God who is a great king over nations died when Jesus did. Jesus' death had left an empty throne where God once sat, and Peter and the men were trying to fill it again. Instead, a new God was to be born in their hearts, one that would teach them to make heaven and earth equal, a new world of equality without masters and slaves or rulers and subjects, without men ruling over women. This was Jesus' message, according to Ruether.

Understanding Ruether's method is crucial to seeing the importance of this work in modern theology. She says that all theology starts and ends with experience. For Ruether, even Scripture and tradition are just codified collective human experience. The problem, she says, is not that we only have experiences available to us – this is just everyone's position – but that women's experience has not been heard and that this needs to change. The established authorities in Christianity of Scripture and tradition are just the religious experiences of others – the transmitters of these (the institutional church) is corrupted by patriarchy, and the authoritative sources themselves are corrupted by patriarchy. They must be thoroughly critiqued, although residue of genuine insight from the original revelation will likely still come through as useful. These should be critiqued by the principle of the promotion of the full humanity of women. Anything that takes away from this, even in the slightest, is not redemptive and does not reflect God, but anything that promotes the full humanity of women is from God. In this way, feminist theology represents a tradition that is necessarily contextual – it is concerned with women in the contemporary world, as, say, liberation theology is concerned with the Latin American world.

It is clear that Ruether breaks with the Christian tradition in several ways. The first and most significant is this: for her, patriarchy is the distinguishing mark of a sinful, fallen world; it is almost entirely what is wrong with our world. It is not just one symptom among many of the world's sin-sickness, one aspect among many that finds redemption in the gospel. No, for her, patriarchy – the deeply rooted domination of women by men in culture and society – is the most basic and egregious form of oppression and sin. Patriarchy is not limited simply to the dynamics of males ruling over females, but on that basis extends to masters over slaves, kings over subjects, the ruling class over the oppressed, and the colonizers over the colonized: these are all male-oriented forms of oppression and abuse. The world works on the principles of male domination. This comes from a flawed anthropology, one that places femaleness as an inferior aspect of human nature. The patriarchal nature of theology deeply harms and oppresses women in society and in the church, and thus women need to offer a corrective voice in theology.

Ruether has another complaint about the Christian tradition: women and women's experiences are ignored or marginalized. To correct this, the feminist definition of women's experience must be the source and norm for theology today. Feminist theology puts women's experience in pride of place, making it the touchstone by which everything else is judged.

She offers three minority traditions in Christianity that provide an alternative to the dominant patriarchy that has characterized theology. First, eschatological feminism awaits the equality found in Eden to be realized in the final redemption of humanity and divine consummation of the world. While the world will be stuck in patriarchy as it awaits its redemption, the church should be the breaking in of the eschaton into this age – part of which is to have equality of men and women. This eschatological feminism can be found in early Christianity and also in certain extreme Congregationalist movements such as the Quakers. Second, liberal feminism, a product of the Enlightenment, championed the equal rights of all human beings, regardless of race, age, or gender. This tradition is fully committed to bringing this equality to this world in the here and now with regard to society, politics, and economics, and this very much includes women. Third, romantic feminism sees a complex and mysterious human personality that has masculinity and femininity as equal yet complementary aspects – we are not to downplay maleness and femaleness, but embrace them as equal and necessary aspects of a diverse and rich humanity. Ruether wants a combination of liberal and romantic feminism, one that insists on the equality of all persons while recognizing femininity as unique and valuable, all without walking down any road that suggests a woman's role is subservient in any way to a man's. Men and women both fully have the essential human nature – the differences between maleness and femaleness are important, but they do not justify the categories of 'male nature' and 'female nature', as if these are two different kinds of humanity.

What is divine revelation, according to Ruether? For her, it is the prophetic and liberating tradition of which Jesus is the highest example, a tradition that calls for a complete egalitarian society free of all patriarchy and oppression. She says that all sorts of sources can be used – Scripture, Pagan religions, theologies condemned as heresies by the Christian church, Marxism, liberalism, and personal narratives of women's oppression and liberation – and will be judged by this prophetic tradition. She contends that this tradition is not ad hoc or arbitrary, but is rather the central tradition in the Bible. It has four key themes. First, God sides with and vindicates the oppressed. Second, systems of power and those holding power are critiqued. Third, a new vision for the future is offered where injustice is defeated and justice and peace reign. Fourth, the Bible and especially the prophets denounce any religion that upholds the unjust power system. Thus, even certain biblical texts can be criticized, and many aspects of the Bible are to be outright rejected. The patriarchy in the Bible is to be denounced, not explained. In the tradition, all the categories of classical theology have been twisted by a male orientation and need radical reinterpretation.

Ruether complains that Christian theology is too tainted by patriarchy. The male domination of theology has brought problematic dualisms into theology, such as nature/spirit, transcendence/immanence, soul/body, creation/redemption, good/evil, and male/

female. These dualisms divide what should be together and serve to oppress and dehumanize women. While she does say that men do not have completely unique capacities for evil that women lack, she also claims that men are more prone to these dualisms than women, and because theology has been dominated by male-oriented thinking, these dualisms have run rampant and have been deleterious for women. Ruether says this male-oriented approach, with the dualisms it brings, has led to connecting women with the 'lower nature' – matter, body, creation, evil – and men with the 'higher nature' – spirit, soul, reason, good. This lower nature is linked with sin, and thus femaleness is somehow more sinful and maleness more connected with the image of God.

The highest point of all this, and the place to start the corrective work, is with the doctrine of God. Obviously, feminist theology must criticize the traditional male imagery for God such as 'Father'. God is not male. He is, in fact, both male and female, and neither male nor female. To understand otherwise is to commit idolatry. Thus we need to speak of God by using female metaphors as well as male ones. However, even this falls short for Ruether because any parental image of God is inherently patriarchal and dualistic.

To find the right way to talk about God, Ruether uses Paul Tillich's concept of God as the ground of being, using the terms 'primal Matrix' or 'God/ess'. God/ess is not a transcendent personal being, but rather that which supports all that exists and all that might be. All the dualisms are held together, with the goal that neither side has priority over the other. Because of this unity with God/ess, every aspect of reality is radically equal. God/ess is not sovereign, powerful, or free. He/she is united with all things in such a way that they are part of his/her being.

A problem for feminist theology is Christology, as Ruether recognizes. Jesus Christ is clearly central to Christian theology, yet how can a male saviour and redeemer be beneficial to women in feminist theology? Her answer to this question shows a radical reinterpretation of the tradition. She rejects any sort of Chalcedonian Christology that says Jesus Christ is the divine Logos, the second person of the Trinity, taken on human form. This sort of theology, she says, is a mistake driven by patriarchy and the male attempt to exert power and domination, where the church controls access to

Christ through the apostolic teaching, and only males can hold church office and represent Christ. Instead of this Christology, Ruether says Jesus was a liberator, who spoke against the oppressive power structures in the world. As a prophet, he proclaimed the new humanity to come, one that is free of all dualisms and inequalities. This new humanity is 'the Christ' for Ruether. In this way, Jesus was not really the Christ, but was the ultimate representative and founder of this new humanity. The traditional mythology about Jesus being the Logos is loaded with masculine imagery that must be stripped off, and when feminist theology does this, Jesus becomes a mere human, a prophetic critic of power who frees us from all hierarchical relations – a figure very compatible with feminist theology. There is no significance in Jesus being a male, except that he is a male who is criticizing patriarchy!

Finally, Ruether argues that feminist liberation theology should form Christian communities that work to free members from the ideologies and roles of patriarchy and also to remove them from society more broadly. More liberated denominations might be able to accomplish this – particularly those that ordain women for ministry – but even in these contexts, congregations will need to give feminist ministers great resources and freedom to advance the feminist cause and educate the laity. It is a revolution in the local church led by clergy, but one that must also empower the people to take ownership of the feminist cause for themselves. In church contexts where hierarchy is strong, where there is a central authority, and where patriarchy is deeply engrained (e.g. the Roman Catholic Church), revolutionary reform seems impossible, and the only alternative is to break off and form autonomous feminist communities. Regarding reform of the church, from these bases efforts will be launched to reform the historical institutions of the church along the lines of feminist theology. For example, Ruether believes these groups should work to take the administration of the sacraments out of the hands of male clerics and allow any Christian to preside over baptism or the Lord's supper. Regarding reform of society, the world must be told that sin is not limited to an individual's moral agency, but is present in social and economic structures. Piece by piece, starting at the local level, the feminist vision for society must be enacted from the ground up.

CRITICISMS

Feminist theology has rightly called out sinful practices and dynamics of patriarchy and misogyny that are all too present in our world. Theology, which historically has disproportionately been done by males, is certainly neither unaffected by nor innocent of sexism. However, some substantial criticisms have been raised against Ruether's diagnosis of the cause of this problem and the solutions she has offered.

First, if revelation is solely our religious experience and parts of Scripture and the tradition can be set aside, then we have no standard to judge truth claims, and only relativism remains. When different sets of experience conflict in ideology and application, whose religious experience wins and why, if there is no authority beyond our experience? If, as Ruether claims, Scripture and the tradition are hopelessly distorted by patriarchy, on what grounds can we 'cut through' this distortion to get at the original religious experience of revelation recorded in the Bible? Such a highly subjective approach appears to collapse under the weight of its own architecture – how can the experience of women (or the experience of any group, for that matter) be the norm that interprets what is and is not normative in Scripture? Has not the feminist consciousness merely replaced the old patriarchy ideology? The Christian tradition has claimed that divine revelation – the Word of God – speaks to all of our experiences, calling us to God and allowing the authoritative divine voice to make sense of ourselves. Ruether, it seems, has reversed this.

Second, while she claims to be rejecting various dualisms that are the product of male-oriented thinking in theology, in the end, her synthesis usually seems to actually amount to an affirmation of the opposite of the supposed male emphasis. While she accuses traditional theology of prioritizing spirit, transcendence, soul, and maleness, her theology seems to prioritize nature, immanence, the body, and femaleness. The world becomes part of God; a person goes back to undifferentiated oneness with the 'primal Matrix' after death, ceasing to consciously exist. The theology produced in the end becomes difficult to recognize as 'Christian' when judged by Scripture and the tradition. Ruether has no problem with this, but many others understandably do.

GUSTAVO GUTIERREZ
A THEOLOGY OF LIBERATION

INTRODUCTION

Gustavo Gutierrez (b. 1928) is a Peruvian-born Catholic priest. From 1951–1959 he studied in Europe, in Lyons and Rome. He was ordained in 1959, and in 1960 he began teaching at the Pontifical Catholic University of Peru. He quickly became a theological advisor to the Roman Catholic Church in Peru, which led to him playing a crucial role in establishing a new priority for the poor in Latin America in Catholicism that started in 1968. His mature description of liberation theology was published in 1971 and is the topic of this chapter.

Gutierrez studied theology in the Western world for several years. He became convinced that Western theology has been unduly under the influence of the questions posed by non-Christians. The liberation theology he envisaged does not want Western theology like that imposed on it – rather than starting on non-Christian terms, he wants to start with the poor, the oppressed, the 'non-person'. Liberation theology begins with poverty because that is the dominant dynamic in Latin American contexts. There is widespread poverty and suffering, with a small elite ruling class perpetuating it – yet the majority of people in Latin America claim to be Christians: how can this be so? The emphasis he developed in response is 'God's preferential option for the poor'. God particularly identifies with the poor and sides with the poor in a special way, and the church must do so as well.

Gutierrez calls for a new way of doing theology in response to the problem he diagnoses. It takes to heart the idea of 'God's preferential option for the poor' found in Scripture and particularly in the teachings of Jesus. It was a theology that did more than reflect on the world: it was to contribute to the transformation of the world, and this was to be accomplished by freeing theology from the sphere of the intellectual elites and putting it in the hands of the poor themselves. Theology is a truth to be done, not merely believed.

A major presupposition of Gutierrez and of liberation theology in general is that theology must be contextual. This is not to say that Gutierrez tends towards relativism, but to point out that we all come from social-economic and cultural backgrounds that substantially influence our thinking. Since we all have a situatedness in the world, we cannot presume to do 'universal' theology that applies to all contexts, as the Western tradition has done to the detriment of the Third World. Theology can only be contextual.

Gutierrez advocated some form of democratic socialism in Latin America as well as public and social ownership of the means of production, for which he was accused of compromising the gospel to Marxism. He was not deterred by such charges, which he believed to be further attempts at oppression by the ruling elites. He also received scrutiny from the Catholic authorities in Rome and responded with a sustained defence. In 1986, he published *The Truth Shall Make You Free*, clarifying for his critics what he cautiously accepts from Marxist philosophy and what he rejects (such as atheism and the inevitability of historical progress).

In short, Gutierrez's work brings a Marxist philosophy of history along with a social analysis of the state of affairs in Latin America to classic theological themes such as liberation, exodus, and redemption, producing a powerful and influential new way of doing theology. He made the poor a legitimate theological priority, especially in Catholicism, in a way that had not been true before in modern theology.

SYNOPSIS

Gutierrez opens by raising the question, What is theology? He answers that the task of theology is to reflect on the actual faith of Christians. Early on in Christian history, it was connected to spirituality and was about wisdom; around the fourteenth century, theology becomes detached from spirituality and becomes about rational knowledge. He says theology should ultimately be critical reflection on Christian practice, and although this will involve wisdom and rational knowledge, these are secondary and subservient. In his estimation, this method is missing from modern theology and needs to be embraced. It will serve as a foundation for theology from a Latin American perspective and provide a new way of doing theology – a theology of liberation.

Liberation in this picture has three aspects. First, it is about external liberation – a freedom from oppression and injustice in the socio-economic realm. Second, it is about internal liberation – freedom from overcoming the effects of an unjust society on the individual, things such as fear, guilt, and shame. Third, it is about freedom and liberation from sin that comes through Christ. Liberation in its fullest always comes from Christ, Gutierrez says, although as we will see, this looks somewhat different from the traditional picture. These stages are not sequential stages or distinct stages – they are a single, complex process which has the saving work of Christ at the deepest part. The idea is that we cannot single out a personal or spiritual liberation, a salvation of the soul, and neglect other areas of human well-being such as the socio-economic realm or the psychological realm. These are all interdependent.

He then tries to put the theological problem as precisely as possible, raising several key questions. What is the relationship between liberation in the sense of salvation and liberation in the sense of making mankind free in life and in society? What does the Kingdom of God have to do with the building up of this world? What does the gospel mean for politics, economics, and society?

Gutierrez mentions three failed answers to these questions. First is the Christendom mentality, which says that only what goes on in the church truly matters. There is no salvation outside the church, and temporal matters such as politics and economics are to be used for the benefit of the church. The second is labelled 'New Christendom', the view that temporal matters are valid, but since the church is very much the centre of things, creating a just and democratic society is only a means to achieve a favourable situation for the church to accomplish her goals. The third is known as the 'two planes approach': the planes of the world and the church are made distinct, each having its own ends in God's plan. The church should evangelize and inspire the temporal sphere, but its independent integrity should be respected. Both the church and the world contribute to the building of the Kingdom of God, which unifies these planes. Gutierrez says that this third model has won the day over the other two, which have passed away, but that this third is now in crisis. It leaves the laypeople, who are not priests, feeling alienated and impotent as Christians. It also leads to secularization. This approach develops a sacred-profane, temporal-spiritual, natural-supernatural dualism that is dangerous and harmful. He sees this dualism being challenged in theology and in the concrete world of Christian life – it too is dying, if not dead, and a new solution is in order, one that he will offer in liberation theology.

Since all theology is contextual, Gutierrez spends no small time and attention on his context in Latin America. He analyses the current situation like this: the developing Third World was being economically and politically structured to eventually grow into the mould of a Western First-World country – a new sort of imperialism. Multinational corporations from the First World were, through government diplomacy, foreign aid, and investment, grooming Latin America for their own ends. This is seen as a tremendous problem because these forces would have at heart neither the best interests of the people of Latin America nor the independence of these economies and political states. In other words, the system was rigged to keep the Western wealthy countries rich and the peripheral countries in poverty, and that gap was not shrinking, but growing. Gutierrez points out that the problem is not limited to international issues – there is a powerful and wealthy elite class in Latin America, whose position depends on inequality and keeping the poor oppressed through the instrument of modern capitalism. From all this, Latin America is in dire need of liberation, and the church should stop perpetuating oppression and be involved in social and political revolution for liberation. For Gutierrez, to truly understand liberation is ultimately to understand the meaning of Christianity and the church's mission in the world.

Gutierrez then presents his theological answer to these questions and problems. He first talks about the concepts of liberation and salvation. Salvation is the central theme of the Christian faith, but in modern theology it is underdeveloped, he says. Salvation has been thought about in binary terms — either a person is saved or not — and salvation is a cure for personal sin in this life in virtue of a salvation to be attained in the next life. This way of thinking is passing away, he says, as the universality of salvation and the possibility for it in this life have risen to prominence. In this way, the understanding of salvation is moving from quantitative to qualitative. Salvation extends to everyone and to all aspects of human life; it embraces and transforms all human reality in the here and now. There is not a sacred and a profane history — the two are one and will both be assumed by Christ. Salvation embraces all men and the whole man, he says.

This point of view can be seen in two biblical themes — the relationship between creation and salvation, and the eschatological promises. On creation and salvation, he says the two are linked by the Exodus experience. Creation in the Bible is seen through the lens of the deliverance from slavery, as the beginning of God's salvific process in the world. Creation begins history, and history is about salvation. As God created the world, so he created a people he politically liberated from Egypt. From the Exodus, God's people, who came from an act of re-creation, were to be a liberated covenant community where God dwelled. This liberation movement is fulfilled in Christ, who re-creates people in him — as Paul says, anyone in Christ is a new creation.

On creation and salvation, the Exodus experience is paradigmatic for Gutierrez. On the eschatological promises, he says that the Bible is a story of promises, starting with Abraham. This promise unfolds into many promises that God makes in history. These promises enter the 'last days' in the New Testament in an 'already/not yet' tension, and Gutierrez thinks we have not fully appreciated the 'already'. In liberation theology, eschatology in the Bible (when understood rightly) manifests itself in a radical concern for the present — and not just spiritually but temporally — in society, economics, and politics.

In liberation theology, Christ is the liberator, and not merely or even primarily for matters of personal ethics. Sin is not just an individual or private reality — it is, first and foremost, a social and historical fact, resulting in the breakdown of relationships with God and with others. Sin is at the root of injustice, oppression, and alienation. Christ redeems from all sin and all its consequences. The salvation that Christ brings entails the process of liberation in society.

The purpose of the liberation process is to 'create a new man' in several different senses, including the development of a just society that contributes to man's well-being. How does this work? Gutierrez tells us that, since in salvation history God has been for man and has dwelt with man – the climax of which is God *becoming* man in the incarnation –, not just Christians, but every man is the temple of God, where God dwells. God is no longer limited to dwelling in tents in Israel, he now dwells in the whole of human history in the hearts of all the people of the earth. This means that we must encounter God in our encounter with our fellow man and with humanity as a whole. The implication is that God is in the historical process of mankind. To love God is to bring justice to the poor and oppressed, and – importantly for Gutierrez – to bring justice to the poor and oppressed *is* to love God, and this is the essence of the gospel. He reads the parable of the sheep and the goats in Matthew 25 to teach this. It is not just that love for God will lead to love of one's neighbour, but that love for God *must* be expressed through love of one's neighbour. Importantly, love for neighbour is not just love for a collection of individuals who happen to contact your daily life, but is also love for humanity – for all of mankind in society, in all economic, political, and racial coordinates. In liberation theology, love for neighbour is not ultimately individualistic, it is corporate.

This has some profound implications for politics. In fact, says Gutierrez, Jesus is hardly apolitical. He chose many zealots – those who politically and religiously resisted the Romans – to be his disciples, and like the zealots, emphasized the coming Kingdom of God, although not in the narrowly nationalist way that they did. He confronted and challenged those in power, including Herod, the Jewish religious leaders, and the Pharisees. He was put to death by the political authorities on the grounds of being King of the Jews. Jesus was interested in the universal revolution against all oppression by addressing concrete instances of such in his day. In short, in liberation theology there is a direct connection between faith and political action, a working towards realizing the Kingdom of God in the here and now.

The meaning of the mission of the church needs to be broadened to include the task of building a new society. Since God wants everyone to be saved – not in the sense of 'guaranteeing heaven', but in the sense of deliverance from sinful systems and institutions, injustice, and poverty in the present – the church must rethink her mission. In the first few centuries of Christian history, the institutional church did not see itself as the exclusive centre of God's saving work in the world. Around the fourth century, a shift took place and Christendom was born, where the church enjoyed the support of political authority and largely defined the various aspects of society. In the modern period, this Christendom has collapsed from the inside out. In this context, then, a new ecclesiastical vision is required.

The way forward for Gutierrez is to think of the church as a sacrament to the world. A sacrament is the revelation of God's salvific plan, where the world encounters God in history. In answering this call, we have communion with God and also unity with all mankind. A sacrament, then, is not really a church ritual such as the eucharist or baptism. The eucharist is a celebration of the cross and resurrection of Christ, which brings liberation from sin – and this is the basis of political liberation. Communion with God and unity with all mankind cannot happen apart from the defeat of all oppression and injustice. Thus, in Latin America, to be the church means to denounce the current state of social injustice and announce liberation – which means to join the revolution, already begun, to abolish that injustice and build a new society. The truth of the gospel is a truth that must be done, especially in the political realm.

This unity with all mankind, this Christian brotherhood, as Gutierrez calls it, means to side with the oppressed class in the Latin American context. However, he does not think that preference for a particular social class is incompatible with a universal love for all mankind, including the oppressors. He recognizes this as a potential problem for his view, but it must be faced – the class struggle is a reality about which Christians cannot be neutral. In his view, to truly love all men is to side with the oppressed and remove injustice, liberating the oppressed, but also liberating the oppressors from their own power and selfishness. Only then is genuine unity possible, which is a gift from God and the task of mankind to realize in history. Unity in the church cannot be achieved without unity in the world.

Gutierrez has said that God has a preferential option for the poor. He then finishes this work by clarifying what it means to be poor. The term 'poverty' is a bit vague and has different meanings. First, it can mean material poverty, lacking the economic goods and means required to have even a basic human life. This condition is scandalous and contrary to the will of God for creatures made in his image; it must be prevented. After all, provisions to care for the poor are at the heart of the Mosaic Law; poverty is contrary to God's mandate in Genesis to be fruitful, multiply, and 'dominate' nature; and poverty undercuts man's call to be the sacrament of God to the world. Second, it can mean spiritual poverty, which many have taken to be an interior anti-materialism of being detached from the material goods of the world. This, however, is misguided in his view. Being 'poor in spirit' is to be humble and open to God. Part of being open to God is to be willing to fight against injustice and oppression, and to build the Kingdom of God in history, and this extension constitutes a third meaning of the word 'poor'. Poverty, then, is an act of liberation in solidarity with those suffering misery and injustice.

CRITICISMS

Liberation theology has been controversial and has earned great praise and harsh criticism. For one, Gutierrez is criticized for focusing too much on the social and economic aspects and for neglecting to relate them well to Christian redemption. In places, it seems like Gutierrez thinks the redemption of a Christian is not much more than the realization of Marxist ideals in society. This is not quite his position, but at times he seems to be liable to this overemphasis. Gutierrez seems to recognize the need for individual repentance and faith, and a personal relationship with God through faith in Jesus Christ, but critics have said he gives mere lip service to this important theological idea. They say that in his liberation theology there is no room for a transcendent God, for a Kingdom to come in the future when Christ returns, or for the need for personal faith and trust in the gospel message.

A second criticism comes from his analysis of the problem in Latin America. Are the economic troubles of Latin America *entirely* the fault of Western governments and corporations? What about the conditions in specific Latin American countries, such as corruption, or the economic policies of Latin American governments? Certainly, the West is not innocent, but it is hard to see how Western institutions are the *only* guilty party or how they are *fundamentally* the one in the wrong. There is enough blame to go around for all parties involved.

A third criticism comes from liberation theology's insistence that theology must always be contextual. If this is so, how can theology be a basis for global condemnation of injustices such as war or torture or genocide? Context is always important, for theology is done by humans in a specific context, but problems arise if context is made to be too much of a criterion.

A fourth and serious objection comes from Gutierrez's use of Marxism. Marxism is at root atheistic and sees its ideals as the inevitable outcome of the unfolding of history. Both of these seem antithetical to Christian thought, and it is not clear whether Gutierrez has genuinely forged a valid synthesis of these two worlds of thought or whether he has capitulated too much to Marx.

A final and perhaps most serious objection comes from his method of beginning with practice and then forming theology. Can theory and reflection ever be second to praxis? If so, how do we determine what 'right praxis' actually is? Should we build a theory/theology to support whatever we do, whatever gets the results we want? This is not what Gutierrez actually argues, of course – he has a vision of right praxis he exhorts the reader to embrace and supports it through theological theory and reflection. How is this consistent with his stated method?

GEORGE LINDBECK
THE NATURE OF DOCTRINE

INTRODUCTION

George A. Lindbeck (b. 1923) is a Lutheran theologian. The child of missionary parents, he grew up in China and Korea. His working life was spent at Yale, where he was a faculty member from 1952 until his retirement in 1993. He is known as one of the founders of the 'Yale School' of theology, or 'postliberal theology' as it is sometimes known, along with Hans Frei. Postliberal theology is influenced by Barth** and (through Lindbeck) by Thomas Aquinas**; its newness came from a fascination with cultural and linguistic analysis, and how theology, and the Bible, each functioned in creating a distinctive Christian community. Lindbeck has not published widely, but his slim volume *The Nature of Doctrine: Religion and Theology in a Postliberal Age* (1984) is one of the most significant works in recent theology.

As the title suggests, *The Nature of Doctrine* offers a proposal about how to understand what we are doing and saying when we make a theological claim. If we say 'Jesus is Lord', is this fundamentally a claim about a reality external to us, like 'Barack Obama is president', a claim about an internal orientation of who we are, like a lover saying 'I am yours', or something different? Conservative theology, on Lindbeck's account, would tend towards the first of these: doctrines describe reality. Liberal theology tends towards the second: religion is an orientation of mind and heart. Lindbeck's postliberal proposal is looking for another direction.

Lindbeck was committed to ecumenical* work throughout his career. He was an observer at the Second Vatican Council**, and for nearly twenty years a member of the Joint Commission of the Roman Catholic Church and the Lutheran World Federation. This ecumenical involvement helps to explain the context of his proposals about the nature of doctrine. Doctrines become fixed within Christian traditions and exist as forms of words that cannot be changed without leaving the tradition. In dialogue between Lutherans and Roman Catholics, the most difficult questions were the formal dogmatic condemnations on both sides. In the sixteenth century, binding dogmatic assertions were made by both churches that announced that positions held by the other were unchristian and unacceptable. In the face of this, it would be possible to continue in polemic mode, insisting that 'we' are right and 'you' are wrong; equally, it would be possible to ignore or reject the traditions, effectively insisting that both sides were wrong in what they said. The ecumenical way, though, is always to try to find a way of allowing both traditions to be right, to maintain their integrity, but still to make some progress towards reuniting divided churches. Lindbeck needed, for his own work, an understanding of doctrine that took this seriously, but allowed the problem to be addressed. This is his core issue in *The Nature of Doctrine*.

SYNOPSIS

Lindbeck begins his book with an acknowledgement of the ecumenical context of the problem (Foreword and Chapter 1). He introduces his analysis of what doctrine is in Chapter 1, suggesting that there are three common accounts of the nature of doctrine: 'cognitivist' accounts, which claim that doctrines are fundamentally attempts to tell the truth about reality; 'experiential-expressivist' accounts, which see doctrines as symbols that describe inner feelings; and attempts to combine the two. He suggests that the first approach is traditional, the second begins with Schleiermacher**, and the third is familiar in recent Roman Catholic theologians such as Rahner**.

None of these approaches make ecumenical advance possible. If doctrines are propositions about the way things are (the 'cognitivist' approach), then two conflicting doctrines are just incompatible. If I claim 'right now, George Bush is president', and you claim 'right now, Barack Obama is president' then, at best, only one of us can be right (we could both be wrong, of course). The same is true if I claim 'the bread on the altar remains bread' and you claim 'the bread on the altar is changed into the body of Christ'. The 'experiential–expressivist' approach appears to fare better at this point (Lindbeck will discuss its problems later): the doctrinal claims are, on this understanding, attempts to express feelings and commitments. It may be that both are valid, if inadequate, attempts to express the same feeling. The combined approach is promising, but the details of how to combine these two accounts are endlessly complex and often profoundly unconvincing, on Lindbeck's view.

Lindbeck therefore introduces his alternative model, which he calls a 'cultural–linguistic' approach to theology. Doctrines, on this understanding, are primarily rules, which govern speech and action within a tradition. Clearly, different rules can apply in different contexts (Lindbeck's own example is the rule 'drive on the left' that is operative in Britain, compared to the rule 'drive on the right' that is operative in America). We can remain faithful to both rules by carefully specifying where or when they apply. The doctrinal claim 'the bread on the altar is changed into the body of Christ' is primarily here a rule about how to speak and act properly: the bread should be treated with respect; it may be held up as an appropriate object of worship; and so on. Lindbeck claims (the demonstration comes later) that this will help the ecumenical problem of 'reconciliation without capitulation'.

Lindbeck claims that this 'cultural–linguistic' approach to the study of religion has become common in sociology, anthropology, and religious studies. Why then has it not gained more ground? Because, claims Lindbeck, the picture of religion given by the 'experiential–expressivist' approach, as an account of our deepest feelings and orientations, is profoundly attractive. Religion as learning to inhabit a culture, and as mastering the complex grammatical rules of a new language, might be more accurate, but it is harder to sell!

In Chapter 2, Lindbeck offers a 'non-theological' case for his approach. He argues that it makes better sense of historical and anthropological accounts of religion than the alternatives. The chapter proceeds by a comparison of 'experiential-expressivist' and 'cultural-linguistic' models. At the heart of the former is a claim that all religions are attempts to express a common experience (see Chapter 17 on Schleiermacher**). This, however, seems difficult: decades, if not centuries, of scholarly debate have tried, and failed, to find a way of expressing what is common to all religions, so why should we assume that this commonality exists?

The 'cultural-linguistic' model, by contrast, is happy with diversity. Indeed, it assumes that different religious traditions will give rise to different practices and ways of speaking. A religion shapes the life and thought of its followers in its own ways. It is also shaped, of course, by what those followers bring. (Lindbeck suggests that both Christianity and Buddhism lost their original pacifism through their inculturation into warrior contexts – Teutonic and Japanese cultures, respectively. The examples might not be historically convincing, but his point is clear.) Religion, thus understood, gives us the language to tell the story of our experiences. This approach can thus account for the strengths of the 'experiential-expressivist' model as well as offering its own strengths. It ought to be taken seriously, then.

In this generic account of religion, the question of the truth of any particular religion has been ignored. Lindbeck turns to this in Chapter 3. It is the case, he notes, that claims to superiority or finality are common in religious traditions, and any adequate account of religion will have to deal with this. The 'cognitivist' approach clearly manages this well; how does the 'cultural-linguistic' approach fare? Lindbeck discusses three themes: 'unsurpassability'; dialogue; and salvation of those of other traditions.

By 'unsurpassability', Lindbeck means the claim that one religion is more adequate than any other that exists (or could exist). The 'cognitivist' approach can narrate this very easily: this religion is true; everything else is (in some measure) false. For the 'experiential-expressivist' approach, unsurpassability means that a religious tradition interprets our shared religious experience better than any other (cf. Schleiermacher**). From the 'cultural-linguistic' perspective, religions are not comparable in the light of a more basic reality, in that they are proposing competing and incommensurable explanatory schemes. Lindbeck illustrates this by comparing philosophy of religion with traditional Christianity: on the one hand, 'God' is defined by narratives of Abraham, Moses, and Jesus; on the other, by arguments about causation (say); we might choose to believe that both discourses are referring to the same object, but there is no requirement that we should.

This might seem to make it impossible to decide between religions on a 'cultural-linguistic' account, but Lindbeck points out that this is not the case. In its strongest form, the 'cultural-linguistic' view could assert that one religion only gives its adherents the language and categories to describe reality successfully. Other religious claims are not so much false as meaningless, mere babbling. On the other hand, some of the claims made within such a strongly unsurpassable religious tradition might still turn out to be false: even if I have language adequate to describe God, I might still say things that are wrong.

Turning to inter-religious dialogue, Lindbeck suggests that each view allows dialogue, but of a different sort. The 'cognitivist' account will compare truth claims in an attempt to convert; the 'experiential-expressivist' account will seek common religious experiences underlying the different expression; and the 'cultural-linguistic' account will attempt to understand the differing perspectives and languages of the different religions, perhaps with the result of helping both parties in the dialogue to inhabit their own traditions more faithfully.

What, then, of the possibility of salvation for those of other faiths? Lindbeck takes up, and reinterprets, Rahner's** account of 'anonymous Christianity'. How can someone who is trying to be a faithful Buddhist (say) in fact be turned to Christ? Lindbeck's answer is to reflect that, in a 'cultural-linguistic' scheme, what matters is the language one is learning to speak, not how well one has learnt it. The speech of a Buddhist – and the speech of a Christian – may both be like the first halting words of two toddlers, sounding very different, but ultimately directed towards the same mature expression.

Lindbeck closes the chapter with a lengthy and technical excursus on religion and truth claims. He is not opposed to the idea that theological claims might correspond to the way things actually are, but this on its own is inadequate. To confess 'Jesus is Lord' is to behave in certain ways, not just to believe that Jesus stands in a particular relationship to all other beings. Religious truths must be performed, not just believed. Indeed, Lindbeck wants to claim that performance is far more important than mere belief, a claim which leads him to suggest that a person demonstrates his/her belief in Christian doctrine through his/her participation in prayer, praise, and preaching, not through his/her formal affirmation of a doctrinal statement. With this claim, Lindbeck returns to flesh out his account of 'theories of doctrine' in Chapter 4.

'Doctrines' are 'communally authoritative teachings regarding beliefs and practices that are considered essential to the identity or welfare of the group' (74). Doctrines may be formally stated or they may be tacit, but operational. In most Christian traditions, he claims, doctrines are not just normative, but permanent, and in Roman Catholicism they are also infallible. For any theory of religion to work, it must be able to account for these three aspects. Lindbeck rapidly dismisses the 'experiential-expressivist' account on this basis: the claim that Christ rose from the dead cannot be reduced to some generic account of religious feeling. He also dismisses hard propositional claims, which insist on a fixed verbal formulation of a doctrine. The live options, for Lindbeck, are his 'cultural-linguistic' account and a softer propositional view which acknowledges that the same reality might be expressed in rather different ways.

Lindbeck's account views doctrines as rules of speech and practice. This does not deny propositional truth, but asserts that *as doctrines* they function not as truth claims, but as rules, rules on how to describe and act in accordance with reality. The rules may be prescriptive, but most are descriptive, illustrating the ways in which speech and practice may be faithful (compare the teaching of verb conjugation through a particular example – *amo; amas; amat* etc. in Latin grammar). Rules – and so doctrines – might be unconditionally necessary ('love your neighbour as yourself'), conditionally necessary (you must not drink from this river until the chemical spill is cleared), or even accidentally necessary (Lindbeck returns to driving on the left: the rule could have been different, but once established is very difficult to change).

What might it mean for a doctrine to be 'conditionally necessary'? Lindbeck offers the example of belief in the immortality of the soul: if one believes in soul-body dualism (which not all Christians do), then the proper Christian way of so believing is always to affirm that the soul is immortal. For an 'accidentally necessary' doctrine, he turns to church order: the papacy, in his view, was not necessary in its actual form, but arguably some lasting, universal, and authoritative teaching office was necessary, and once the papacy had evolved, it necessarily fulfilled this role.

In the final chapter, he turns to three more doctrines to test his theory more fully, pitting it against propositional accounts. He turns first to the Trinitarian* and Christological* decisions of Nicaea** and Chalcedon**. These doctrines are held to be normative within the Christian tradition, and yet are expressed in a very particular local technical vocabulary. This recalls the point made in the previous chapter that the only live options are doctrines-as-rules or a soft propositionalism that acknowledges multiple ways of describing the same reality. However, we must ask how we can know that an alternative description is in fact adequate? Propositional theories offer us no help here; rule theories are much better: an adequate alternative is one that obeys the rules. Athanasius**, indeed, formulated doctrines as rules; he narrates the homoousion* as the claim that 'whatever is said of the Father is said of the Son, except that the Son is not the Father' (p. 94; Lindbeck relies on Bernard Lonergan for this interpretation). We can obey this rule with or without the technical Greek language of ousia* and hypostasis*, and so we can write a different account of the Trinity which remains faithful. If we do so, however, we cannot rewrite the creed or the conciliar decisions: the rules, doctrines, are necessary and unchangeable.

His second example concerns Roman Catholic beliefs about the Blessed Virgin Mary, such as the immaculate conception* or the assumption*. These are relatively recent, but irreversible dogmatic developments in Roman Catholicism. How can the 'cultural-linguistic' account of doctrine explain such developments? Lindbeck suggests that we can easily imagine a process of discovering new rules, which, post-discovery, are seen to be natural and inevitable. He offers mathematical exploration as an example: we can discover rules that were always there, but never before noticed. In the case of doctrinal development, in the constant exploration and evaluation of speech and performance, the time can come when a new criterion of faithful speech is discerned.

The Marian dogmas are irreversible because of the confession of papal infallibility*, which serves as Lindbeck's final test. Clearly, it is easy to assert that infallibility is a proper doctrinal rule within Roman Catholicism, but Lindbeck returns to his ecumenical issues: Eastern Orthodoxy would see only the consensus of the whole church as authoritative; and Reformation traditions would look to Scripture alone. At present, these accounts are irreconcilable, and the communions must remain divided; we can hope and pray for a time, however, when there will be sufficient confidence that the consequence of obeying each of these different rules is identical that reunion may be achievable.

The final chapter is entitled 'Towards a Postliberal Theology'. Lindbeck believes he has demonstrated the superiority of the 'cultural-linguistic' approach; now he attempts to analyse what a theology built on this method might look like. A postliberal theology will understand faithfulness primarily as 'intratextuality'. Meaning is located, and faithful performance validated, by successful inhabiting of the texts that make up the tradition. The primary reference is not beyond the language used to narrate the religious tradition, but within it. Lindbeck returns to the practices of anthropology to validate this, and then draws on the work of his colleague Hans Frei to suggest that this practice, of interpreting the world through the categories of the (biblical) text, was normal through most of Christian history. Frei demonstrates that this practice fell apart in the eighteenth century; Lindbeck acknowledges the problem, but suggests that a postliberal theology needs to find a way of returning to the primacy of the biblical narrative.

CRITICISMS

Lindbeck's essential claim is that we need to re-evaluate how doctrine functions and see it as a set of rules for inhabiting a culture well, rather than as a set of truth claims or an interpretation of religious experience. He acknowledges that he sets out on this journey to make ecumenical dialogue possible. Criticisms of the book have focused on both the intended aim and the main thesis.

On the first, there is a question of appropriateness and a question of interpretation. An unsympathetic reader might ask whether the quest for ecumenical unity should be elevated to the point where the nature of theology is redefined to serve it? Lindbeck would respond, we think, that he is not doing this; he is observing genuine, if limited, successes in ecumenical understanding and struggling to explain how this has happened. This raises the question of interpretation: is Lindbeck right to think that ecumenism has had some successes, or are the claimed agreements merely illusory, clever forms of words that conceal, rather than solve, old disagreements?

The main thesis of the book has sometimes been misunderstood as a 'postmodern*' claim that theology is only ever an account of the practice of the churches, not a description of reality, created or divine. Lindbeck's claim concerns the status of 'doctrine', the formal or informal authoritative teachings. He does not dispute – indeed in several places he clearly affirms – that theological statements are truth claims, but maintains that when they are functioning *as doctrines*, their role is regulative, not referential.

Lindbeck is unapologetic about the status his proposal gives to routine Christian practice, but silent about a necessary consequence of this: if he is right, then a theologian who is not at least moderately faithful in Christian practice is going to be unable to do serious doctrinal work. He is hardly the first writer in the tradition to make this claim, of course, but in the context of the modern academy, it is somewhat controversial and perhaps deserving of more discussion than it has been given. That said, locating theology primarily within the practices and speech of the local worshipping and witnessing congregation would be seen by many, the present authors included, as a welcome correction to an unhappy detachment and professionalization of the theological academy.

GLOSSARY

Allegorical reading — An interpretation where characters and events represent ideas and concepts, often seemingly disconnected from a straightforward reading of the text.

Apostolic succession of bishops — A purportedly unbroken lineage of ministers of a Christian church to the apostles of Jesus Christ.

Arianism — The teachings attributed to Arius stating that the Son of God is a lesser being than God himself (the Father) and that the Son was a created being. They were deemed heretical in 325 and again in 381.

Arminianism — The teaching associated with Jacobus Arminius that God's election is resistible, and so that salvation is open to any who choose to have faith in Christ.

Aseity — The absolute independence and existence of God. He exists in and of himself; he is uncaused or perhaps the cause of himself. God is '*a se*'.

Assumption — The belief of the Roman Catholic and Eastern Orthodox churches that Mary the Mother of Jesus was taken directly into heaven after completing her earthly life (it is debated whether this also means she avoided physical death).

Atonement — The work of Christ in his life and death to bring salvation to sinners and to defeat sin and evil.

Begotten — The attribute of the Son that distinguishes him from the Father; see **generation**[*].

Christology — The area of Christian theology that addresses the person and work of Jesus Christ.

Council — A meeting of church leaders and theological experts to settle matters of doctrine and practice.

Doctrine of God — The area of Christian theology that speaks of the divine life: God's attributes, his existence, the Trinity, etc.

Ecumenical — Pertaining to the entire Christian Church.

Election — The sovereign choice of God in eternity past, where he lovingly and freely chooses those who will receive salvation.

Eschatology — The area of Christian theology dealing with the end of history and the complete realizing of God's purposes in the world.

Exegesis — Explanation or interpretation of a body of text, usually Scripture.

Existentialism — A system of thought which focuses on an individual person's existence and his/her discovery or creation of meaning regarding life, free choices, and values.

Fall — The entrance of sin into human existence and the effects for mankind and all of creation, as recorded in Genesis 3.

General resurrection — The resurrection of all the dead in the **eschaton***, including both the righteous and the wicked.

Generation — The eternal relationship of the Son to the Father. The Father always generates the Son, and the Son is always generated by the Father.

Gnosticism — A system of belief which says that the material world is evil, the spiritual world is good, and there is a secret knowledge of salvation reserved only for certain elites.

Great Schism of 1054 — The break in the Christian Church which formally severed the connections between what would become the Roman Catholic Church and the Eastern Orthodox Church.

Greatest conceivable being — The approach to the idea of God that works from the basis that he is the greatest possible being, and thus must have certain attributes. Often connected with the **ontological argument***.

Heresy — Any belief or doctrine that is unacceptably deviant from the core of Christian tradition, often deemed so on the criteria that (at least by implication) it threatens the possibility of salvation from sin. It is often believed that an idea can only be formally determined to be heretical by a competent church authority, such as a **council***.

Hermeneutics — The science and art of interpretation, usually of Scripture.

Historical Jesus scholarship — Attempts by scholars to reconstruct the life of Jesus of Nazareth using accepted historical methods; these are usually critical of the gospel texts.

Homoiousios — 'Of a similar substance', an alternative explanation of the relationship between God the Son and God the Father to that which was recognized at Nicaea in 325. The Son is of a similar but different substance than the Father, which raises problems for the Christian commitment that there is only one God.

Homoousios — 'Of the same substance', a technical word used at Nicaea in 325 to articulate the idea that God the Son and God the Father are of the same substance and are both fully and equally God.

Hypostasis — One actual existence.

Idealism — A system of thought which says that reality is fundamentally mental and/or immaterial.

Immaculate Conception — The teaching of the Roman Catholic Church that Mary the Mother of Jesus was kept free of original sin from the moment of her conception.

Incarnation — The event in history in which the second member of the Trinity, the Word, took on flesh and became a human being in the man Jesus Christ.

Justification — The freedom of guilt from sin before God.

Liberation theology — A political movement in Roman Catholic theology which attempts to interpret the Christian faith through the plight of the poor (usually in Latin America).

Logos — The 'word' or 'reason' in Greek philosophy; in Christian theology, it is the Christ.

Marxism — An economic, social, and political system of belief which is atheistic and which views history as necessarily unfolding towards socialism.

Neoscholasticism — A revival in Roman Catholic theology of medieval critical thought which emphasized inference and resolving apparent contradictions.

Nicene faith — The doctrine taught at the Council of Nicaea that the Father and the Son are equal in deity and are of one substance, in short, the orthodox Trinitarian doctrine.

NRSV — New Revised Standard Version of the Bible. Unless otherwise noted, all translations of biblical passages in this book are from the NRSV.

Ontological argument — A type of argument for God's existence usually arguing that God exists necessarily and that God's existence is inherent in the definition of God.

Ontology — The study of the nature of being and existing, and the relationships between things that exist.

Ousia — 'Substance', a technical term involved in debates about the Trinity.

Pantheism — Everything composes God; the universe is part of God's being.

Papal infallibility — The doctrine in the Roman Catholic Church which states that the Pope is preserved from error when, acting in his office as Pope, he makes a doctrinal or moral pronouncement.

Piety — Reverence for and worship of God and an earnest devotion to obey and serve him.

Platonic forms — The highest reality in Platonic philosophy is the realm of forms, which are abstract ideas like chair-ness, kind-ness, circle-ness, etc.

Platonic philosophy — Philosophical ideas and systems indebted to Plato.

Pneumatology — The area of Christian theology that deals with the Holy Spirit.

Postmodern — A broad set of sensibilities (not a defined position or world-view) that resist absolute truth, hold a suspicion of authority, and reject modernism's crowning of human reason as the ultimate authority.

Procession — The eternal relationship of the Holy Spirit to the other divine persons. The Western churches teach that the Spirit proceeds from the Father and the Son; the Eastern churches say simply 'from the Father'.

Providence — God's relationship to and action in the world begun with creation, where he guides, sustains, and directs.

Purgatory — Taught in the Roman Catholic tradition, but rejected by most of Protestantism, it is a place of purification in preparation for heaven, where those who die in a state of grace are temporarily punished and purged of any remaining sin and guilt.

Realism — A system of thought which says that at least some aspects of reality exist apart from our mental interaction with them.

Reformation — Usually refers to the Protestant movement in the sixteenth century calling for correction of church doctrine and practice with an emphasis on Scripture in the original languages and the Church Fathers.

Reprobate — Those who refuse to repent and will be condemned to eternal punishment.

Revelation — God's disclosing of truth and knowledge through divine communication to creatures.

Rule of Faith — The core doctrinal beliefs which the Christian tradition has firmly held, often used to evaluate theological positions and religious practices.

Sacrament — A rite in which God especially acts to confer grace.

Sanctification — The freedom from all that causes guilt before God, where a person is conformed into the image of Christ.

Soteriology — The area of Christian theology that deals with salvation.

Theodicy — An attempt to explain and reconcile evil and suffering in the world with a God who is all-powerful, all-knowing, and morally perfect.

Transcendent — God is beyond all created things, qualitatively greater than all else without limit.

Trinity — God is one being who exists in three persons: Father, Son, and Holy Spirit.

Universalism — The idea that all sinners will receive salvation and that hell will be empty.

INDEX

Ambrose of Milan 55
Anselm of Canterbury 4, 61–9, 82,
    91, 105
apologetics 2
Apostles' Creed 45–53, 72, 77
Aquinas, Thomas *see* Thomas
    Aquinas
Aristotle 5–6, 8, 70
Arius, Arianism 23, 30, 31, 47
Athanasian Creed 45–53
Athanasius 3, 4, 29–37, 39, 46
Augustine x, 4, 54–60, 73, 84, 158

baptism 75, 101, 105, 109, 115,
    118, 174, 196, 205
Baptists 7
Barth, Karl x, 11, 172, 173, 182,
    191–8, 200, 267
Basil of Caesarea 3, 4, 38–44, 48
Bible 9, 12, 15, 18, 19, 21–3, 24,
    26, 39, 40, 70–1, 95–6, 97, 99,
    105, 115–16, 124–5, 161–2,
    171, 207–15
Bonhöffer, Dietrich 11, 182,
    199–206
Bultmann, Rudolf 11, 181, 207–15,
    225

Calvin, John 6–7, 53, 95–102, 113,
    114, 118, 121, 242
Cappadocian Fathers *see*
    Basil of Caesarea; Gregory
    of Nazianzus; Gregory of
    Nyssa
Chalcedon, Council of 36, 46,
    50–1, 66, 124
Charlemagne 46
Christology 4, 25, 29–37,
    38–9, 46, 49–50, 61–9, 74–5,
    83, 154, 162, 170, 175–6,
    187–8, 191–8
Church of England 7, 9, 112–120,
    138
Congregationalism 7
Constantine 3, 38, 129
Constantinople, Council of 3, 4,
    44, 46, 48, 55, 58
councils, ecumenical 45–53,
    233; *see also* Council of
    Chalcedon; Council of
    Constantinople; Council of
    Nicaea
creation 3, 17–19, 20, 24, 26,
    27, 30–1, 32, 41, 48, 63, 72,
    73, 98, 195

creeds, ecumenical 45–53; *see also* Athanasian Creed; Apostles' Creed; Nicene Creed
Cyril of Alexandria 49–50

Daly, Mary 13

Eastern Orthodox theology *see* Orthodox theology
ecclesiology 12, 48–9, 100–1, 117–19, 157–64, 233–41
ecumenical creeds *see* creeds, ecumenical
Edwards, Jonathan 8, 130–7
Enlightenment 9
Ephesus, Council of 49–50
eschatology 19, 24, 27
Eucharist 75–6, 101, 109, 114, 118–19, 205, 238
Eutyches, Eutychianism 50–1
evil 3

Fall 32, 59, 97, 98, 105
Feuerbach, Ludwig 10, 155, 165–72
filioque clause 49, 52

Gnosticism 14–15, 21, 23, 25
Greek philosophy *see* philosophy, Greek
Gregory of Nazianzus 48, 58
Gregory of Nyssa 48
Gutiérez, Gustavo 12–13, 258–66

Harnack, Adolf von 11, 182–90, 199
Hegel, G.W.F. 10, 174
Hell 53
Holy Spirit 2, 3, 8, 24, 26, 38–44, 73, 77, 97, 99, 130–7

Irenaeus of Lyons 2–3, 14–20
Israel 1, 88

Jesus 1–4, 29–37, 74–5, 182–90, 242–9; death of 5, 34, 79–80; deity of 4; resurrection of 1, 34; *see also* Christology
Julian of Norwich 6, 78–85

Kempe, Margery 78
Kierkegaard, Søren 10, 173–81, 220, 221

Leo I, Pope 50
liberal theology 10–11, 147–56, 159, 182–90, 191–2, 207, 210
liberation theology 12–13, 240, 248, 258–66
Lindbeck, George 12, 267–75
liturgy, worship 39–40, 43
Locke, John 130
Lodge, David ix
Luther, Martin x, 6, 86–94, 114, 138, 201, 220, 242

Maccabees 1, 105
Methodists 8
monotheism 2, 3

Nestorius 49–50
Newman, John Henry 9, 157–64
Nicaea, Council of 4, 30, 31, 46, 47, 58, 124
Nicene Creed 45–53, 57, 58–9
Niebuhr, H. Richard 11, 216–23

Origen of Alexandria 3, 21–8
Orthodox Theology 4–5

philosophy, Greek 1, 21, 23, 27–8, 174, 188–9
prayer 83
Presbyterianism 7–8, 121–9
Providence 3, 195

Quakers *see* Society of Friends

Rahner, Karl 12, 224–32, 268
Reformation 5, 6–7, 12, 54, 86–120, 164

resurrection 19, 24, 34, 140; *see also* Jesus, resurrection of
Romanticism 9, 148
Ruether, Rosemary Radford 13, 250–7
Rule of Faith 16–17, 24

sacraments 75, 101, 109–10
Schleiermacher, F.D.E. 9, 11, 52, 148–56, 165–6, 167, 193, 219, 268
Scripture *see* Bible
Second Vatican Council *see* Vatican Council, Second
Society of Friends 7
soteriology 5, 19–20, 33–4, 41–2, 59, 61–9, 73, 86–94, 98–9, 105–9, 116, 191–8
Spirit, Holy *see* Holy Spirit

Thirty Nine Articles 7
Thomas Aquinas 5–6, 7, 8, 70–77, 219, 267

tradition 9, 18, 43, 105, 115, 124–5
Trent, Council of 7, 103–11, 136, 206, 233–4
Trinity, Doctrine of 2–4, 12, 18–19, 27, 38–44, 46, 54–60, 73, 84, 98, 115, 154–5, 198, 224–32

Vatican Council, Second 12, 103, 225, 233–41, 250, 268
Virgin Birth 52–3

Wesley, John 8, 138–46
Westminster Standards 8, 121–9, 206

Yoder, John Howard 12, 242–9

Zwingli, Huldrych 114